P9-CEN-666

About the Author

Dr. Agnes Grant worked with the Native Teacher Training programs at Brandon University, Manitoba, for thirty years. She travelled extensively in remote and isolated communities, both as an administrator and as a professor. As she listened to the students and community members, she learned of the tremendous effect residential schools have had on members of First Nations and Canadian society in general. Her painstaking research and interview methods ensure that it is the women's voices we hear in *Finding My Talk*. These women are not merely presented as history but as contemporary members of today's global society.

Dr. Grant is the author of *No End of Grief: Indian Residential Schools in Canada* and three other books. She lives in Winnipeg.

...IS COLLEGE LIBRARY
100 Wellesley Street West
Toronto, Ontario
Canada M5S 2Z5

Finding My Talk

How Fourteen Native Women Reclaimed
Their Lives after Residential School

REGIS COLLEGE LIBRARY
100 Wellesley Street West
Toronto, Ontario
Canada M5S 2Z5

Agnes Grant

FIFTH
HOUSE

E
96.5
G73
2004

Copyright © 2004 Agnes Grant

All rights reserved. No part of this publication may be reproduced, stored in a retrieval system, or transmitted, in any form or by any means, electronic, mechanical, recording, or otherwise, without the prior written permission of the publisher, except in the case of a reviewer, who may quote brief passages in a review to print in a magazine or newspaper, or broadcast on radio or television. In the case of photocopying or other reprographic copying, users must obtain a licence from Access Copyright.

Published in Canada by Fifth House Publishers
195 Allstate Parkway, Markham, ON, L3R 4T8
www.fifthhousepublishers.ca

Published in the United States by Fifth House Publishers
311 Washington Street, Brighton, Massachusetts, 02135

The publisher gratefully acknowledges the support of the Canada Council for the Arts, and the Ontario Arts Council for their support of our publishing program. We acknowledge the financial support of the Government of Canada through the Canada Book Fund (CBF) for our publishing activities.

ONTARIO ARTS COUNCIL
CONSEIL DES ARTS DE L'ONTARIO
50 YEARS OF ONTARIO GOVERNMENT SUPPORT OF THE ARTS
50 ANS DE SOUTIEN DU GOUVERNEMENT DE L'ONTARIO AUX ARTS

Canada Council   Conseil des Arts
for the Arts   du Canada

Cover and interior design by Kathy Aldous-Schleindl
Front cover artwork "Pow Wow Dream" by Joane Cardinal-Schubert
Edited/copyedited by Meaghan Craven
Proofread by Lesley Reynolds

Library and Archives Canada Cataloguing in Publication
Grant, Agnes, 1933–
Finding my talk : how fourteen Native women reclaimed their lives after residential school/Agnes Grant
ISBN 1-894856-57-0
1. Native women--Canada--Biography. 2. Native women--Education--Canada History. 3. Native peoples--Canada--Residential schools. 4. Native children--Abuse of--Canada. I. Title.
E96.5.G718   2004   371.829'97071   C2004-904870-8

Printed in Canada by Friesens

13 / 5 4 3 2

Contents

To all the children
of residential school survivors,
may your lives be filled with
understanding,
forgiveness,
healing,
peace, and love.

Foreword

We survive,
and we do more than survive.
We bond, we care, we fight, we teach,
we nurse, we bear, we feed, we earn, we laugh,
we love, we hang in there, no matter what.[1]

The words of Paula Gunn Allen, a Laguna Pueblo/Lakota poet, writer, scholar, and professor of English succinctly describe the essence of the women who are featured in this book. The resistance and resilience displayed by these women is awe-inspiring, as are their achievements and phenomenal successes in their chosen careers. There are many women who did not survive the residential schools, women who still lead lives of quiet despair, and many have suffered premature deaths. They are a continuing shadow on our souls, but we must remind ourselves there also are those who have survived, the ones who are examples and an inspiration to us all. The stories in this book attest to the fact that there is life after residential school, and that life can be good.

I am an Ojibway from Sandy Bay First Nation in Manitoba. My formal schooling began in Sandy Bay Residential School in 1963. I did my time for seven years, and there were four significant lessons I learned in that institution. I learned how to be silent and how to be obedient to authority. I learned that being "Indian" is to be inferior. I also learned how to read and write.

During those years I witnessed many incidents of humiliating punishments for minor "sins." In her biography Shirley Sterling points out that we were punished, not for being bad, but for being children. Running away and insubordination were mortal sins punished in secret. Otherwise, every punishment was formally displayed in front of all students. Public humiliation was always a part of the punishment.

My memories of life in residential school are sporadic, as are my memories of my life as a child in general. I remember two incidents of severe child abuse; one in which I experienced physical abuse, the other in which a classmate was the victim. She was an adolescent girl who was humiliated in the worst possible fashion. Sister Theresa, a formidable woman, forced her to stand in full view of the rest of us girls for hours with her blood-stained panties over her head. While she stood there, we treated her as if she were invisible. We saw it as a way of maintaining the dignity of the victim, whereas in truth we were validating the unjust treatment by simply accepting it. We were well trained to ignore it and remain silent. I would dearly love to have memories of abuse blotted from my mind, but they remain there, firmly etched. Today I view these memories as validation of claims that abuse occurred in this particular school. I saw it and I felt it.

I shelved the manuscript for this book for many days before I summoned the courage to start reading it. I had to prepare myself; actually, I felt I had to armour myself so that I would not succumb to depression while I read these biographies involving residential school experiences. I was afraid my old scars, which I have struggled so long and hard to overcome, would be excoriated by these testimonies.

I did experience myriad reactions, but none that evoked any personal emotional turmoil. I did feel compassion and empathy, but neither anger nor anguish. Perhaps that is a testimonial to the progress of my personal journey of healing, but, more accurately, I believe my response shows that this book is not just another book about abuse in residential schools. It is a triumph over the emotional, physical, mental, and spiritual abuses experienced by so many, a book that demonstrates success in spite of adversity. This is what makes this book unique. It offers hope to those who endured abuse in residential schools because evidence of healing is found in the lives of these remarkable women.

I began to read eagerly, hoping to find explanations of some issues that had long perplexed me. My generation was the last to attend these schools. My mother spent her childhood years in residential school, as did some of my siblings. As a family we have been devastated by the experience, but we also have had our share of successes. I believe that today I am a survivor. For many years I harboured feelings of anger at those who had gone through the residential school system before me. Much was known about the devastating effects of the schools because children returned to reserve communities unable to function normally. Our languages were rapidly disappearing, and our ties with the Elders had been broken. Abuse—physical, sexual, psychological, and spiritual—was never mentioned, though there were people in my community who had suffered from it all. People suffered in silence and isolation, believing they alone had been singled out for hell on earth.

It is true that the aftermath of abuse was not a phenomenon that was as fully understood then as it is today and that the discipline of child psychology was still in its infancy. But the gut-wrenching knowledge of what it was to be abused was present in my community, and yet no one took steps to prevent it from happening to other children. Why did those who had experienced the same system not move to stop it? Why did no one warn me? Why was I not given strategies to cope with what was in store for me? Though my mother was a kind and loving person, until the day she died she was of the opinion that nuns could do no wrong. How could she accept the infallibility of the church when it was hurting her children? Why did my mother not challenge the system? Why did our leaders, our grandmothers and grandfathers not fight for us? A nagging thought preoccupied my mind: Could it be that we, as a race, were really so inept and incompetent that we simply rode the waves of colonialism, unconcerned about the welfare of the children we were bringing into this world?

I approached these biographies with great trepidation, afraid that my worst fears would be realized. I feared that the women in this collection would gloss over the hardships of their lives and would attribute their current successes to the fact that they had adequately adopted the value systems of the colonizers. This, I feared, was what would have enabled them to find a niche in society where their token "Indianess" served them well. I worried that their attitudes would salvage the conscience of society at large and absolve it of guilt.

I soon found exactly the opposite to be the case. The residential school experiences of these women encompass a wide spectrum, from that of being the favourites or "pets" to that of being brutally abused. It is not surprising that their perspectives on residential schooling are just as varied. However, there are certain commonalities. There is a feeling that the inevitable must be endured, but it must not be accepted. Though they may sometimes have felt that their incarceration would go on forever, these women knew that eventually it would end, and what they did with their lives after residential school was up to them. Whether they went on to doggedly relearn the skills denied them by the system, like Alice French was required to do, or whether, like Sister Dorothy Moore, they were able to sort out the good from the evil and find solace in the church, the decisions they made were made as autonomous human beings, not as brainwashed puppets. I found similarities to my path to healing mirrored in the experiences of some of these women. Though many questions remained in my mind, my anxiety evaporated as I read on.

An exceptional feature of this book is its scope. It includes many different angles and points of view, which is different from the first-person accounts of one particular school, such as those other testimonials that have predominated the market until now. Nor is this a documented overview based on the protocols of colonial institutions, such as have been provided by non-Aboriginal historians. Though the author of this book is non-Aboriginal, the voices are ours. I want to thank the author for her involvement in our lives and the painstaking methods she used to ensure that it is our voices that are heard in the telling. Often additional information drawn from the author's research is included in order to put individual experiences into a broader context. I also want to thank Brandon University in Manitoba, a leader in educating Aboriginal teachers, for providing research money for Dr. Grant's work.

Included in this book are women from the four directions and from across the entire country. The north is represented by the Northwest Territories, the west by British Columbia, the east by Nova Scotia, and the south by southern Manitoba and Saskatchewan. The women come from many different language groups: Ditidaht, Nlakapamux, Woodland Cree, Plains Cree, Dakota, Ojibway, Mi'kmaq, and Inuvialuktun. Different religious denominations are also represented. Most of the women attended schools that were run by the Roman Catholic Church, which is not surprising since it operated approximately half of the schools. However, those run by the United, Presbyterian, and Anglican Churches are also represented. Also included are first- and second-generation survivors, who attended schools from the 1930s to the 1970s. Dr. Grant deliberately selected women from the professions, but another category of women that must not be overlooked are those who remained in the homes, raising and nurturing children effectively in spite of the austerity and pain of their own childhood years. One need not be a professional in order to nurture children, and success is not limited to, nor should it be defined by, a professional career.

This book is not a history or documentation, rather it is a reflection of how the residential school phenomenon impacted on fourteen representative women. It came as a great relief to me that finally there is a book that does not treat us as "history" but rather as living, breathing human beings who still exist today. In traditional Aboriginal societies women had a role equal to that of men; this role was destroyed by colonialism and especially by the Indian Act. In residential schools we were carefully tutored, through both direct teaching and role modelling, to accept inequality of the sexes as right and just. The "might makes right" philosophy of the residential schools has done immeasurable harm to our communities, and it will take years of resocialization for us to regain our equilibrium. Progress is being made in the political realm, which is almost exclusively the right of male Aboriginals. However, more than control of political structures is needed in order to restore a culture. This book demonstrates how progress is being made by women who are working to restore the underlying tenets of our cultures, knowledge that has been denied us for too many years. Without the essential understanding of our own cultures we cannot hope to take our places as fully contributing Canadians.

The final chapter answers another question that has plagued many of us. Even today there are those among us who argue that without the residential schools there would not have been the opportunity for us to learn to read and write and subsequently participate in contemporary society. But is this true? One Ontario father, at least, did not accept this premise. Sara and Beverly Sabourin, a mother and daughter team, did not go to residential school. They describe an alternate life experience that shielded them from the excesses of the colonizers but still taught the skills they needed for survival in outside society. Both are grateful that they were spared the devastation the residential school experience wrought. However, both also recognize that they personally have been affected by the aftermath of the schools, as have all members of Canadian society.

I feel it is an honour to write the foreword to this book. I feel privileged to have come to know these women through their writing and hope that I will meet some of them in the future. I would personally like to say, "Megwetch! Thank you for sharing your stories so we all can understand better what happened in our lives. You are an inspiration to us all."

Marlene Starr

Acknowledgements

Credit and gratitude needs to be extended to those who provided invaluable assistance as the book was being compiled. To the women who are included in the book—a heartfelt thank you for your time, generosity, and good humour. Thanks to Colin Wasacase from Kenora for his assistance with the chapter on his twin sister, Ida Wasacase. I had the good fortune to meet Eleanor Brass in Regina and carried on a correspondence with her for several years. Thanks to Bev Jackson of The Pas, who augmented the story with memories of her "Auntie" Eleanor. Dolores and Levi Sock from New Brunswick were generous with time and transportation as the chapters on the Mi'kmaq women were complied. Thanks to Sister Dorothy who invited me to "tag along," and to Caroline and Roddy Gould who offered generous hospitality on more than one occasion. The visit to the Joeyaskans at Merritt, BC, was a great pleasure. I had the honour of meeting Sophie Sterling, before it was too late, as I participated in the daily activities of the close-knit family. I will remember to bring some good Manitoba, smoked farmer sausage when I return.

I extend heartfelt gratitude to Brandon University for financial assistance through the Brandon University Research Committee, which made the extensive travel possible.

Last, but not least, I want to thank Helen Giesbrecht and Nancy Grant for their detailed comments, questions, and suggestions and for keeping my focus and enthusiasm alive in spite of the numerous drafts, delays, and revisions.

Introduction

The residential school era spanned the years between 1830 and 1988, but the histories of the schools vary in different times and different regions of Canada. The first schools opened in Ontario in 1830, where First Nations welcomed the move, envisioning their own teachers, ministers, and interpreters. They supported the schools in principle, as well as financially. When they realized that total renunciation of their cultures and languages was the price the government and the churches exacted at the residential schools, First Nations withdrew their support. They were, however, unable to save their children from the system. The greatest number of schools existed across the country at the turn of the twentieth century when the west was opening up for settlement. Even as the viability of the system was being questioned and some schools were closed, others were opened in different areas. No region of Canada was spared.

At no time were all First Nations children educated in the residential schools, but the aftermath of the system was such that few communities have been left unscathed. Catholic, Anglican, Presbyterian, and Methodist Churches, and later the United Church, were involved in this school system. The Catholic Church consistently operated just over fifty per cent of the schools so appear to have been the most neglectful and abusive; however, neglect and abuse have been documented at all schools, regardless of denomination or historic time frame. Nor did all the abuse come from "white" people; some residential school students learned the lesson of "might makes right" well and tormented fellow students mercilessly. Parental abuse and neglect took a further toll, as some students raised in the loveless environments of the schools themselves became parents.

It was my hope that I would identify women in a wide variety of occupations as my research took me across Canada. This was not to be. Several women featured in this book are writers leaving records of their experiences. One woman was a journalist and one is a community worker. The other women are educators. This is not surprising since

1

education, along with nursing and stenography, were the only acceptable occupations for all women when these women were training for careers. However, I soon found that there is a deeper reason why so many of these women focussed their considerable energies in the field of education. There is a fierce undercurrent of determination: *Never again will people from outside the culture determine how First Nations children will be educated. Never again will people from outside the culture be given the opportunity to destroy what the people themselves value.*

Eleanor Brass

Eleanor Brass was born on the Peepeekisis Reserve near Balcarres in southern Saskatchewan in 1905. Her parents, Walter Dieter and Marybelle Cote, were both products of the residential school system. When it came time for Eleanor to go to school, she, too, was forced to attend the residential school, in spite of her father's strong objections. Eleanor was one of the first babies to be born on the File Hills Colony, the most comprehensive social engineering experiment with residential school graduates that Indian Affairs had undertaken up until then, or ever would again.

Eleanor's father was born on the Cree Okanase Reserve, the grandson of Chief Okanase, one of the signatories of Treaty #4. During the North-West Rebellion of 1885 Chief Okanase and some other chiefs pledged their allegiance to the Queen and then fled to the Dakotas in order to avoid the conflict. Though the Métis cause was just, they did not believe it would benefit their people if they became involved. Those who did, like the Cree bands of Big Bear and Poundmaker, paid a very high price for their participation. Walter Dieter was very young at the time of the rebellion but remembers riding a dog most of the way to the Dakotas.[2]

A Presbyterian residential school had been built on the Okanase Reserve near Balcarres, and a Catholic school had been built at Lebret in the Qu'Appelle Valley. Both principals bribed parents to send children to their schools. Competition for souls was intense, but, more importantly they needed bodies to justify keeping the schools open. Walter Dieter's father accepted the bribes from both schools and then sent Walter to File Hills, the Presbyterian school, because it was closer to home. When Walter was in his teens he was sent to the Regina Industrial School.

Eleanor's mother was born on the Saulteaux Cote Reserve near Kamsack and attended the Crowstand Residential School, which was situated on the reserve. Her grandfather was Chief Gabriel Cote, another signatory to Treaty #4. When the Crowstand School closed she attended the Anglican school at Prince Albert and then went to the File Hills School for one year. Here she met her future husband. Later she attended the Brandon Residential School for grade twelve.

The Regina Industrial School existed for nineteen years, and once it was firmly established it housed approximately 120 students a year. There was great resistance to this school because the government expected parents from as far away as the Manitoba parklands to send their children to Regina. They objected because the school took the children too far from home. Eventually it closed for lack of support from parents and because it was plagued by a continuous mismanagement of funds. While in existence, however, it was a successful vocational school and produced many outstanding graduates in areas such as farming, gardening, carpentry, cabinet making, painting, glazing, blacksmithing, steam fitting, steam engineering, shoemaking, and typesetting. The girls excelled in housekeeping skills, including sewing and laundry work. The "showpiece" brass band was made up of boys from the school and played an important role in non-Aboriginal community events.

Recreation at the Regina school consisted of singing, social evenings spent in games and dances, swimming, skating, lacrosse, baseball, soccer, and camping. There was friendly interaction between the community and school, and students were often invited to the homes of Regina residents for evening visits. Lecturers and entertainers visited the school frequently. The students were well equipped to interact with the outside world upon graduation, and it was from these graduates that much of the leadership for the early Indian organizations, such as the Association of Saskatchewan Indians, came.

Eleanor's father worked for a farmer during the summer months, as did many of the older students. If they were paid wages they usually did not see the money; it went directly to the schools. The farmer Walter worked for had acquired large amounts of land by buying Métis scrips for next to nothing. This was a "legal" move that had involved high-ranking officials and had effectively defrauded the Métis of most of their land. The farmer offered to help Walter Dieter get established on a farm of his own when he graduated, but he preferred to go back home to the reserve. Upon graduation Marybelle Cote returned to the File Hills School to work as a laundress, a common practice since female graduates were expected to work at household chores either at the schools or for settlers until they married.

The local Indian agent, W. M. Graham, founded the File Hills Colony. His dream was to continue the agricultural training of the students once they left school since too many of them were lapsing into shiftless, unproductive lives, a phenomenon Indian Affairs termed "retrograding." A part of the Peepeekisis Reserve was set aside for this experiment, and only school graduates could qualify for the eighty-acre lots. As time went by the graduates demonstrated that they could handle six or seven of these lots each.

Walter Dieter was among the first farmers of the colony. Like the others, he built a one-room home of logs and finished it with lime and plaster. Later, as the men married, they added lean-tos and kitchens. The school principals and Mr. Graham put careful thought into the selection of these young farmers, and they thought it equally important to select good farm wives for them. Though this may sound outrageous today, the practice of arranged marriages was not uncommon in Aboriginal cultures at that time. Indian agents and school principals exerted such control over Aboriginal people that choosing marriage partners seems to have been accepted as an extension of their powers. In any event, there was little anyone could have done to stop it. In some cases the marriage partners did not even know each other, and, in one case, Father Hugonnard at Lebret married six couples simultaneously.

Aboriginal languages were strictly forbidden at the schools, and it was no accident that Walter Dieter was Cree and Marybelle Cote was Saulteaux. That would ensure that English would be the language of the home and the children would learn neither Aboriginal language. In later life Eleanor tried to learn to speak Cree but she was unsuccessful, though she could always understand it reasonably well.

Eleanor was one of the first babies to be born on the colony. Her grandmother from the Cote Reserve was the midwife. Her home was a cosy and comfortable log cabin with curtains at the windows and patchwork quilts on the beds. Eleanor spent most of her babyhood in a hammock suspended from the ceiling. Fortunately she was a very good baby because her sister, Janet, who was fifteen months older than Eleanor, was sickly and required much of her mother's attention. Her mother continued to nurse Janet and put Eleanor on a bottle. She had not even had time to prepare a layette for the new baby. When she was born, her father wrapped her up in one of his shirts, saying, "poor little darling."[3] Eleanor recalls a very happy childhood because their parents loved them dearly and gave them the best of care. She believes they were very fortunate children.

Eleanor grew up in a family of nine boys and three girls. Her youngest brother was born the year she got married. They had a happy but strictly regulated life. Eleanor described herself as a lively, curious, and outspoken child who caused her mother considerable anxiety in public because of her unguarded comments. Spankings and pinches were the usual forms of punishment, especially for children who did not behave well in church.

During the first twenty years the Indian agent kept tight control of the File Hills Colony. This appeared to be acceptable to some of the young farming couples since they had all been institutionalized throughout their childhood years. Some, however, left soon after they arrived when they realized they were as controlled as they had been in the school. There were benefits to staying. Graham's vision for the colony involved paternalistic support in decision-making but also education in the form of lectures and demonstrations by agricultural authorities. There were no handouts, but loans were available. However, small sums of money were given to brides to set up housekeeping.

Agricultural exhibitions were held to encourage competition and, consequently, more productivity. Money prizes were not given but useful farm and household items were acquired in this way. The Indian agent controlled every aspect of their farming practices, and since the Indian Act mandated the "permit" system, no produce could be sold without the agent's permission. Consequently, Mr. Graham controlled most of their expenditures as well. The farms became highly successful and were the envy of the community, which created problems both on and off the reserve.

Graham also controlled the social life of the colony. All couples had to be legally married according to non-Aboriginal customs; women were not allowed to visit each other since that would encroach on house-keeping time. Fiddle and powwow dances and other tribal ceremonies were forbidden since they cut into farming time. Eleanor did, however, remember secret fiddle dances away from the prying eyes of the agent. At the agricultural exhibitions foot racing and ball games were allowed, but horse racing was not.

Parents were allowed to attend some Indian feasts and some-times funerals. Eleanor recalls that these funerals upset her and the other children because they knew nothing of their Indian heritage, and the wailing and keening was frightening. Soon the parents attended funerals without the children, leaving them at home in care of their *kokooms,* the grandmothers; these are times that Eleanor remembers fondly.

The children accompanied their parents to town where they met with open racism, but they did not yet understand the implications of being considered inferior. Eleanor felt that as a child she had many experiences, both good and bad, in both cultures. The title of her book, *I Walk in Two Worlds,* exemplifies her philosophy of life.

The colony thrived at first, and both Catholic and Presbyterian churches were built. A small hospital followed. Community halls were scenes of teas, suppers, bazaars, and sales, mirroring the social life of the non-Aboriginal community. Youth organizations, also based on non-Aboriginal models, flourished. Many of the men continued to play in the brass band that began at the Regina Industrial School. This band served a significant function in recruiting military personnel in both white and reserve communities for the First World War. When many of the reserve and colony men enlisted in the war, they joined military bands. In fact, enlistment from the colony exceeded that of other communities, both reserve and non-Aboriginal, in proportion to the population.

In 1918 Graham left File Hills, which was the beginning of the end of the colony. Three more agents followed before the colony was disbanded. The personality of the agents, the farmers' desire for more freedom, the conflicts with surrounding communities, and farmers' gradual understanding that they were forced to give up their culture totally, led the colony members to slowly reintegrate themselves into the Peepeekisis Reserve. Colony farmers lost their separate identity with the collapse of File Hills, but the schisms the experiment created on the reserve remained for several generations.

It is noteworthy that in spite of all the experimental and progressive attitudes in the colony that a day school was not established. That would, of course, have negated government and church insistence that residential schools were the only acceptable form of education for Status Indian people. It was to be another fifty years before the church and government stranglehold on Aboriginal education began to be questioned by non-Aboriginals. Eleanor's father had no use for the residential school and wanted his children to attend the provincial schools nearby, but Mr. Graham forbade it. The Presbyterian residential school was only nineteen kilometres from Eleanor's home but it might as well have been a million. The children suffered acute homesickness and cried themselves to sleep until they realized that there was no alternative to their situation and adjusted as best they could.

Eleanor had a few happy memories of the school. When she started school Mr. Sweet was the principal and he lived up to his name, as did his wife, who mothered the children. No one got strapped as long as he was principal. But when he left life changed. Eleanor never forgot the many severe strappings she received. She recognized that there were favourites at the school who were never punished, those who went out of their way to please the staff, but her personality did not lend itself to conformity. She referred to the strap as an "instrument of torture." She suffered from back pains all her life, which she attributed to the severe beatings she received.

Nor did she forget the unbearable pain she endured as a nurse probed around in her swollen mouth to find an abscessed tooth and then pulled it without giving Eleanor a painkiller. She recalled being locked in a closet all day with nothing to eat and then beaten mercilessly when she was let out because she had wet herself. This beating went on for so long that the boys, who could hear her cries through the ventilator, began to shout for the matron to stop. She recalled the beating a twelve-year-old boy received, which was so severe that he could not bear covers on his back for a long, long time. No doctor was called in to tend to his wounds. Nor could she forget the seventeen-year-old who hung himself in the school barn. His misdemeanour had been relatively minor. They all were afraid, and fear led to apathy and depression. Eleanor believed the staff's reaction to the normal behaviour of children was invariably overblown.

For example, when Eleanor's shoes were so worn out that they were almost falling off her feet she asked for new ones. The supervisor told her that there were none in her size. Eleanor was raised in a household that met physical needs in a compassionate manner, so when she found the storeroom door open she decided to check shoe sizes for herself. She was caught and consequently was given a pair of men's size-nine boots, which eventually got so dry they curled up and constantly tripped her.

Eleanor pointed out that the worst atrocities happened during the winter when the children were quarantined to prevent sickness. No parents were allowed to visit. On one occasion, however, her father came by just as his niece had been punished for attempting to run away. Her hands and arms had been beaten so they looked like boxing gloves, and her ankles were shackled together. Walter Dieter's face became deathly pale when he saw the child, and he took the steps in a few leaps, burst into the principal's office, grabbed him by the scruff of his neck and dragged him downstairs. Though the shackles were removed immediately nothing else came of the incident.

Eleanor recalls that apples were stored in the school attic but the children never got any because they were reserved for staff. The children found a way to hook them with a line but were discovered when a staff member noticed that almost all of the apples were gone. They all were strapped, a few every day; the principal did not have the energy to hit them all at the same time. When Eleanor howled loudly the principal laughed and said, "The Cotes are good singers." He was referring to her mother's fine voice and to her cousin who was a professional singer.

Eleanor's frustration and indignation was still palpable when she recounted the incident over forty years later.

The children were sick and undernourished at the school. The food was inadequate and unappetizing, though it was supplemented with cod liver oil and iron. Sunday walks were fun in the summertime but the inadequately dressed children suffered greatly in winter. The walks were four to five kilometres long. The little ones, especially, suffered. They often wet themselves and then walked back with clothing that was frozen stiff, knowing a beating awaited them upon their return.

In summertime, when the children experienced a little more freedom, they often met away from the staff's prying eyes. Then the older ones would attempt to teach the younger ones their language as well as some cultural practices. The children from the File Hills Colony were especially unaware of their heritage, and they were routinely picked on by staff, accused of thinking they were better than the rest. Eleanor pointed out that most of the colony people had some degree of non-Aboriginal ancestry. She thought perhaps that was what made them less passive than the reserve students and consequently singled out for punishment more frequently.

Eleanor's first teacher did little but draw diagrams of heaven and hell. The next year they had a young musical teacher, and she did little but play snappy music. Again they did not learn to read or write but they did learn all the latest pop music. The teacher was very popular with the principal and the Indian agent, both of whom were married men. The agent frequently picked her up after school, and the children instinctively understood that this was questionable behaviour. Finally, in her third year, Eleanor began to read. They had a no-nonsense English woman for a teacher who immediately recognized how far behind the children were and set to work teaching them how to read. They liked her though she made them work hard. Eleanor's father eventually made arrangements to place Eleanor in a provincial school at his own expense and the English teacher was invaluable in helping Eleanor get caught up and preparing her for the "white" school.

When she was twelve Eleanor began school in Abernethy, Saskatchewan. She met with considerable discrimination, especially from the boys. The non-Aboriginal students were totally ignorant about Indian people though they all lived near reserves. She boarded with a family that was kind to her, and her father took her home for the weekends. She completed grade seven and eight in one year. When she got the highest marks in the class she was tormented by the other students. Eleanor got sweet revenge, which she still relished years later, when her father picked her up in his new blue Ford. One boy yelled at her, calling her a dirty Indian and demanding that she get out of the car. The boy's face fell when he discovered her father owned it! None of the people in the community were as well off as the Dieter family.

Eleanor went to Canora for high school and stayed at a Presbyterian boarding home with twenty other girls of different ethnic origins. They ranged in age from seven to eighteen. The matron was friendly but the senior girls stared at Eleanor because she was the only Indian student there. The matron put Eleanor with the younger children who were friendly and accepting, and eventually the seniors got used to her. They explained later, after they had become friends, that they had been afraid that she would scalp them. Eleanor went home for holidays and long weekends. Soon she had a boyfriend, Hector Brass, whom she had known since childhood, and her schooling became less important to her.

Eleanor did not finish high school. Instead she left to earn her own living and assist her parents on the farm. Her younger siblings had attended the village school in Lorlie but there was a lot of discrimination. When an outbreak of lice happened the Dieter children were automatically blamed; however, when the nurse came to their school she found that they were the only unaffected family. Even so, after that incident the school board told her father they would no longer accept any Indian children. The only other option was the residential school. Eleanor believes that one of her younger brothers died of neglect at the residential school. The others were sent to the Brandon Residential School for their higher grades because the school in Regina had closed. The principal at Brandon was what Eleanor described as a "fearsome" man and even after they left the school her brothers were afraid of him. One sister, Edna, became a teacher and taught in various Indian Affairs schools. None of the boys were interested in farming but Eleanor was proud of her family, whatever paths their lives followed. She believed they all had to overcome great adversity in order to be successful adults. This she attributed to the examples set by both her parents.

Eleanor worked at various housekeeping jobs as well as on her father's farm. She enjoyed working with her father at whatever tasks needed to be done. They raised pork, beef, and chickens, milked cows, and had a huge garden. Eventually she took a job as a waitress in Balcarres. When she was nineteen she and Hector were married at his parents' farm. His parents had a house with a big lean-to that served as a kitchen/dance hall. These were the prohibition years and a major problem for all communities was bootleg liquor, but Eleanor remembers her wedding dance fondly because nobody got uproariously drunk. The dance was lively and peaceful and guests had great fun.

Eleanor and Hector began married life in a big seven-room house with a veranda. She was thrilled with the space and enjoyed furnishing it with the necessary items. She described Hector as good-natured, humorous, and a talented musician. Though they were farmers she admits that they were not very good at it. Perhaps they compared themselves to the exemplary model her parents set. They also experienced considerable difficulty in their farming practice because of the capricious behaviour of the Indian agent. Eleanor admitted that her non-conformity likely exacerbated the already strained relationship she and Hector had with the man. The agent handled all their finances, and they were not allowed to sell anything without his permission. On one occasion Eleanor needed housekeeping money and drove the fifteen kilometres with horse and buggy to get some from their bank account, which was also controlled by the agent. The agent said, "What's the matter with that good for nothing husband of yours? Why doesn't he get out and earn something, he's so darn lazy."

Eleanor replied, "Just a minute, sir, he's busy working on the summer fallow and if it isn't done you'd be bawling us out, and furthermore, my husband is an honest man. He'd never think of stealing money from anyone and he's never been in a penitentiary."[4]

This comment was really hitting the agent below the belt because his son was in jail for defrauding farmers at the Qu'Appelle elevator. However, the agent did not give her any money. The next day she went to borrow money from her father but the agent had already been there and left some money for her. He had told her father that she was very "sassy" but her father had replied mildly that she was only standing up for her rights. On another occasion, when Hector sold a horse without permission, the agent threatened him with jail. Hector hired a lawyer and the case was dropped.

After that event the reserve community formed an organization to study the rights of Indians. Their aim was largely to get out from under the domination of the Indian agent. At this time the difficult Depression years and the drought were hitting the reserve community especially hard. The agent did not give families any welfare. When a child starved on the reserve, the official investigation report stated that the child had died of "natural causes."[5] The people who met to plan strategies for gaining more control over their own lives were labelled as agitators, and their activities were dismissed as inconsequential.

Eleanor's people survived the Depression as best they could by bartering firewood, digging seneca roots, and growing their own food. Racism increased as the Depression deepened, and they had to be on guard constantly so they were not cheated by the farmers who bartered food for firewood. Eleanor said they received so many pigs' heads instead of the good pork roasts that had been agreed upon that she became an expert at making headcheese. To her dying day she could not ever again stand the sight of headcheese.

Though life was very hard they always had a rich social life on the reserve. The Presbyterian Church was the focal point of their activities. Eleanor and other family members sang in the church choir while her mother played the organ. Eventually Eleanor replaced her mother as organist, but she claimed she was never a very good musician. She also accompanied Hector, who was an outstanding violinist. Visits to the Motherwell farm, which was situated near the reserve, were a source of constant pleasure. Mrs. Motherwell had been a beloved teacher and principal at the residential school, and she and her husband always welcomed former students with open arms. Mr. Motherwell was a stonemason and had built a beautiful home. Today the Motherwell homestead is a museum and popular tourist attraction.

In the 1940s Indian political action spilled from the small community groups which had sprung up and become a regional organization called the Association of Saskatchewan Indians. Hector Brass represented the Peepeekisis Reserve. In 1946 political groups across the province amalgamated to form the Union of Saskatchewan Indians. The union decided to present a brief to the Joint Committee of the Senate and the House of

Commons, which was established to examine the Indian Act.

Hector Brass was one of the committee members selected to work on the brief. He spent long hours on the task but enjoyed the challenge of the intellectual rigour and research it required. Eleanor felt that she was an "Indian Affairs widow" at times but realized how important change was for the future of Indian people.

This political action exacted a financial toll on the activists and their families. There were no funds of any kind available for political activity so expenses had to be defrayed by participating members. In some cases band funds were used but in most cases the women stayed home and eked out scarce funds so that their husbands could participate in the meetings.

One of the biggest concerns the activists put forward was that Indian people did not have the vote. They were not to be enfranchised until 1960. The Indian agent had informed them that they were not allowed to write articles for publication. One day Eleanor asked a newspaperman who had come to interview Hector if this was true. He told them they had been misinformed.

By 1949 Eleanor felt that her husband should be writing and publishing the many speeches he was making on behalf of the cause. He agreed it would be a good idea, but when he did not do it, Eleanor began to put the words down on paper herself, believing she was helping him with his work. He saw it differently. Hector suggested that she send her writing to the *Regina Leader Post,* and thus Eleanor's career as a journalist began. She entitled that first article "Breaking Barriers," and not only did the *Leader Post* publish it, they paid her ten dollars, which was a lot of money for them. Later it was published in a small booklet called *Saskatchewan Digest.*

Hector told her not to stop writing, and soon she had a regular column in the *Melville Advance* that she entitled "Teepee Tidings." She reported on news from both the reserve and off-reserve communities and augmented her column with commentary and legends.

As Hector and Eleanor became more and more immersed in Aboriginal issues they felt they needed to broaden their horizons and become more knowledgeable about off-reserve life. They were free to move because they had no children, so they took jobs on a dairy farm where the owner had hired them sight unseen. When they arrived she told them that if she had known they were Indian she would not have hired them. However, the job worked out well, but they stayed only a few months because the physical demands on Eleanor, because of her weak back, were just too great. In spite of an offer of a pay increase they left, taking a chance on finding work in the more northerly regions of the province. A difficult period followed as they could get only the most menial labour and at one point were reduced to eating berries and sleeping in the bush. Eventually they gave up and returned to the reserve. They felt that they had not wasted their time because they had gained valuable experience and had much information to pass on to other reserve members. The most important lesson they learned was that it was impossible to survive off the reserve without money.

The Indian agent who had caused them so much grief in the early years of their marriage had left, and the hated permit system had been discontinued so they attempted farming again. At first they subsisted largely on rabbits, but they worked hard to get their farm established. Then a tornado smashed the log cabin they had built with such great labour, and several days later an electric storm killed Eleanor's favourite horse. They took it as a sign that perhaps they should not be farmers after all.

They moved to Regina, this time better equipped to cope with the outside world. Hector immediately got a job as a buttermaker for the Eaton's dairy department and Eleanor did housework. Their first landlord was racist, and the rooms they had were infested with cockroaches. Their second apartment was clean, and Eleanor got a job as second cook at Regina College. This job did not work out because the head cook could not accept working with an Indian. Undeterred, Eleanor kept on searching and soon got the job of second cook at the YWCA. It was not long before the executive director recognized that Eleanor's talents were wasted in the kitchen and suggested she move to the front desk as receptionist. Her pleasant, friendly manner was just what was needed as women sought help at the only safe haven for them in the city.

An aspect of integrated life that was very difficult for both Hector and Eleanor was that they faced a continual barrage of negative comments about Indians. A report from the United Church, published by the *Leader Post* in 1956 began, "Most reserve Indians are lazy, immoral, non-social and unambitious." This report aroused such indignation among Indian people that Hector and Eleanor were asked to write a rebuttal. They compiled information, citing facts and figures, which discredited the whole United Church report.

As time went on they found themselves more and more involved in working with Indian people who had come to the city. They were especially concerned about the young people who seemed lost. The young adults could not cope with reserve life since the residential schools had alienated them from their own culture, but they did not have the skills to cope in non-Native society either. With the co-operation of the YWCA Eleanor and Hector began a club that held meetings and social events. They did much of their work with young adults at their own expense so rarely had any extra money for themselves.

They travelled to Winnipeg to visit the first Friendship Centre to have opened in Canada. They returned to Regina determined to open one there too. They established a committee to work on it, made speeches and wrote articles, and finally received enough funding to open a few rooms and hire a director. Those few rooms were the nucleus of the Friendship Centre that exists to this day, even though there were a few years when it was closed. Instrumental in getting the centre established was Mrs. W. B. Clipsham, whose husband was a deputy minister in the civil service. As Eleanor so succinctly put it, Mrs. Clipsham knew "what strings to pull."

Eleanor took great satisfaction in watching the progress made at the Friendship Centre. She remained on the board of directors and, not surprisingly, she began a newsletter. She continually encouraged other people to write. She was invited by CBC in Regina to do a school broadcast on Cree legends. She began to collect stories about old Cree people in southern Saskatchewan, as well as other stories and legends. Ultimately she published the book *Medicine Boy and other Cree Tales*.

When Eleanor had worked at the YWCA for about ten years as receptionist, switchboard operator, and general clerk, her husband's health began to fail. She felt badly that she could not stay home with him but someone had to bring in some money. The work at the Y also became more stressful as she became more successful in her other activities. One woman, who had supervisory responsibility for Eleanor, was particularly hateful and made comments about how she could not understand how an Indian person could know enough about the English language to write articles. Eleanor became discouraged and depressed and did not have the energy to fight the racism.

She applied for other jobs and was hired by the Department of Agriculture as an information writer. She took a week off work before she was to begin her new job. It was on the last Sunday of that week that Hector died of a massive heart attack while sitting in his chair. Though she called an ambulance, it was too late. They held funeral services in the city for their friends there and then took Hector home to the cemetery on the reserve.

Eleanor had often cried when other young married families were having babies but Hector had always reassured her that she was all he needed, affectionately calling her *Wanapuss* (Little Rabbit). Now she was all alone.

At first Eleanor was very lonely, but soon she was surprised at how well she could cope alone. A niece moved in with her, and she really enjoyed her job with the Department of Agriculture. She interviewed specialists in order to write her information articles and spoke on various agricultural issues on the radio. She learned how to write news releases, stories, and editorials. She wrote about everything from producing honey to rat control. The *Western Producer* reprinted her rat control article. Even though she worked for the province, she never forgot her role as advocate for her people and kept the reserves, which were not a provincial responsibility, informed about what information was available from the department.

After a year with the Department of Agriculture she asked to be transferred to the Indian and Métis Branch as a placement officer and counsellor for girls and women. She became an outspoken advocate for affirmative action. Her first move was to contact all government departments to ask them to hire at least one Aboriginal woman. When one department head refused she merely stated, "Fine, I'll just include this in my report to the premier."[6] He changed his mind quickly, and before long every government office in Regina had at least one Indian employee. Then she broadened her work area to include rural government offices as well.

Eleanor enjoyed her work, taking great delight in the successes of the young people she was able to help. They became like children to her. In 1971, when she reached the age of mandatory retirement, she asked for an extension because she felt her work was so important to the welfare of young Aboriginals, but it was not granted. And, indeed, thereafter the numbers of Aboriginals employed by the government in Saskatchewan steadily decreased.

Not content to be a "retired" person, she applied for and was accepted as executive director of the Friendship Centre in Peace River, Alberta, where she stayed for the next twelve years. By then she was seventy-eight years old. The centre was relatively new, and Eleanor found the people there to be more shy and unaware of the outside world than her clients in the city. She became fascinated with northern customs and social life. In 1975 she was asked to be a news correspondent for the Alberta Native Communications Society. Eventually she resigned from the Friendship Centre in order to be a fulltime news correspondent, undaunted by the fact that her territory included the whole Peace River region. In spite of the difficulty of winter travel and the considerable distances involved, she covered her area by car during both winter and summer. She overcame every obstacle until she had an eye operation and her activities became restricted. She could not write regularly but she still did some freelance writing and soon went back to the Friendship Centre as an evening volunteer.

In 1985, when she was eighty years old, Eleanor left the Peace River region. Her health was deteriorating, and her family wanted her to move closer to home so they could look after her. In 1987 she published her memoir *I Walk in Two Worlds*. In the last six years of her life she took great pride in the accomplishments of her siblings, her nieces, and her nephews. She became an ardent supporter of Native Studies programs when they were established at the universities, believing that was exactly what young Aboriginals needed. Eleanor always regretted that young Aboriginals had been denied knowledge of their vibrant and honourable history and had lost so many cultural teachings as a result of the residential schools.

At age eighty-six, her vision significantly impaired, she passed away. She received many honours in her later years, among them an honorary doctorate from the University of Ottawa. Unfortunately, the records of her achievements and all her memorabilia were lost in a house fire in 2000.

Her extended family has always taken great pride in her accomplishments. Her sister Edna's granddaughter, Bev Jackson, from The Pas, Manitoba, herself a survivor of the Prince Albert residential school, recalls what an inspiration "Auntie Eleanor" was to them in their formative years. She was independent; she was talented; and she never ceased to make use of her talents to make a difference in people's lives. She liked to dress meticulously and had a particular love for hats. They were fascinated by their auntie because not only did she have a reputation for wearing elegant hats but also she often dyed her hair!

But most importantly, the younger generation realized that Auntie Eleanor had risen above the pettiness of the racism that she encountered since she was a child, secure in her own self-worth. She felt that bitterness would only interfere with the important things she needed to do with her life. She taught the younger generation that they were worthwhile Canadian citizens with a rich cultural heritage to sustain them. She taught them to be justly proud of their ancestors and the role they had played in making Canada what it is today. She taught, by word and deed, that young Aboriginals could have control over how they live their lives. She demonstrated that it was possible to live in both the Aboriginal and non-Aboriginal worlds and be a valued member of Canadian society at a time when tolerance of minority groups, especially Aboriginals, was rarely found.

Though *I Walk in Two Worlds* has been in print since 1987, few residential school survivors or their descendants have known of its existence. With increased focus on the residential school era, however, young Aboriginals today are astonished and delighted to find this indomitable feminist pioneer who refused to bow to the constraints placed on her, both as a woman and as a member of a First Nation. In her unassuming way she lives on as an inspiration and role model for all who learn of her history and her accomplishments.

Ida Wasacase

The Saskatchewan Indian Federated College was established in May 1976, and a powwow was held in a foyer at the Regina university campus to honour the occasion. The event marked the beginning of a new relationship between an institution of higher learning and the First Nations of Saskatchewan. A powwow at a university was a unique event, and approximately one hundred people were in attendance at the 1976 opening. For the twentieth anniversary celebration of the college, the powwow had to be moved to a stadium because over twenty thousand people were on hand to participate. Sadly, Ida Wasacase, the founder and first director of the college, did not live to take part in the celebration.

Ida was born on the Ochapowace Reserve near Broadview, Saskatchewan, in 1937. She, her twin brother, Colin, her sister, Laura, and brother, Alfred Jr. (Bud), were raised in traditional ways. Their mother was Cree, their father Saulteaux. Cree was the language of the home. Their grandfather, Walter Ochapowace, was a medicine man and spiritual leader. The children were raised with models of commitment to service of others, and Ida followed this model all her life.

Both of Ida's parents attended the Round Lake Residential School in the beautiful Qu'Appelle Valley. The Reverend Hugh McKay, a

Presbyterian minister, first established a mission in 1884 on the north shore of the lake, since he was not allowed to build on the reserve. Within a few months he had built a school, which had been promised to the band in the treaty of 1874. He hired an Aboriginal couple, Jacob and Nancy Bear, to assist him and act as interpreters. However, Rev. McKay learned to speak Cree quickly and immersed himself in the history of the area, even joining in traditional feasts. Students recalled the stories he told about their people as part of their education at the residential school.

Ida's father had not stayed in school beyond the mandated time but her mother, Florence Ochapowace, was an enthusiastic student. When Round Lake had no more to offer, she went to the school at Brandon where she took grades seven to eleven. She finished grade eleven when she was only fifteen years old.

A common practice was to keep students in the residential schools until the mandatory age of sixteen. Many students never achieved more than a grade-six level, or even less. Others were deliberately slowed down in their progress, forced to repeat grades so they remained with their peers, or they were simply kept in grade eight until they reached age sixteen. Florence Wasacase, however, left the school after grade eleven because a family crisis required her presence at home.

Numerous reports from across Canada identify students who performed very well in the early residential schools. Their parents clearly understood that education was essential in order to cope with the new lifestyles imposed on them by reserve life and encroaching settlement. They were encouraged by their parents and were highly motivated to learn in order to cope with a changing society. They were challenged and intrigued by the new ideas schooling presented.

Another factor that influenced early school attendance was the devastating poverty First Nations experienced with the coming of European settlers. On the Plains, buffalo herds were disappearing much faster than had been anticipated; government rations were inadequate and slow in the coming. It was government policy to keep rations to a minimum in order to impose a new agrarian lifestyle on First Nations as quickly as possible. The combination of this niggardly ration structure, graft, and unscrupulous suppliers led to starvation on many reserves. Ottawa was deaf to repeated requests for more rations from the civil servants in the field. As a result, some parents reluctantly sent children to residential schools where they would at least be warm and fed. Though the schools have been severely and justly criticized for not providing adequate diets for the children, in truth, the children in the schools during this era were at least guaranteed a regular supply of food, however inadequate, which was not always the case for the children who stayed at home.

The early schools were run by dedicated missionaries like Rev. McKay at Round Lake, Father Hugonnard at Lebret, and Father Lacombe, who had some Indian ancestry himself, at the Dunbow School in Alberta. These were missionaries who did not set themselves apart from the people they served, who respected the Cree language and, to some extent, the traditions. Father Hugonnard showed an insight into sound educational practices when he instructed the nuns who taught at the primary levels to not only learn to speak Cree but also to make it the language of classroom instruction until the students could learn English. This practice continued until 1909, when the federal government outlawed the use of any language other than English in the schools. These missionaries understood that in order to successfully teach the children, parental co-operation was necessary. They also understood the dire consequences for Indian people if they were not educated to participate in mainstream society.

This same level of understanding did not exist in Ottawa. The high success rates at the schools were viewed as more of a problem than a triumph. The prevailing assumption was that Indians would soon die out or they would assimilate to the point that they would no longer identify as Indians, consequently the "Indian problem" would be a temporary one. It soon became evident that Indians were not dying out, that federal aid was essential for rations and health care during this transition period, and that the promise of schools as guaranteed in the treaties was becoming a costly proposition.

The success of Indian students came as a surprise to many bureaucrats. Canada, like much of the world at that time, was a racist society. Equality for Aboriginals was a concept that was not even entertained, not only in Canada but all over the world where Christian, European empires held sway. Frank Oliver, Liberal Member of Parliament for Alberta, told Parliament in 1897:

> We are educating the Indians to compete industrially with
> our own people, which seems to me a very undesirable use
> of public money, or else we are not able to educate them
> to compete, in which case the money is thrown away. [7]

No one challenged the underlying racism in his statement, and Oliver was later to become the deputy superintendent of Indian Affairs, playing a major role in implementing the hated half-day system. Under this system, once they reached grade four, students were expected to work half the day in an attempt to make the schools self-sufficient. Farms had become an integral part of the schools in areas where farming was viable, and for older students, especially the boys, this often meant hard labour and little schooling. Some girls, too, spent more time in the kitchens and laundries than in the classrooms. Predictably, academic performance dropped. When questioned in Parliament in 1905, Minister of the Interior and Superintendent of Indian Affairs Clifford Sifton explained, "You cannot press the Indian children as you can the children of white people, you cannot require so much of them."[8] The die was cast, and even today First Nations struggle to obtain adequate school resources, often leading to substandard education programs.

In spite of the odds against them, some students, like Florence Wasacase, did remarkably well. Rev. McKay was a strict disciplinarian and attempted to inculcate the children with his particular value system. However, he also acknowledged the traditional practices of the Cree and worked with community leaders rather than discrediting them, as was the norm later. Rev. McKay had established a pattern where Indian leaders were invited to participate in school ceremonies, and it was Ida's grandfather, Walter Ochapowace, who prayed in his own way in Cree at the residential school, sharing the platform with Rev. McKay. This practice continued when Ida and her siblings were in school, even though the children were not allowed to speak the language themselves. In Florence's time the Cree language was not forbidden. However, her children were affected by the terrible cultural discontinuity that was to destroy so many residential school students because they were denied the use of their languages at school.

Florence Wasacase raised her children to be well grounded in both Christianity and traditional beliefs. She remained active in the

Christian church all her life but her devotion to Christianity did not preclude traditional ceremonies and practices. The children were raised with an intimate knowledge of the ceremonies and rituals of their culture. Ida grew up with a mixture of traditional beliefs and Christianity without any expectation of conflict between the two.

Florence always regretted that her education had been cut short so she enrolled her children in the school at age five in order to maximize their opportunities. The children never questioned the decisions made by their mother. They had learned English in their home; Ida and her brother recall climbing the fence of the horse corral in order to count the horse's legs, in English. School was presented as a positive and important experience.

Ida's parents always delivered the children to the school personally and picked them up at Christmas time and at the end of the term. This was relatively easy, as long as they were at Round Lake, since the school was directly across the lake from the reserve. The extreme poverty of the home did not impact on the children, but, at one point, their parents had to sell the children's pet pony, a sacrifice that was greeted by wails of protest when they learned what had happened. When the Round Lake School closed the children were dispersed to various schools in Manitoba. Ida was sent to Teulon where she stayed for a year, living in a student residence and taking classes in a provincial school; Colin, Laura, Bud, and a foster sister, Patricia, were sent to the school at Portage La Prairie. Not satisfied with the turn of events, Florence made every effort to have her children reunited. In this she was successful and they all attended the Portage school the next year. From there, they attended the residential school at Birtle because the school at Portage did not offer high school. Ida graduated from grade twelve in 1955 at the age of eighteen, winning the Governor General's Award for Highest Achievement in French.

Ida's experiences at the various schools were generally positive. She was highly motivated to do well, and she had an outgoing personality. She had a great deal of love and support from her parents, who actually had adopted some non-Indian practices, such as letter writing and celebrating birthdays with parties. Florence wrote to her children constantly, and Ida became a prolific letter writer exchanging long missives with her mother regularly. Her mother was Ida's closest confidant and support. Though their parents were not directly involved in the children's academic performance and school activities, the children felt very strongly that everything they were doing at the school was done for their mother. Her expectations of them were high and they met these expectations admirably. They wished, above all else, to meet with their mother's approval and follow her guidance. When, as adults, the children became leaders in their own fields, it gave them a great deal of pleasure to have their mother as an honoured guest in their midst.

It is hard to tell whether the children looked forward to or dreaded going to school in the fall. The adults in their lives made the decision and they never questioned it. Since the Round Lake School was situated just across the lake from their home the feeling of separation from their parents was not as great for them as it was for some of the other children. It was easy for the boys to sneak home, especially in winter when it grew dark early. The time between the end of the school day and supper was chore time. The boys hurried through their chores and then sped home for a quick visit and a bite to eat, then hurried back to the school before they were missed at suppertime. Such stolen visits were not an option for the girls because their chores inside the residence were more closely supervised.

Every second Sunday was visitors' day, and the parents brought food. As in all other residential schools, the children were not fed adequately and the Wasacase children have fond memories of the delicious bannock and venison sandwiches their mother brought. Though the children missed their parents and looked forward to seeing them, it was also the thought of food that kept their optimism alive between visits. It was not until they were at the Birtle School that food was reasonably adequate. The Birtle School operated a model farm, so a greater variety of food was available. The school also received more media attention than most other schools and the principal, Mr. Rousseau, was highly conscious of public reaction to the school.

Though Ida did not dislike the schools and did well academically there were some negative consequences to attending residential school. She lost her first language, which she attributed to a particularly traumatic experience. One day she forgot about English and spoke Cree. Punishment was swift and gruesome. She was hit over the head with a board. Tragically, there was a nail in the board, which the supervisor had not noticed, and the nail was driven into her head. After that incident she never spoke Cree again. Even as an adult, she was struck dumb when she attempted to speak in Cree. She could always, however, understand the Cree that was spoken around her. In later years Ida became a strong advocate for the restoration of traditional languages. She was convinced that the first step in improving education for First Nations children was to resurrect language teaching. She firmly believed that once a language is lost, culture loss will follow, and with culture loss comes loss of identity and sense of belonging.

A record of Ida's experiences at Birtle exists in a student newspaper in which she had co-authored an article with Elsie Crate. They described the daily life of the school, mentioning the school routine, sport and social activities, piano and vocal lessons, sewing, and exhibiting articles they had made at the Brandon Fair. Ida participated enthusiastically in United Church activities, such as Canadian Girls in Training, and in the choir. She continued this involvement with the church all her life. The girls concluded their essay as follows:

> As one can see, life in our school follows much the same pattern day by day. However, one cannot expect tranquility at all times around a crowd of spirited boys and girls, but with the help of our principal and using our own common sense trivial disturbances are soon overcome. All in all, life in the Indian school is quite interesting and we know that after we have left, each and every one of us will miss our days here. [9]

Even taking into consideration the fact that the essay would have to have been approved by staff, the up-beat tone reveals much about the personalities of the writers.

The greatest drawback to the schools for Ida was the loneliness, which increased when the children were sent to Manitoba schools. Visits from their parents became less frequent. The subsequent loneliness greatly increased the psychological stress with which they lived. The loneliness that residential school students experienced could be so extreme that they were often in despair, wondering how they could possibly cope. Many children who reached this stage ran away. Ida and her siblings, however, never considered running away because that would have gone against their mother's wishes. Instead, Ida became a role model for younger children at the school and often provided strength and support for despairing youngsters. She set an example for other children on how to survive the residential school experience without being broken by it.

The children at the residential schools turned to each other for comfort, and friends became surrogate parents. Lifelong friendships developed for most residential school survivors since their friends helped them through very impressionable periods of their lives. For the Wasacase children, school staff played a relatively minor role in their lives. Now adults, they have difficulty remembering names and faces of even one staff member. But even though they cannot recall positive role models, they do not harbour any particular bitterness.

A particularly negative aspect of residential school life was the presence of gangs and bullies. Among the boys especially, organized gangs were common. Staff made virtually no attempt to control these gangs unless they threatened each other with violence. To really come to terms with the bullying, staff would have been forced to examine the very philosophy upon which the schools were established, and it is unlikely that they had any desire to do that. There is some evidence that the staff secretly welcomed the gangs since they took care of a lot of the discipline in the school.

Reports from all schools indicate that staff had favourites who often acted as informers. This practice indirectly established a control system, and the gangs emulated this system. The bullies regulated activities within the overall structure imposed on them. If younger children had older siblings to protect them they were, indeed, fortunate.

Ida's twin brother, Colin, did not belong to a gang nor did he bow to gang pressure in spite of the fact that he had lost an arm because of improper medical attention from residential school authorities. He suffered in many ways for his independent spirit, not the least of which was severe beatings from bigger boys as well as from staff. Because he only had one hand, he received double the strokes on that hand. He was sexually abused by bigger boys, but he knew that to report any of this abuse to staff would have been useless and would have led to drastic retribution. Colin often deliberately courted detention because it removed the threat of violence from bullies. Often this detention took the form of eating in isolation at a table in the corner, in view of the other students. It was intended to humiliate but for Colin it was a safe haven—the only place he could be assured that his food would not be taken away from him.

Though there were bullies among the girls, as well, gang activity was not as drastic. Ida also did not bow to the demands of the bullies and at times suffered physically because of it. On one occasion the girls caught her in the bathroom, wrapped towels around her neck, and pulled viciously in two directions. By and large, however, she was not molested. She had a strong, independent spirit that brooked no interference, but largely she relied on her charm and peaceable nature to defuse situations. Unlike Colin, the staff never punished her because she was an excellent student and a co-operative, cheerful worker who accepted the inevitable with good grace. Rather than fear bullies, she was more likely to assist those who were being harassed, so she was rarely bothered. She would threaten to report bullies to staff though she never followed through on these threats. She was well liked by staff, and the bullies were cautious about pushing her around, fearing that she would actually report them. But Ida was not what could be termed a "favourite" because she did not succumb to bullying and manipulation by the staff either. Both she and her brother spent a lot of time in CB (confined to barracks) because they questioned the system. They also wrote out a lot of lines where they promised not to talk back to staff again.

Colin believes that he became cunning and manipulative as a result of his treatment at the school, and he certainly became a thief, as did many children in the schools, because of the chronic food shortages. Whether Ida also stole food is unknown, but it was easier for the girls to obtain forbidden food. They had more access to the kitchen and staff dining rooms and were able to hide their misdeeds more easily. Ida simply did whatever she had to do so well that no fault could be found with her, controlling her anger at injustices with an "I'll show you" attitude. She was largely successful, remaining, even in adulthood, the kind of person who virtually never antagonized or upset people.

Ida and her siblings went home for summer holidays and Christmases when they were younger, but as they grew older they began to make decisions about their own lives. Other activities presented themselves so they did not always go home for the summer. Ida, along with other girls from the school, worked at Clear Lake at jobs arranged for them by the principal of the Birtle School. Ida did everything from chambermaid tasks to working in restaurant kitchens and waitressing.

Though there was no alienation between the parents and children, in later life Ida admitted to some feelings of superiority as her parents clung to traditional ways while she became more acculturated and learned to function in the society outside the reserve. She attempted to influence her parents to become more like the "outside" world. This phenomenon, perhaps, is not unique to residential school children since most children of immigrant parents also struggle with the culture conflicts that Canadianization can create.

A negative influence in Ida's home environment was that her parents instilled in their children the belief that if they were to amount to something in life they would have to find success off the reserve. However negative, this faith in off-reserve success was an accurate reflection of the times because Indian people were bound by the constraints of the Indian Act and a stifling bureaucracy that controlled virtually every aspect of their lives. On-reserve jobs were held by non-Indians; in fact the "Indian industry" provided employment for many mainstream Canadians, a system that did not effectively change until the 1980s. Though Ida's relatives were honoured and influential people within their own culture, the underlying message the children received from their parents was that life was changing and their future lay in another lifestyle. Their parents insisted that their education had equipped them for something better in another milieu. It was not until Ida was well along in her career that the dynamic between Indian Affairs and the people it was established to serve changed so that Indian people could begin to be involved in decision making regarding their own affairs.

After Ida graduated from the Birtle School she attended the Manitoba Teachers' College in Winnipeg, receiving a provincial interim and later a permanent teaching certificate. Her first job was in a one-room provincial school at Ebor, Manitoba. From there she went to Spence's Bridge in BC and taught grades one to three. She continued her studies over a thirteen-year period, and, in 1964, was awarded a B.A., majoring in calculus and French. In 1971 she received another B.A., with majors in anthropology and sociology. In the meantime she had moved north. Ida worked as an elementary school teacher in the Yukon for twelve years, followed by a year as an exchange teacher at a military base in Germany. Upon her return to Canada she worked as curriculum consultant and cross-cultural consultant for the Manitoba Department of Education and then moved on to a job as the Native language coordinator for the Department of Indian Affairs in Ottawa.

Her message as a consultant was always clear: Aboriginal students have to be allowed to develop a sense of their own identity before they will flourish in the public school system. She pointed out that people have to understand their own culture, and be comfortable with it, before they will operate successfully in mainstream society. She drew parallels between Aboriginal children and immigrant children, such as the Chinese and Japanese, who adapt relatively quickly to Canadian education systems. She attributed this to the grounding they have in their own cultures and languages. Though they, too, suffered discrimination, their sense of self-worth had not been destroyed by years of negative indoctrination. She pointed out that Indian students were never taught to understand themselves; they were not taught that, as Indians, they were once proud people with rich cultures.

Throughout her career Ida became involved in many organizations, too many to mention, frequently in an executive position. To name some, she was active in both the Yukon Teachers' Association and *Soest* (the Germany Teachers' Association), the Canadian Indian/ Eskimo Association, the Canadian and American Bilingual Association, the International Reading Association, the International Indian Education Association, the Institute on Higher Education and Learning, and she was on the planning committee for the first World Assembly of First Nations that took place in 1977. She was a council trustee for the Institute for Research on Public Policy and a member of the International Who's Who in Education.

She also served in appointed positions with bodies such as the Saskatchewan Board of Teacher Education, the Regina Urban Native Committee, as senate member for the University of Regina, and the education committee established by the Yukon Tribal Office in 1989. She served on numerous other boards dealing with Aboriginal education at the local, provincial, national, and international levels.

In 1975 Ida began a new phase of her life as she began to work for the Federation of Saskatchewan Indians, first as the education consultant before moving on to the arduous task of establishing the Saskatchewan Indian Federated College (SIFC) under the auspices of the Federation of Saskatchewan Indians (FSI). She laid the groundwork for the first Indian-controlled university program in Canada.

The Indian Teacher Education Program (ITEP) had been established by the FSI in Saskatoon, and it was because of this initiative, which strongly demonstrated the commitment of First Nations people to establish viable education systems, that the idea of the Federated College was born. Cecil King, the first director of ITEP, stated in 1995:

> I would be remiss if I did not mention the drive and enthusiasm brought to the Federated College by Ida Wasacase. She threw herself into the task of making Indian controlled university education a reality.[10]

At the twentieth anniversary of SIFC, notable speakers, such as Allan Blakeney, former premier of Saskatchewan, and Dr. Lloyd Barber, former president of the University of Regina, paid tribute to Ida's contributions, noting especially her vision and tenacity during the early years of the college's inception.

Ida did not believe that separate First Nations schools were necessarily the best solution to the under-education of Aboriginal people. She did believe, however, that no significant changes would take place until trained Aboriginal professionals were hired in all Canadian schools that teach Aboriginal children. Moreover, these professionals would have to receive a university education that incorporated their own values, beliefs, languages, and cultures. Unless they received this kind of relevant training, she feared, First Nations teachers would simply be inclined to perpetuate the colonial systems that had been so damaging to First Nations students in the past. She was confident that institutions like SIFC could make significant changes to the future of Aboriginal education.

Though Ida had two arts degrees she did not have the postgraduate degrees usually expected of people holding university positions. However, she was a dreamer who would never accept second-class status for her people, and her particular talents and commitment were recognized. Once an idea caught her attention she visualized her goal and worked unremittingly toward its achievement.

As the first director of SIFC, Ida was largely responsible for negotiating terms of the relationship between the FSI, the government, and the University of Regina. In May 1976 the FSI entered into a federated agreement with the University of Regina and SIFC was created. The agreement provided for an independently administered university college whose mission was to serve the academic, cultural, and spiritual needs of First Nations people. The programs were academically integrated with the University of Regina and followed all university regulations respecting admissions and development of new programs. Courses were open to both Native and non-Native students. By 1997 enrolment in the introductory Indian Studies course was almost equally split between the two groups. In 1998 SIFC became the first degree-granting tribal college in Canada with full membership in the Association of Universities and Colleges in Canada.

The mission statement of the college has remained unchanged over the years. The SIFC calendar states:

> The mission ... is to enhance the quality of life and to protect and interpret the history, language, culture and artistic heritage of the First Nations. ... [SIFC will] provide opportunities for quality bi-lingual and bi-cultural education under the mandate and control of the First Nations of Saskatchewan.[11]

Culture is considered an essential component of the Indian Studies program and Elders are an integral component of the institution. The calendar goes on to state:

> Indian Studies programs complement the knowledge and traditional teachings of the Elders, competencies in the standard of western educational accomplishments are stressed as only one part of balanced personal development, and students are encouraged to seek cultural growth as a vital part of their education, within the broad-based meaning of university higher education. [12]

Ida loved her years at SIFC, and she remained as director for six years. However, the work was highly stressful, made more so because she was one of the few women in administrative positions in Canadian universities at the time. Always generous to a fault, Ida was known to dip into her own financial resources, especially to bail out students in crises. She never did keep records of what she spent, but later in life she ruefully explained that the money that had been in her bank account for her "old age security" was no longer there. She estimated her personal expenditures at approximately eighty thousand dollars. She likely also suffered additional stress because she did not have the formal university qualifications, and increasing numbers of First Nations members with more acceptable credentials became available to replace her. She moved on to other things in 1982, and her tremendous contributions to the college became history.

For several years she worked as a consultant for the Indian Language Institute, Saskatchewan Indian Nations, and First Nations Holdings, and as head of the Commission of Indian Education Inquiry established by the Assembly of First Nations. She also became involved with the Program for Educating Native Teachers (PENT) at Brandon University and taught courses at the University of Saskatchewan, Laurentian University in Ontario, and McGill University in Montreal. In 1988 she became education consultant for her home reserve of Ochapowace and later became the director of education as the band moved to take control over its own education systems.

Ida threw herself into the Ochapowace project with her usual enthusiasm and was highly successful in her endeavours. She established not only the usual elementary school programs but also nursery-school, kindergarten, and high-school programs at a time when these were not yet common in First Nations communities. The stresses of this job, however, were no less than in her former job so she left the position after a year. She took a job as a centre coordinator at Lynn Lake in northern Manitoba with the Brandon University Northern Teacher Education Program (BUNTEP). BUNTEP was established to provide teacher training in remote northern communities, and, again, Ida threw herself into the task energetically.

However, in May 1993, after less than a year on the job, she passed away after a sudden heart attack. Many of the bereft BUNTEP students travelled to the funeral in southern Saskatchewan to show the love and respect they had for Ida even though her time at the centre had been cut so short. A commemorative plaque was placed on the wall of the Lynn Lake School in her honour.

Ida never married or had children but her brother, Colin, describes her as "a wonderful mother to everyone." She never forgot her early teachings of service to others, and her greatest gift to others was her sharing of herself. In keeping with her desire to share and teach, when she returned to work on her home reserve she combined traditional ways with new customs. Her grandfather's feasts were a part of her cherished childhood memories. Added to her love of traditional feasts was Ida's great fondness for beautiful art objects, such as fine bone china. She became a gracious hostess to the old women of the reserve who dropped by for tea served in bone china cups. She brought a taste of the outside world to reserve customs and was loved and appreciated for the experiences she shared.

The residential schools she had attended were very austere and even cruel. They were highly regimented and demanded conformity. In spite of the stifling environment she endured for thirteen years Ida did well and went on to become one of the very few Aboriginal teachers of her time. But she achieved her success only by accepting that she would have to do it the way mainstream society dictated, and she was driven from her home reserve by lack of opportunity. When she finally went back home she undertook onerous tasks, more onerous because society was not only watching but was sharply critical of all moves made by First Nations people toward even a modicum of equality. Band members themselves harboured a deep-seated distrust of all education systems and some found it hard to accept that one of their own was a part of the system they despised. Ida was a trailblazer, not only as an Indian but also as a woman. On both counts she had to perform better than her peers or be found wanting. She often mentioned the "fish bowl" in which she lived and particularly related to a poem by Cree poet Sheila Erickson:

> if the game is over
> why doesn't someone tell me
> if I won
> why won't anyone applaud
> if it was never called in the first place
> why is everyone watching my moves? [13]

Ida Wasacase

Though she may have felt that she lived a life in a fish bowl, and felt she was judged harshly if she did not meet the standards others set for her, her accomplishments did not go unnoticed. In 1980 she won the Notable Saskatchewan Women Award and the Who's Who in Education Award. In that same year *Chatelaine* magazine listed her among the ten top educators of the year. In 1982 she was made a member of the Order of Canada. The citation stated:

> Ida Wasacase is a Cree who, in the course of a teaching career in the Yukon and elsewhere, equipped herself by advanced study for a wider service to her people. She became a consultant on Indian education and languages; but more recently her main task has been the first and only institution of higher learning controlled by Indians: the Saskatchewan Indian Federated College at the University of Regina. Under her directorship it has strongly encouraged the emergence of the Indian people.

In 1990 the SIFC gave her the Outstanding Educator of the Year Award.

She continues to live on in the hearts of her people, and in October 1998, five years after her death, she was among those especially remembered with a Women's Honour Song at a powwow in Saskatoon, Saskatchewan.

Ida's personal life suffered severely from time to time as the stresses of her situations overwhelmed her. But she was a survivor; she recouped her losses and began again. Her spirit was never broken because she had been raised with sound values and was confident in the love and support of her family. She took great pride in her Cree heritage and would never settle for second place, not for herself or for her people. She was a spiritually strong person, both in the traditional Cree and Christian ways. She is fondly remembered by many who cherish her memory as one of the most generous and thoughtful human beings they have ever known.

Rita Joe

Rita Joe spent a highly stressful childhood in various foster homes. Finally, at age twelve, she requested that Indian Affairs officials place her in the Nova Scotia residential school at Shubenacadie because she felt it would be a safer place for her to be. But residential school life was not much happier than her earlier experiences had been, and soon after she left the school she entered a turbulent marriage. In spite of her difficult life, or perhaps because of it, she eventually was to discover her poetic voice and leave a record of not only her own experiences but also the experiences of many other women like her. Her three books of poetry, *Song of Eskasoni*, *Song of Rita Joe*, and *Lnu and Indians We're Called*, have received much critical acclaim. Rita Joe has received many honours, among them the title of "Poet Laureate of the Mi'kmaq." Her poems touch the souls of Native and non-Native readers alike. Her poetry reveals her deepest feelings, and her gentle voice carries a profound message.

Today Rita Joe considers all Canadians her "family," and she writes for those who wish to know more about her Mi'kmaq culture and understand more about the history of the Mi'kmaq people. She records her personal life, and the history of the Mi'kmaq people of Nova Scotia, in her writing. Her book *Song of Rita Joe: Autobiography of a Mi'kmaq Poet* is dedicated to her children, her children's children, and "all the people who read and identify with my life." She concludes the dedication with the words: *Alasutmay ujit kilow* (I pray for you).

In 1998, when I interviewed Rita Joe for the last time, Parkinson's disease was taking its toll on her body, and she was no longer the energetic activist I had first met. She often closed her eyes as she talked and her words came slowly. She was very emphatic, however, that she still was "today's" Indian. The recognition she has received for her poetry reassures her that she was right in putting her innermost thoughts on paper. She has received many awards and honours but the one she values the most is the Aboriginal Achievement Award presented by her own people. She says, "Finally, after twenty-eight years, my people are saying: Thank you for your words."

Rita Joe feels it is her role to correct how Indian people have been portrayed in literature, the media, and popular culture. She points out that even today, whenever anything is said about Indians in the Maritimes, it is usually negative. She says of herself, "I am always the one who has to tell our story." With the economy of words that is her trademark, she does so very effectively.

She believes Aboriginal history and the role of Aboriginals during and after colonization would have been different if they had been able to express themselves. She points out that the distortions created by biased and incomplete documentation have done more harm than can be imagined. Today Rita Joe passes on the gentle message of healing and believes that, in order to heal, Aboriginal people will have to search out and dwell on the positive. She knows that being a stranger in one's own land is very sad, but she is hopeful that as Aboriginals speak out this can be turned around.

Her strength has come from the teachings she received from her father when she was a young child. She remembers that even during her years at the Shubenacadie School, when she got "mixed up and flustered about the spiritual part of things," it was her concentration on the teachings she received in childhood that gave her the strength to endure and triumph.

When she first began to research her culture she visited the Nova Scotia Museum in Halifax. The curator, Ruth Holmes Whitehead, remembers Rita Joe's first visit vividly. She wrote in the introduction to *Song of Rita Joe*:

I recall she had the quietest way of speaking—she made about as much noise as an ant's foot. Who would have thought that this woman, who looked as if she had been made out of rose petals, could manifest such a powerful voice? [14]

The years and a difficult life have taken their toll but the powerful voice has not been stilled. Rita acknowledges that she can no longer do all she once did and must rely on help from family and friends, but she is also aware of the important role she plays as a female Elder in Aboriginal culture. In one poem she wrote:

I join the dance, sometimes closing my eyes,
Dancing the elderly woman dance,
My feet flat, close to earth. [15]

Rita was born at Whycocomagh, Cape Breton Island, to Joseph Gould Bernard and Annie Bernard, one of seven children. One brother died in infancy and another died at birth, along with his mother. Rita was five years old when her mother died, and today she says she has been grown up since that day. There were some grown-up half-siblings from her father's two previous marriages in Rita's family group as well. Rita recalls her early childhood as being gentle and loving. Everybody in the community was very poor, but they survived by helping one another. She remembers no violence or even anger in her early years.

There were rumours that Rita's great-great grandfather had been a white sailor and Rita recalls stories about her great-grandmother's light features. The rumour was never proven but Rita thinks it was likely true because she has many family members with blue or hazel eyes. Sometimes Rita wonders about her mixed ancestry. She would dearly like to know where she came from but can only be sure of her Mi'kmaq identity.

Rita's father was a handsome man, strict, persuasive, and soft-spoken. He was in his late fifties or early sixties when he married Rita's mother, who was sixteen. Rita cannot remember much about her mother except for her laughter and her very white teeth. Rita believes that she likely was somewhat fat because she remembers resting on a bosomy cushion. Her mother loved to chew spruce gum, laugh, tease, and sing.

Rita fondly remembers her oldest brother who took good care of the younger children and was favoured and adored by his parents. The next two boys were at the Shubenacadie Residential School so Rita hardly knew them. Her sister, who was pretty and had long braided hair, was raised by their grandparents. Rita was the youngest and describes herself as "skinny with constantly sore eyes—the ugly duckling of the family."

Rita recalls the sadness and confusion surrounding her mother's death. Worst was when her grandmother, a rather cross woman at the best of times, pointed a finger at Rita and told her it was all her fault. Five-year-old Rita could not think of anything she might have done except that she had slept with her mother and she thought, perhaps, she had inadvertently kicked her in the stomach. The midwife told her not to worry about her grandmother's accusations. Her mother had been fishing for smelt through the ice and the midwife believed she had become too cold.

After their mother's death the children lived with their grandmother for a while but there was conflict between her and Rita's father so he removed the children from her home. Rita was placed in a succession of foster homes. For the next seven years of her life she was to hear the words "she is an orphan" frequently. The homes were in nearby Mi'kmaq communities and the stays lasted from two weeks to a year. There was a strong belief among the Mi'kmaq that if they were kind to orphans, good things would happen. Rita recalls:

> I always remember the mothers. Native women every-
> where are loving towards children. They would give me
> what I call indifferent love: no touching except on the
> head. [16]

Usually she was adequately cared for physically but missed greatly the real love of her own parents. She had to work very hard to receive even a little bit of affection. She also recalls, however, that at times she had to beg for food, and she became very effective at being quiet, humble, and acquiescent. She learned how to be a survivor, a skill that helped her throughout her life.

Her first foster home was with her stepsister where she was well cared for and was accepted by both the home and the community, but her sister's husband was mean and sadistic. Her father then placed her with his cousin where Rita was happy though the father punished his fourteen-year-old son so severely that Rita was often frightened.

During this time Rita met an old man on the reserve who taught the children Mi'kmaq prayers and talked about their culture. Rita wonders what her identity as an Aboriginal person would be today if she had been allowed to continue living there. This was not to be, however. One day her father came to take her away. She recalls that it always happened that way. Suddenly her father would appear to pick her up and take her to another home without any warning or explanation. Much later she learned that she had to leave this home because of an incident that she had all but forgotten. She had wandered into a bog and become trapped in mud up to her armpits. She waited patiently until she was rescued. Her foster mother was reported to the authorities for not caring for Rita properly, and Rita was moved to a new home.

In her next foster home the father abused Rita sexually. She allowed him to continue the abuse because it brought her a measure of approval, something she craved desperately. She spent much of the time hiding in a tiny crawl space, but she kept quiet about the abuse because her foster mother was kind and Rita loved her dearly. Eventually Rita told another girl at school about what was happening to her. The girl told her mother and Rita was removed to the sounds of her foster mother's accusations. She called Rita an ungrateful liar. Rita was seven years old. Now she says of her childhood:

> Some of the hurt was too great, so I just bundled it up
> and put the little bundles away. Those bundles are still
> on the shelf today and I cannot open some of them.[17]

Two more foster homes followed, but when she was nine Rita went back home to live with her father and three other siblings. The older children looked after her and she was very happy. For a year she experienced love, family support, celebrations, and she remembers her father reading to them from a book of Mi'kmaq syllabics. All this was to end when her father died of pneumonia. His last words to his family were: "Do not let your sister go to Oxford." Her siblings, however, were young adults, engrossed in their own lives, and Rita was sent to Oxford to live with her half-brother, William.

Life at Oxford introduced Rita to many new experiences. It was a non-Aboriginal community, and she faced racial discrimination daily. She stayed home the first year, but the second year she went to school and did make some friends. Her friends, however, were never allowed to come to her house, nor did their parents allow her to visit them. Her brother was a bootlegger and not only did she experience drinking for the first time in her life, but she soon became "the best underage home-brew maker in Cumberland County."

Many frightening things happened to Rita when she was living in Oxford, surrounded as she was by alcoholism and violence. She was exploited by the adults who frequented her brother's house, and on one occasion was forced to get drunk. She received no teachings of any kind but she was expected to do all the manual labour. If they asked her if she wanted to go to residential school she said no because that was what she thought they expected her to say. On one occasion a Mountie came to look for her but they hid her under a couch. She could have touched the Mountie's foot but was too afraid to try.

Finally, when she was twelve, she understood that she had to get out of her situation and she wrote a letter to the Indian agent. She mailed it with the help of the woman at the community store. A week later, the agent and a Mountie picked her up at school and took her to Shubenacadie Residential School. They fed her a good dinner along the way and even bought her a chocolate bar. Rita recalls that her first impression of the school was of its beauty and elegance, so different from the foster homes she had been in.

She calls her four years at the school "memorable." She recognizes that very bad things happened at the school, and in one poem she calls it a "deluge of misery," but for her it was no worse than what she had already experienced. In fact, she received some small kindnesses from several sisters and responded with love and gratitude.

She was very eager to please. She had learned many survival skills before she entered the school so she knew how to adjust to the routine. But as a neglected foster child she had experienced unusual freedom so she found the regimen of the school galling. On the other hand, she was anxious to learn the skills children learn in normal homes and approached tasks like cooking, sewing, knitting, cleaning, and laundry with great enthusiasm.

She found the relentless pressure to conform hard to bear. In one of her poems she refers to the "mind mistreatment" the children experienced. Her spirituality, language, and culture were taken from her, and her most widely anthologized poem is entitled, "I Lost My Talk":

> I lost my talk
> The talk you took away
> When I was a little girl
> At Shubenacadie school.

The poem ends:

> So gently I offer my hand and ask
> Let me find my talk
> So I can teach you about me.[18]

One particular kindness she remembers was an anonymous Christmas parcel she received. Other students received gifts from their parents but there was never a parcel for her. Rita understood that a compassionate nun had provided her with a small gift package of fruit, candies, hand lotion, handkerchiefs, and pretty hair pins. Rita accepted the gift with exquisite grace and gratitude.

Rita did not leave the school, even for a holiday, until she was sixteen. About thirty girls had to stay for the summers because they had no place to go. The school did make an effort to make the summers more enjoyable. She remembers a special summer treat was Corn Flakes for breakfast! Whether in summer or winter, above all activities, Rita enjoyed spending time in the school library. Access to the library was restricted and library privileges were rewarded for good behaviour. Since Rita was highly adept at determining what behaviours were expected of her, she was allowed into the library once a week.

When she was sixteen, the nuns presented her with two options. She could continue at the school and become a nun, perhaps even go to college, or she could get a job at the Halifax Infirmary. Rita did not hesitate; she chose the job. She wanted to get away from the nuns, and she was aching for freedom. The nuns said good-bye and put her on the train with one change of clothing. As the train pulled away, Rita cried. The school had been her home for four years. She had no home to return to and, at sixteen, she felt she was truly all alone in the world. However, she also felt great freedom and vowed that never again would anyone else regulate her life. Most of all she vowed that her spiritual life would be her own, and for years after she left the school she never went near a church.

She was met at the station in Halifax by a nun from the Infirmary and it was only then that she realized the place was run by nuns. Not much had changed in her life; she fell into the routine easily and worked hard. She celebrated her first paycheque by buying red shoes. Friends suggested she buy a brassiere, as well, since her strip of folded flour sack held in place with elastic snaps was not very chic. She learned about shampoo, make-up, and all the other things her peer group valued. She was also very vulnerable and naïve and her experiences with boys and alcohol were disastrous. The school invited her back to talk about life after leaving the school but Rita was too ashamed to go. She had become exactly what the nuns had predicted, a girl who leaves school and is corrupted by the world.

Rita left the hospital for what she believed would be a less onerous waitressing job, but waitressing turned out to be even more difficult because of customer abuse. As well, at this time a relationship with a boy resulted in pregnancy. She gave her son, Eddy, to her sister to raise. She became pregnant a second time and left for Boston, where her brother lived. She immediately got a job in Boston at Beacon Hill Hospital and then looked for her brother only to find that he had left for Canada. His friends, however, were happy to meet her and they helped her. She was comfortable with the Mi'kmaq people she met in Boston.

When her pregnancy was advanced she supported herself by babysitting her friends' children and then went on Mothers' Allowance when her daughter was born. Friends offered to adopt the baby, but Rita could not part with her. Soon she was pregnant again, thinking she had found the man she would marry. The relationship did not work out, so she became engaged to an easy-going Mi'kmaq widower with children of his own. Before they could get married, however, she met Frank Joe, who was also engaged to be married. It was not long before Rita and Frank wrote "Dear John" letters to their partners. They married shortly thereafter.

Rita says today, "Frank Joe was a good man. I loved him so deeply ... I am not sorry to have chosen him." The early years were good, but then the storybook version she had hoped for faded. No matter how hard she tried to make the marriage work, Frank mistrusted her. He had a severe drinking problem. She was a battered woman for many years, but the eight children she had with her husband gave her the courage to persevere.

When Frank was seven, his father had died. He was sent to residential school. For him it was a very negative experience, and he was very bitter. He was a very bright thirteen-year-old in grade nine when his mother took him out of school to help support the family. He had to work much too hard for his young age. He was bitter because he felt he had potential that he had never had the opportunity to fulfil. During all their married years Rita attempted to build up his fragile ego.

Rita now says that she put up with a lot of things during her marriage, always hoping for a better tomorrow. Poverty dogged their footsteps; Frank eventually became an operating room technician but the pay was still inadequate and they were always strapped for money. That Frank drank on payday made financial matters even worse. Although he loved his stepdaughter, he insisted that Rita give up for adoption the son with whom she was pregnant when she met Frank.

They moved to Halifax, and because they had such difficulty making ends meet, they decided to send Rita's oldest daughter, Phyllis, to the residential school at Shubenacadie. Rita took the other children and moved to Eskasoni to live with Frank's mother. Today Phyllis understands why her mother had to send her to the school. The care Phyllis received at the school was good and her experience was not particularly negative.

Living with Frank's family was difficult for Rita. Her mother-in-law was a bossy, assertive woman who used loud, foul language, but eventually Rita did come to love her and even won her respect. It was a hard-drinking and smoking family. Rita worked very hard to look after her children and do the housework. On the positive side, she fit into the reserve life easily and today she says:

I have been sharing problems and jokes with friends, especially other women on the reservation, since I arrived in Eskasoni in 1956. The friends I made then are still my friends. That is why I like living on a reservation, even today. [19]

After ten years of marriage Frank built a home for them. Phyllis came home from the residential school and life would have been good if it had not been for Frank's drinking and womanizing. Rita's reaction to his womanizing sometimes turned violent. Once she smashed all the windows on his car; another time she assaulted the other woman. As a result she spent a night in jail and was fined twenty-five dollars.

Frank was a hard worker and supported the family but when he drank he was abusive. Eventually Rita stopped trying to hide the abuse and often ran to others for help. Once, his mother hit him with a piece of wood and told him to leave Rita alone, but it was not until Rita went to the Elders for help that Frank gradually began to control his temper.

Rita began to write when she was in her thirties. Fortunately her husband and family supported her efforts. She was heartsick at the portrayal of Aboriginal people in the material her children were learning at school. She felt they were being immersed in an alien culture and wrote in one of her poems:

Let us trade places just this once
And you listen while I go on about my culture
Important just like yours
But almost dead. [20]

At first she was very cautious about what she wrote. She told her children not to accept stereotypes, but at the same time she told them not to make waves. She did not want to offend the educators who, she assumed, must have known better even though that fact was not readily apparent.

Her first poem was about Eskasoni and was published in a Mi'kmaq newspaper. The response was so positive that soon she was writing a monthly column in the *Micmac News*. Many of the stories were about traditional ways and medicine and information she got from the

Elders. Gradually Mi'kmaq words began to creep into her poetry. Soon she dropped her regular column and wrote occasional stories, writing in a loving and respectful way, especially about people who had passed on. She wrote poetry about her various life experiences, except for the battering. She did not wish to step on "live toes."

In 1974 she entered a literary contest in Halifax. She recalls that her poetry was a collection of frustrated and angry words, crying out for communication. She won, and was invited to an awards ceremony in Halifax. When she told her husband she recalls that his face lit up; she believes it was because he was thinking of all the free booze and women at the ceremony. She hardly cared because she was so elated, seeing the poetry as her own accomplishment and triumph.

Rita attended the ceremony in borrowed moccasins and a Native dress made of polyester with leather fringe. The Writers' Federation found a publisher for her and assigned a professional writer to help her polish her work. He told her she cried too much in her poetry so she tried to be more assertive. She also came to realize that though Indians have been researched to death, non-Aboriginals know virtually nothing about them. She still calls her first book, *Poems of Rita Joe* (1978), her "cry and look at me" book.

Her publication led to speaking engagements in schools arranged by the Nova Scotia Department of Education. She could hardly afford to do this since the individual schools were responsible for paying her and her honorarium was usually a book or a small craft item, the best the cash-strapped schools could afford. Then the Canada Council for the Arts contacted her and her financial situation improved; soon she was booked six months in advance.

She spoke to a wide variety of audiences, but one memorable occasion still stands out in her mind. It was a police function. A young Indian man spoke ahead of her and the audience did not listen. Then a drummer, a young woman, performed and met with the same fate. By the time it was Rita's turn she was angry. She slapped the podium with a resounding crash and said, "You guys never listen! You never listen! Have never listened for five hundred years and you're still not listening!" Needless to say, they listened that day.

After Rita's first book was published she felt she needed to upgrade her education in order to live up to the praise and accolades she was receiving. She completed grade twelve and took a business course, finally learning to type properly. She was considering college when Frank expressed a desire for university education as well. Optimistic as always, Rita decided to support his aspirations. Meanwhile, their daughter's marriage had ended and she expressed a desire to go to university, too. Rita put her own aspirations on hold and looked after her grandchildren so her daughter and her husband would be free to study.

Both her daughter and Frank got bachelor of education degrees. Frank got a job with the Micmac Children and Family Services and immediately began working on a sociology degree. His studies seemed to meet a need that had never been met before. He quit drinking and began to understand his past behaviour. Rita recalls that after this turnaround his expressions of love for her were never-ending, and in the last years of their life together there was love and peace. One conversation with Frank is etched in Rita's memory. Frank told her he had gone to university in order to be better than she was. Once they had talked all that through, she says, they laid all the old demons to rest.

Rita believes her children felt fear, love, and respect for their father. Later they felt great admiration for him when he turned his life around. They also learned not to accept abusive relationships. All her daughters, except one, had abusive relationships with men, but they ended their marriages quickly when the abuse started.

Rita's second book, *Song of Eskasoni*, was published in 1988. During the intervening years Rita had spent much time researching her history and consulting with others about how the early missionaries and explorers might have misinterpreted the Mi'kmaq sounds. They speculated on what might have taken place. Rita says she was "at war" in her second book, but it was a gentle war as she attempted to correct historic wrongs. Some called her the "Warrior Poet."

Between 1980 and 1989 Rita was busy with many speaking engagements and Frank accompanied her. They called these trips their "little honeymoons." While on one such honeymoon in Maine, content and at peace with each other, Frank died of a heart attack. The day after the funeral one of her sons drove Rita to a speaking engagement. She viewed it as the beginning of a new life without Frank. She also made a vow to speak and write only the truth from then on. She warned her children that the truth might be hurtful to them. When her third book, *Lnu and Indians They Call Us,* was published in 1991, it included a poem about wife battering.

Rita believes she has grown along with her poetry. In *Lnu* she felt free to analyse her language and she began to write about her spirituality. Her autobiography, published in 1996, contains many details about her life that she had never divulged before, many details that her children did not know.

In 1989 Rita received the Order of Canada. An experience in a store just before the ceremony dampened her exhilaration but she soon regained control of herself. She was looking for a hat to wear and the clerk asked her if she was the same woman whom she had been hearing about on the radio. Rita offered her hand but the clerk did not take it. Instead she challenged her with, "Where did you go to university?" "The dreary war never ends," Rita thought to herself, but nevertheless, she explained courteously that she had never gone to university but spoke at many of them. She concludes a poem about the experience with:

> She does not know I sense ill will
> So gently I turn around and walk out,
> Looking for another store.[21]

The ceremony at Rideau Hall, however, was all that Rita had hoped for. She realized that she had crossed a bridge and no longer felt insecure as an Aboriginal person. She knows the honour was given to her as an individual but believes that the significance of the honour is that it will have meaning for all the coming generations of Mi'kmaq. With gracious courtesy she wrote in a poem:

> To me, the medal is for my people, the coming generation.
> The greeting of the hand over the heart has earned a
>   merit.
> Thank you, my country, for accepting my salutation. [22]

In 1991, on Prime Minister Brian Mulroney's recommendation, she was flown to Ottawa to meet Queen Elizabeth. She had been briefed on protocol and knew she was to wait for the Queen to make the first move and not speak until spoken to. When she stood in front of the Queen, however, Rita saw only another woman like herself, and she experienced good feelings emanating from her. Impulsively she asked, "How are your grandchildren?" The Queen was a bit flustered because Rita had broken protocol, but then she gave Rita a big smile and replied eagerly, "Oh, they're fine!" Rita says of the incident, "She acted like a grandma. I felt happy after that." Later, others asked her what she had done to make the Queen smile like that and she knew she had done a good thing.

Rita operates a craft shop in the summers, which she calls *Minuitagn* (Recreate), from the basement of her home. After Frank died, the shop, along with her writing and many speaking engagements kept her busy until ill health forced her to slow down. Many honours continued to come her way, including an honorary doctorate degree from Dalhousie University, and the Aboriginal Achievement Award.

Rita believes she has always kept her traditional Native spirituality alive. She walks two paths, one "begging you to understand how good my people are," and the other, her own spiritual path. She got a solid grounding in her spirituality from her father and other Mi'kmaq people when she was very young, and though traditional ceremonies were not performed like they are today, she did hear Native singing, hymn singing in Mi'kmaq, and Mi'kmaq talk.

When she was in her thirties she began to have prophetic dreams and other experiences that reassured her that spiritual forces exist. Today she is acutely aware of these forces around her. All her life, whatever befell her, she would talk to her Creator in Mi'kmaq. She regrets that there has not been a greater melding of Christianity and traditional spirituality today. She is saddened by the fact that residential schools taught people to be afraid of their own traditional spirituality. For herself, she is convinced of its goodness.

Rita believes there is a reason for her writing; it is to bring honour to the Mi'kmaq people. She feels that Aboriginal people are survivors with much to offer society but that often mainstream Canadians are bored by Native concepts. They know so little about Aboriginals that they absorb the negative images without realizing that they are only one aspect of Aboriginal life. Many remain indifferent to other aspects of Aboriginal life. A recurring theme in her writing is that Aboriginal people are still strangers in their own land.

Rita's poetry is being put to music. Her "Oka Song" has been translated into Mohawk, and she was especially moved when "And Then We Heard a Baby Cry," a Christmas carol, was sung by the Eskasoni choir at midnight mass. In 1996 a Dutch musician composed a symphony based on her work.

Rita lives peacefully in her Eskasoni home overlooking beautiful Bras D'Or Lake on Cape Breton Island. She is an honoured Elder in the community, called "Granny" or "Auntie" by most. One of her daughters passed away after a very difficult marriage, causing the family great sadness, but Rita says, "my love overflows for my children and my twenty-two grandchildren." She looks forward to the great-grandmother phase of her life.

Today Rita is content that her words have reached many people and perhaps have helped to correct some of the misconceptions of the past. She explains that in her culture there is a term for a person with a brave heart, *kinap*. She says in traditional times it was men who were referred to as *kinap*, but she thinks that there must have been some women who were *kinap*, too.

Anyone who has had the privilege of meeting Rita Joe, or even those who have only read her poetry, will not doubt that there were and are women who would be called *kinap*. Rita Joe is, indeed, a woman with a brave and loving heart.

Alice French (Masak)

Alice French has written two books about her residential school experiences. She was living in Churchill, Manitoba, with her husband, RCMP officer Dominick French, when she began to record her memories. An artist/writer friend, H. Albert Hochbaum, urged her to submit her writing for publication. Though Alice had written largely for herself and her children, she liked the idea of publishing a book. She felt it was important that her children understand what her life had been like, and she hoped the book might help explain to the world how the lives of the Inuit had been changed and shaped by a culture that was not their own.

Unaware of the finer points of the publishing industry she sent the manuscript for *My Name is Masak* to Hurtig in Edmonton and to Peguis Publishers in Winnipeg simultaneously. Both publishers, Mel Hurtig and Mary Scorer, who then owned Peguis, accepted the manuscript but Peguis' acceptance letter arrived first and consequently they published the book in 1973. This double acceptance was highly encouraging for Alice who interpreted it as a sign that her writing had merit and that she was "doing something right."

The book was successful, more so because it appeared at a time when relatively little had been written about residential schools, and even less had been written from a First Nations perspective. Alice felt the need to write a sequel because in *My Name is Masak* she dealt largely with her childhood, both when she was with her family and when she was at the residential school. It is predominantly descriptive and serves as a fine source of background information for her second book. The sequel, *The Restless Nomad*, which analyses the impact the system has had on her life, took much longer to write.

Alice's life after residential school was fraught with difficulties. Her first marriage was not a happy one and she had to leave her sons behind with their father and grandparents. Writing the post-residential school book created considerable emotional anguish for her as she was forced to come to terms with what had happened to her in the course of her life. As she became more immersed in the writing of the book she became overly sensitive and angry. At first neither she nor her family realized what was causing all the upheaval in the home, but eventually they came to understand and accept that her unpredictable emotions arose from the turmoil she was attempting to sort out. In 1992, after five agonizing years of struggle, the manuscript, *The Restless Nomad*, was published by Pemmican.

Today Alice and her husband, Dominick, live in an attractive bungalow with a large vegetable garden in a typical middle-class city neighbourhood. When I visited Alice at her home we sat formally in the living room for a few minutes, then she suggested we move to the kitchen. Assuming I drink coffee, she asked Dominick to make it because she claims she only knows how to make tea. Then we settled down to serious talk. Alice's answers to my questions were clearly formulated, carefully worded and comprehensive. The relatively simple style of her books is not indicative of her mastery of the English language, the depth and complexity of her thoughts, and the storyteller cadence of her delivery.

Her books are narratives, told as directly as any traditional story teller would tell them. Discussing the more abstract concepts about the effects of culture loss and the difficulty of reintegration are complex issues, and it is very important to Alice that every nuance of her speech be interpreted accurately. She takes great exception to the idea that residential school students were "brainwashed." She feels she was never brainwashed and listeners can not doubt the validity of this assertion for even a moment.

Today she finds life satisfying. She has sixteen grandchildren and three step-grandchildren whom she considers her own. She has three great-grandchildren and admits to having lost track of birthdays, but she does give Christmas gifts to each and every one. Her life revolves around her home, her husband, and her family; however, she feels that she needs to write another book about contemporary issues. Her computer waits patiently as Alice ruminates over exactly what she wants to include in this book.

The dedication in *My Name is Masak* explains the purpose of Alice's writing. She says:

> Listen, listen my children.
> And I'll tell you a story of where I
> was born and where I grew up.
> About your ancestors and the land
> we live on.
> About the animals and the birds.
> So you can see.[23]

Though Alice was born on Baillie Island in the Northwest Territories, her parents were classed as Alaskan Eskimos. Her father, Anisalauk, was born and raised in Alaska. Alice remembers him as a loving, teasing, affectionate person. His father was a Laplander who was fluent in both English and Eskimo. School attendance was compulsory and Alice's father completed grade ten with little difficulty. In 1923 he travelled to Herschel Island on a Canalaskan Trading Co. ship, then to Baillie Island. He worked as an interpreter for the police and augmented his income with trapping.

Alice's mother was also Alaskan Eskimo but after her marriage to Anisalauk made her home on Baillie Island. Here the couple came to be known as Charles and Lily Smith. The sandy point where Alice was born had a trading post, Roman Catholic and Anglican missions, an RCMP detachment, and a small settlement of Inuit. It has been washed into the Beaufort Sea without leaving a trace.

The family lived a very traditional life, and as a result many taboos were avoided during Alice's birth. Her mother had taken no chances in breaking any of these taboos during her pregnancy. As other women gathered around, her labouring mother continued to prepare food for the visitors who would come to celebrate once the baby was born. The women visited and drank tea and talked about anything except the birth; to do so would be to tempt fate and perhaps bring on a disaster.

Once Alice's safe delivery was completed the men were sent for and an oilcloth was spread on the floor on which food and utensils were placed. They gathered around to discuss suitable names for the baby. They decided on *Masak,* after her paternal grandmother, and *Alice,* after her maternal grandmother. During the meal the virtues of the name-sakes were discussed to help Alice grow up to be a worthy human being.

Many taboos were avoided after Alice's birth as well. The ancient time-honoured customs played an important role in Inuit culture. They brought peace of mind and a sense of well-being and belonging. They were adapted and reinvented, as foreign customs and material goods were thrust upon the Inuit people, but still formed an integral part of the culture.

In the Inuit culture, as in many traditional cultures, boys were preferred over girls because they would eventually be the hunters and providers, ensuring the continuity of the families. Girls, on the other hand, were not seen as being able to do much, though in truth, without the support of the women, the hunters and providers would have been a sorry lot indeed. A girl was taught that she had little value until she married and brought home a good provider. The girls were taught to cook and sew and in that way help their husbands. And girls, of-course, gave birth to children, preferably boy children.

However, Alice's life and training for life was profoundly changed as the residential school she attended disrupted her develop-ment in a way that could never be redeemed. Alice's training was dis-rupted when she was taken from her culture at an early age. When she finally left the residential school her chief concern was that she did not have the requisite skills to take care of a young hunter and she would be forced to marry some old man who could no longer compete with the more proficient hunters. But that was many years into the future.

Had Alice been born a boy, a birthday feast with great delicacies would have taken place. Since she was a girl, a simple meal of daily fare like rabbit, ptarmigan, and caribou was sufficient.

When Alice was four years old her parents moved to Cambridge Bay where her father worked as interpreter and clerk at the Canalaskan Trading Co. They lived in a prefabricated house, but their lifestyle continued to be traditional. Caribou and tomcod were their daily fare and Alice was dressed in a traditional parka made of caribou summer skin that had lost its long hairs, trimmed with wolverine. She wore mukluks made of the skin of caribou legs. Most of the Inuit still lived nomadic lives but Christmas and Easter brought large numbers of people to the settlement for traditional games, feasts, and dog-team racing, which lasted a week.

When Alice was five and her brother was three a flu epidemic hit the community and many people died. Their mother, too, took ill and never fully recovered. When Alice was seven they moved to Aklavik (Inuvik) because their mother had tuberculosis and had to be hospitalized.

The children were placed in the All Saints Anglican Residential School while the mother was taken to the Anglican hospital. Alice's father went back to the trapline and the children did not see him for a long time. Alice was allowed to visit her mother freely but one day the minister came to tell her that her mother had died. Alice had visited her mother only that morning and did not believe him. She ran to the hospital to look for her but all she found was an empty room with a carefully made-up bed. With profound understatement she says, "I felt terribly alone."

The school at Aklavik was much like other residential schools across Canada, though some Inuit staff were employed as dormitory supervisors. The house mother was Lily Smith's cousin. This did not afford Alice any special privileges, but it was reassuring to her to have a relative nearby.

The regimen at the school does not seem to have been as severe as it was in some other residential schools. The diet was adequate, if somewhat monotonous by today's standards. Alice was terrified of the ghost stories other girls delighted in telling after the lights were out at bedtime, and she yearned for contact with her younger brother. She was, however, a tractable, sensible child and she adapted quickly to the school routine with good grace.

Rules at the school were more lax than in many southern

schools. Children who lived in Aklavik were free to visit parents on Saturday afternoons; those who were without parents were free to go home with friends. They enjoyed the freedom away from the over-crowded school and took ample snacks back with them when they returned. The school itself gave them seven candies a week, which the children guarded carefully to make them last for seven days.

Alice's memories include both good and bad events. She hated cod liver oil but today acknowledges that it was beneficial to their health. She hated the bone-chilling walks they had to take because their cloth coats did not provide enough protection from the cold; she had experienced the cosiness of caribou clothing in her early years and knew that warmer clothing existed. Today she says: "I hated to be cold. I was never cut out to be an Inuit!" She hated the fire-drills that forced them outside even into freezing cold, but even then she recognized that fire was a worrisome hazard in the wooden buildings. Children were strapped at the school but she feels that the children had an element of choice; to her knowledge, if children were strapped it was because they had broken a rule.

Alice remembers with fondness her first Christmas with Santa, candy and the gift of a new doll. She accepted all the new and different experiences at the school with curiosity. She missed her parents and contact with her brother, but her English was good so she did not feel the frustration and fear many other students experienced. Some staff members were cruel to the more vulnerable students, which Alice found disturbing, but she herself was always well treated.

She did, however, find many aspects of the school puzzling. She was curious about what a toothbrush was and was told it was used to keep one's teeth from getting holes in them. That seemed a strange concept but not as strange as combing her hair with coal oil to kill lice when she did not have any lice in the first place.

Alice experienced difficulty with arithmetic, but she loved learn-ing to read and write. She discovered a vast store of knowledge and developed a love of reading that has lasted a lifetime. However, subject matter in the books they read could be very confusing to her. Humpty Dumpty, sitting on a wall dressed as a human being was bizarre enough, but when the teacher taught them to say "Hey Diddle Diddle," Alice felt something was really terribly wrong. She wrote in *My Name is Masak*:

Now I knew cats could not play fiddles. I did not know whether cows could jump over the moon or not, but I was sure that dishes could not run and certainly not with spoons. I worried about my teacher sometimes. She did not seem to know the difference between what creatures could and could not do. [24]

Alice and her brother stayed at the school without a break for three years. Other students left to go home for the summer but a few children remained to rattle around the almost empty school buildings. It was all very spooky for the ones who were left behind. Most of the staff left for the summer, as well, but some teachers who had come from England could not afford to go home so they attempted to make life more bearable for the children with camping trips and picnics.

Wisely, the school recognized some of the realities the children would face once they left the school. Each child was given muskrat traps and taught how to use them. They sold the skins at the Hudson's Bay store, and, as well, the school paid them twenty-five cents for each rabbit they had snared, which were then used for food. The more proficient students made quite a bit of spending money, and they were given the opportunity to handle this money themselves. Students in some other schools never saw money, and some did not even know how to count change when they graduated.

The fourth summer brought major changes to the lives of Alice and her brother. Their father had remarried and the children spent the summer with their parents and their new extended family. Though Alice would have preferred to spend the summer with her mother's parents, Grandma Susie, her stepmother's mother, ruled the family with an iron hand. She said Alice was now a part of her family and the case was closed.

Alice accepted this, as she did most things, and Grandma Susie was eventually to become a very strong influence in her life. Susie was an Inuit doctor with blue tattoo marks on her chin; her black and grey hair hung to her shoulders. Some of her doctoring methods were highly unconventional, but she saved the lives of many people in the Mackenzie Delta. Alice estimates that at least half the people living in the area came to her for help at one time or another.

Grandma Susie was a strict taskmaster, and Alice had a taste of what lay in store for her as she matured into an Inuit woman. Try as she might, Alice had difficulty mastering the skills she had lost. If her stitches were too big, Susie's finger, encased in a metal thimble, came down on Alice's head with a painful knock. Even at ten years of age Alice knew she had to learn these skills or she would be useless as a marriage partner. It was her Grandfather Amos who acted as a buffer between her and Susie, pointing out that Alice could not be expected to do everything right so quickly.

Basically, Alice enjoyed the summer, except for the dogs. She was mortally afraid of dogs yet had to help with loading and unloading them as they moved up the coastline by boat. Her struggles were exacerbated when Grandma Susie yelled at her father, "You have brought me a grandchild who is clumsy." Struggles with dogs continued for Alice once she left school but she did eventually get to the point where she could drive a dog team. Asked in 1999 if she could still drive a dog team she answered, "I could if I had to," but then added very emphatically, "but I don't want to."

That summer provided the opportunity for Alice to socialize with her own people. Girls were strictly guarded and chaperoned by grandmothers, and Susie was hawklike in her vigilance. Alice's "clumsiness" was again in evidence when she attempted to learn drum dancing. Succinctly she says, "I was not a graceful child."

In fall Alice's brother was allowed to stay home because his family recognized that he had more important skills to learn at home, but Alice had to return to school. She was returned with a generous supply of caribou meat, rabbits, and fish. Reindeer herding had begun in the north as an industry, and the government donated surplus reindeer meat to the school as well. A warehouse was used to store the meat, but Alice recalls it was "a little high" by the end of the school year.

Her parents removed Alice from the school when she was eleven. Unfortunately, she had an accident that summer and suffered severe concussion. It was three months before she was fully cognizant of her whereabouts again. The family had given up hope for her recovery. She did recover enough to participate in camp life but then suffered a severe cold. The family decided she would be better off in town where she would be close to medical help. She returned to Aklavik where she was placed in a boarding home with a young couple in town. Her father promised to pick her up the next summer, and she began a life of babysitting in the morning and going to school in the afternoon. The foster mother was a former teacher from the school, and she and Alice got on well. Then the family was transferred and Alice found herself back in the residence.

Her family did not return for her as promised, so she was able to spend more time with her maternal grandparents. Though she loved her grandparents and she did not dislike school she became miserable and discouraged. She felt she would never, ever be able to leave the school and would, in fact, grow old there. Deep depression overwhelmed her. When she turned fourteen she realized that she had spent seven of those years confined to the school.

She tried hard not to feel unloved and unwanted, envisioning all the unforeseeable problems that had kept her family from her. When a letter finally came from her father saying that he was coming for her, she was sceptical and was a nervous wreck before he finally arrived. At the end of *My Name is Masak* she recalls:

> It was sad to say goodbye to my friends but at the same time I felt a great sense of relief, like a prisoner whose sentence is finally over. When the door closed behind me and my father I felt like a bird flying home to the vast tundra. [25]

In 1976 *My Name is Masak* was a relative novelty. The general attitude toward residential schools at that time was that they were a necessary evil, and people who objected to them were seen as ungrateful complainers. A few schools were actually still operating in 1976. The simple story of a lonesome child was appreciated for its sensitivity, beauty, and humour. Alice appeared to be a well-adjusted child who had suffered separation from her parents, leading to loneliness and alienation, but many children in many different circumstances suffer this same fate. Alice hints at cultural disruption in her first book but this was not a phenomenon that was generally understood. Many other survivors were also suffering from this disruption, but in 1976 their voices were largely silent. Assimilation was still the generally accepted policy, and the prevailing attitudes were that the sooner Aboriginal cultures accepted "white" values and lifestyles, the sooner the problems would disappear.

Alice accepted none of these platitudes. *The Restless Nomad* continues where *My Name is Masak* left off. She dedicated the book to "my people who have gone from dogsled to the mechanized age with some difficulties and with great courage." She also acknowledges the encouragement she received from her family to "continue writing and to put into words all the heartache and happiness of growing up in these changing times."

The Restless Nomad begins when her father picked her up at the school. She felt she was the one who had been lost, having been away from home for so long. She explains, on the opening page, that her name is *Masak*. In the Inuit culture people need to know who they are and what names they are called. She was named after her grandmother but that was taken away from her when the school called her by her second, Anglicized name. When her father came for her he called her *Masak* and she was reassured that her identity as an Inuit was still there. She was going home and she felt it was the happiest moment of her life.

When they passed the school she said a silent prayer that she would never have to see the inside of it again. The people had been kind enough to her but she had been desperately lonely. Her father tried to warn her about the challenges that lay ahead for her. She would have to relearn the language and customs. There would be changes in diet. She was so euphoric over leaving that she paid scant attention to his predictions. A friend of her father pointed out her predicament much more bluntly. He asked her:

> What has the school taught you, except the English language, even to the point where you can not even talk your own tongue? Can you scrape and sew hides for clothing? Do you know how to skin the furs that are brought home? What kind of a wife will you be since you must learn all these things which go into homemaking before you can get married? [26]

What, indeed, was to become of her? She did have great confidence in her ability to learn, and she reminded herself that she was not getting married, she was merely going home. Later, when reality struck, she says:

> I wondered what people would have done if they had been taken away from their cultures into my world ... had been taught our language and culture, and had our phi-losophy of life ingrained into them? Then when they were teenagers, what if we suddenly sent them back to their own people to relearn their own cultural heritage from scratch, and to forget all they had been taught when they were young because it was impractical in the world in which they were living? [27]

Her conclusion was that it would have been just as difficult for white people as it was for Aboriginal people. She goes on to explain:

> Each group of people have their own rules and way of life that are best suited to their own environment. They should be allowed to keep that heritage and not be told it is not the right way to live. [28]

Much as Alice had looked forward to life with her family, she found it was fraught with difficulties. Her father and brother could speak English but her stepmother and step-siblings spoke only Inuvialuktun. She did understand it but her attempts at learning to speak it made her the butt of many jokes and caused her extreme embarrassment. Her people still laugh at her today when she tries to express herself in Inuvialuktun. Her speech is very slow because she has to think in English and then translate her thoughts into Inuvialuktun.

She had to get used to what to her were overpowering smells of muktuk and dog mush. She had to adjust to what the residential schools had called immodesty as mothers nursed their babies, and she had to overcome feelings of revulsion as mothers chewed the food for older infants. She had to learn again the life of generous sharing, a custom that had not been valued at the school.

Most difficult was to learn the many tasks that would make her a marriageable young woman: to drive a dog team, chop firewood, haul chunks of ice, snare rabbits, prepare dog food, shoot accurately, keep a fire going, skin furs, sew clothes. The list of tasks she did not know how to do appeared to be endless. Even routine tasks like cooking were difficult because she had been taught to cook in an institution where ingredients had been measured out for the students to mix. She endangered her own life and the lives of others with her inexperience and clumsiness, and she was afraid of the solitude of the bush. Eventually she did learn all the tasks and most of all she learned to love the out-of-doors. She says:

> If you have never gone out in the moonlight and walked
> in the bush by yourself, you have missed one of the most
> beautiful experiences of your life. [29]

The question of marriage preyed on her mind, and she knew that Grandmother Susie worried about it too. One night when they were camped on the coast, Alice and her young aunt came home from a dance in the settlement later than their curfew allowed. When her grandmother called Alice over to her, Alice assumed it was for a scolding. She was stunned when her grandmother informed her that a marriage had been arranged for her.

The man was a nephew of her grandmother's friend, and the family was willing to give Alice a try in spite of her many shortcomings. Alice mustered many arguments about her ineptitudes and inexperience to no avail. When she was forced to meet the young man she found him "not a bad looking kid," as embarrassed as she was. Alice recalls:

> Having read so many romantic books in which marriage
> followed a courtship filled with love, I had imagined it
> would happen to me. What a shock to find I was at the
> mercy of the old ways of arranged marriages. All my
> dreams of finding someone to love and live happily ever
> after vanished. [30]

Events turned out better than she had hoped. The boy was already courting another girl but the idea of obeying the Elders was as ingrained in him as it was in Alice. By the end of the week he told his uncles he was not ready for marriage, so they were allowed to go their separate ways. Alice was very frustrated. She recalls:

> I had never been allowed to think for myself; first it was
> the school and then it was my grandmother who made
> all my decisions for me. I would not have known
> what to do if I had to decide for myself about anything.[31]

Alice was happy that she had gained more time before marriage, but the event had led to her first argument with her grandmother, which disturbed her. Her grandmother accepted what had happened and even felt sorry for Alice because she had been rejected by "a very good catch."

Alice loved her life with her family, though they were living in an over-crowded driftwood cabin in winter and in tents in summer. They had a busy social life; especially they celebrated religious holidays like Christmas and Easter. She quickly came to love her step-mother and her young step-siblings. Her father, as always, was kind and loving, and she had the companionship of her brother. The work was hard, but as Alice gained proficiency she took pride in her accomplishments. A radio was their constant companion. Alice had to learn to accept the Inuit way of tolerating everyone's behaviour. She was more inclined to spank the little children when they misbehaved, as she had been taught in the residential school, but soon learned that spanking was unacceptable.

Their lives changed dramatically when they were required to move into town. She describes the nomadic lifestyle with nostalgia:

> Being a nomadic people we are ever restless unless we
> are moving about and hunting and storing food like
> squirrels for the winter ahead ... Schedules are not for us,
> not in the sense that white people know them, but
> nonetheless we have our own schedules dictated by the
> seasons. There never is wasted time since we work
> from sunup to sundown. [32]

The family's move to a salaried job came about largely because all children were required to get an education; family allowances were an incentive for parents to send the children to school. During the residential school days only children who could be spared were sent to school, but with changing regulations all children were to receive an education. Alice sums this era up succinctly, "So we moved into town, and, in moving, lost the art of looking after ourselves the way we used to." The move brought welfare payments with it and loss of family cohesiveness as men who did go out trapping had to leave their families behind.

Her father accepted a position at a reindeer station and it was there that Alice met her future husband. She was seventeen years old, and she agreed that it was time she settled down. She remembers, "I was tired of hedging, and thought it was time I found a home for myself."

Friends of Jim Nahogulook came to ask her if she would marry him. She knew him to see him. He was five feet, four inches tall and had black hair and eyes and weighed about a hundred and forty pounds. "Not much to base a marriage on," Alice recalls dryly. Later she learned he was about ten or eleven years older than she was. She consoled herself with the fact that at least she knew of him and knew what he looked like. She recalls that she did not know whether she was happy about her marriage or not and points out they never could discuss anything since he spoke no English and she did not know his language well enough to express the things she would have wanted to say. Nor did they have a common culture. He was a Kukmalik from Cambridge Bay and she was a Nunatakmuit.

The marriage lasted for thirteen years. The early years at the reindeer station were hard for Alice. After their first son, Charles, was born Alice lapsed into deep depression. Finally she went home to her family because she needed the support of her father to help her overcome the profound despair that engulfed her. Jim was not a bad husband, but lack of communication and Alice's inability to meet the expectations placed on her played a major role in her loneliness. They had three more sons, Gerry, Daniel, and Glenn, and a daughter, Bunny. Eventually they moved to Cambridge Bay where Jim's family lived, and Alice came to know and love her in-laws. They knew the marriage was in trouble but never criticized or interfered.

Alice's first major break from the life that had entrapped her came when she was invited to take part in an Inuit way-of-life display at the Pacific National Exhibition in Vancouver. The children's grandparents provided the stability the children would need while she was gone. Alice accepted that this was normal in the culture, and she also accepted that her parenting skills were not all they could be. When Alice left for Vancouver she knew her children would be well looked after, and so she finally felt she was free to follow her own dreams. She believes she looked after the children well enough but she was too unstable. She explains, "I loved my children but I was always running away from my marriage because I had never learnt to cope with it and this caused me a lot of problems."

Upon her return, Alice realized that life could never be the same again. In 1959 she took her children to her parents at the reindeer station, and she went to work at a construction camp at Inuvik as a waitress and cook's helper. She needed time to sort out her life without Jim and in Cambridge Bay there were no jobs. She would have had to depend on Jim's kindness, and he surely would have supported her, but she felt this was unfair because she was the one who had left the partnership. She returned to Cambridge Bay when she felt strong enough to face the outcome of her decision. She got a job at the nursing station and the marriage ended formally in 1960. They parted without bitterness; the boys stayed with their grandparents and Alice took Bunny with her.

Later that year she went to Edmonton to meet an RCMP officer she had grown to love in Cambridge Bay. She says of Dominick:

He had been my best friend and knew the very worst side of me, yet he cared about what happened to me. He made me see myself, not just my bad side, but also the goodness I never thought I had. [33]

In 1961 they were married secretly by an RCMP chaplain in Ottawa because Dominick did not have permission to get married. They lived in Ottawa until Dominick's five years of service were up and then he left the force to join the Deep River police detachment in a small atomic energy town in Ontario. There, Alice says, she learned to play bridge and bingo and "I was content, but when I was pregnant I thought I had the whole world at my feet." Their first child was a son whom they named Barry. They visited Ireland where Dominick's family lived, and

Alice found her new in-laws wonderful.

When the atomic site was built at Pinawa, Manitoba, in 1963, they relocated to Winnipeg where their daughter, Katherine, was born. In 1966 Dominick rejoined the RCMP and they moved to Lac Du Bonnet, Manitoba. Their second son, Kevin, was born in 1966 but died of crib death. One of Alice's older sons had also died of pneumonia in 1966, and three months after Kevin's death her father died. Alice could not afford to attend either of their funerals.

After this grief-filled interlude, Alice's life settled down. With the oldest children in school she found time heavy on her hands so she joined a group of women who drove to Pinawa and worked as cleaning staff, though they were called "housemaids." A job opened at the Pinawa hospital and Alice was hired, and she also worked as a bartender. Next she took a job selling cosmetics by doing demonstrations at a local hairdresser's. She had never worn anything but a bit of lipstick in her life so she went to a charm school in Winnipeg to learn how to apply cosmetics properly.

From Lac Du Bonnet Dominick was transferred to Boissevain, Manitoba, and it was there that that Alice got the news that her son Gerry, an epileptic, had died in his sleep. By this time, Bunny had also left home and it was a lonely time for her.

In 1974 they moved to Churchill and Alice had the opportunity to socialize with her own people once again. It had been thirteen years since she had left the north and moving to Churchill was like coming home again. The food was familiar as they hunted for game and fished for char. To keep herself busy Alice began to work with furs and eventually she made little fur animals for the tourist trade. She was befriended by Jenny TooToo, an Inuit from Rankin Inlet, and even though they spoke different dialects they had little difficulty understanding one another. Class distinctions between the predominantly non-Native town and the Native settlement were severely drawn in Churchill at that time, creating considerable tension. Little did anyone suspect that Jenny's son, George Hickes, was to become an elected official and eventually the Speaker of the House in the Manitoba legislature. He was the first Aboriginal speaker elected in any Canadian province.

The next transfer was to Grand Rapids. By this time *My Name is*

Masak had been published and Alice went on several promotional tours. She hoped that her writing would somehow help others to better understand the impact residential schools had on Aboriginal people. They enjoyed a quiet life in Grand Rapids, but then it was disrupted again with news that Dominick's father was gravely ill. They were afraid that great changes were in store for them and, indeed, Dominick's father passed away before they could reach Ireland. The family farm had been left to Dominick, so the following year they left Canada to take up residence in Ireland. Their stay in Ireland, however, was short-lived. Neither one of them enjoyed the life there. Laws were different and everything was privately owned. Dominick, who loves the outdoors passionately, found it particularly galling that even the fish were privately owned and there seemed to be no animals, no birds. They sold the farm and returned to Canada. Alice said she felt like the Pope when they arrived back, wanting only to kneel down and kiss Canadian soil. They returned to Pinawa where Alice happily worked as a home-care attendant until the estate was settled.

They chose Medicine Hat, Alberta, as their place of retirement. Alice loves the wide-open spaces around the city. The drive to the outskirts of the city only takes a few minutes. The prairie reminds Alice of the tundra, with "no trees to clutter up one's vision." Another reason they settled there is that it is one of the closest points by air, and on the most direct route by truck, to Yellowknife and Inuvik.

After her restless, nomadic life, Alice has come full circle. She goes back home periodically to keep up with her family. If she is away too long she does not recognize names or know who belongs to which family and who the younger generation's parents and grandparents are. It is very important to her to keep in contact with her people.

Her oldest sons had stayed with their father and grandparents and attended day school before going to a residential school for the higher grades. Alice placed great emphasis on the importance of education, and her sons were secure in their identity as Inuit and in their language before they left home. And they did not stay away for long. Much as Alice wanted to raise them herself she could not bring herself to take them south. She herself had suffered cultural disruption and could not inflict a similar experience on her children.

Today Charles works for a housing program, and her youngest

son is a dental therapist who prefers to live off the land. He returns to Yellowknife to practice his profession intermittently. Bunny lives in Yellowknife, as well, and is a housewife and mother while her husband is also employed in a housing program. Kathy is married to a farmer in southern Manitoba, and Barry works in a minimum security corrections institute near Winnipeg. Alice's grandchildren are moving into professional careers because they have had more educational and career opportunities than their parents had.

Alice is justifiably proud of her family. She had many misgivings about her parenting skills as her children were growing up. She had little mothering in her formative years and lost many natural teachings. She learned to repress her feelings at the residential school, and she thinks this is frustrating for her family. Though she loves to hug and cuddle her children she also recognizes that she is often distant, even in their midst. In residential school she learned to shut everyone out; survival in the bush taught her the pleasures of solitude. When she lived with her family in the bush she came to hate it when people came by their cabin. She recognizes that she often prefers to shut out people, and she hates crowds. Her family has come to recognize this and accept that "that is how Mom is."

Her southern children are proud of their Inuit heritage, and Alice is pleased when she is asked to make presentations to school children. She takes along furs, an ulu, a spear point, and a fish hook made of bone with a copper point. She loves to answer questions and correct misconceptions people may have about Inuit life. She wants children to see an Inuk and understand that how they live today is not much different from how other Canadians live. She says that she really does miss the muktuk, and the ribs, backbone, and tongue of the caribou.

She regrets that she is not fluent in her original language but otherwise is not very judgemental about the schools. She says she never believed the "English superiority" myth and learning to read and write opened doors for her. Her knowledge of English helped her cope with Europeans and, in that respect, residential school served her well.

In retrospect, Alice believes that though residential schools were difficult, in her case at least, she did have choices. She lost her heritage in the school, but she gained many other things. She believes that if she is a "rotten person" it has nothing to do with the school; she has to take personal responsibility for what she is. She also acknowledges that the school helped her to become the person she is today. Even her memories of the school are selective. She believes she can dwell on the negatives or the positives; she has a choice. However, she is also quick to point out that she is speaking only for herself and not for other survivors.

Most importantly, she believes that dramatic changes were in store for the Inuit; the residential schools merely speeded up the process. She is grateful that the period of greatest upheaval is behind them as a people. Nothing is stopping the Inuit today because their native resilience has helped them adapt to a new order of things. She has great pride in her people, who have come such a long way in such a short time. Her next book, when it comes, will be about differences between the old and the new. "But," she explains thoughtfully, "it is not good to rush into things."

Sister Dorothy Moore

Ave Maria,
Kuleyin Mali, Sapeutil Wajupenl,
Ksaqmaminu tekweyask

Aq apis wikwiatiek
Alasutmelsewitesnen.

The liquid Mi'kmaq syllables combined with the mellow tones of Sister Dorothy Moore's voice to soar up to the lofty recesses of St. Mary's Basilica in Halifax. Radiant autumn colours saturated the city, so bright that they were almost blinding, and the brilliant sunlight streaming through the richly coloured cathedral windows continued the dazzling display.

Earlier, dignitaries had solemnly taken their seats to commemorate the signing of the Treaty of 1752 between the Mi'kmaq of Nova Scotia and the King of England, an annual event that renews promises of old and strengthens relationships today. The morning of the official commemoration began with traditional drumming and chanting at the basilica. A choir from the Eskasoni Reserve sang, accompanied by a guitarist, as people gathered in the nave.

Mi'kmaq veterans in uniform, their numbers diminishing annu-ally, led the procession into the church. They were accompanied by an honour guard of Mi'kmaq RCMP officers, resplendent in red coats with eagle feathers in the bands of their regulation hats. All the male officers had hair in carefully braided queues down their backs; the only break in the uniformity was the solitary female officer whose hair was closely cropped. The veterans were followed by various dignitaries from the Aboriginal community, and from civic, provincial, and federal govern-ments, including the Honourable Jane Stewart, Minister of Indian Affairs and Northern Development.

At ten o'clock two priests entered and celebrated the Eucharist, then withdrew to the front of the sanctuary and turned their backs to the assembled congregation as two Elders performed the Sweet Grass Ceremony. Then Sister Dorothy Moore stepped up to the podium as guest speaker. She was attired in a long navy skirt with traditional Mi'kmaq patterns embroidered around the hem, a red blazer, and a white blouse. Her topic was "Restoring Mi'kmaq Educational Initiatives."

Legend telling has always been a primary teaching tool for the Mi'kmaq, since time immemorial, and Sister Dorothy began her talk with the following legend:

According to the legend an Indian Brave came upon an eagle's egg, which had somehow fallen unbroken from an eagle's nest. Unable to find the nest, the brave put the egg in the nest of a prairie chicken, where it was hatched by the brooding mother hen. The young eagle, with its judicial strong eyes, saw the world for the first time. Looking at the prairie chickens, he did what they did. He cawed and scratched at the earth, pecked here and there for stray grain and husks, now and then rising in a flutter a few feet above the earth and then descending again. He accepted and imitated the daily routine of the earth-bound prairie chickens. And he spent most of his life this way. Then, as the story continues, one day an eagle flew over the brood of prairie chickens. The now aging eagle, who still thought he was a prairie chicken, looked up in awe and admiration at the big bird soaring through the skies. "What is that?" he gasped in astonishment. One of the old prairie chickens replied, "I have seen one before. That is an eagle, the proudest, the strongest and the most magnificent of all the birds. But don't you ever dream that you could be like that. You are like the rest of us and we are prairie chickens.

She continued, "And so shackled by this belief, the eagle lived and died thinking he was a prairie chicken." The parallels were clear as she explained,

> Each one of us at this gathering is born into this world with a God-given right to be whom our Creator meant us to be—in race, in language, in culture, and in gender. As well, the right to enjoy all the freedoms associated with becoming the best we can possibly be culturally, linguistically, socially, spiritually, traditionally, and educationally.

Her quiet passion held the assembly spellbound, and at the end of her talk she presented the gift of Ave Maria, singing a cappella in her beloved Mi'kmaq. "Peace be with you," the members of the congregation had murmured to each other earlier, and as the commemorative ceremony came to a close and the assembly streamed out into the brilliant sunshine it was hard to believe that there could ever be anything but peace between Aboriginal and non-Aboriginal Canadians. It was tempting to believe that the residential schools, the Donald Marshall Jr. betrayal of justice, the conflict over fishing rights, the Oka standoff, had never really happened, or that Aboriginal people do not need to continue the relentless struggle day after day to reclaim lost rights.

But this glorious October morning in 1998 was no place for acrimony or recrimination. The commemorative celebration was intended to improve communication and strengthen the bonds of friendship. The ritual at the basilica was followed by a reception at city hall, hosted by the mayor of Halifax. Then, pleasantries over with, the assembly moved to Province House for the afternoon. Here the Aboriginal dignitaries sat in chairs normally reserved for provincial legislators, a body that has never included any of them. The Honourable Russell MacLellan made opening remarks following a flag-raising and Sweet Grass Ceremony. There were speeches by the Honourable Jane Stewart and by the provincial minister in charge of Aboriginal Affairs. The packed building had an air of restlessness during the political speeches but a hush descended as Phil Fontaine, National Chief of the Assembly of First Nations, and Lawrence Paul, chair of the Assembly of Nova Scotia Chiefs, spoke. Though the messages were carefully worded and respectful, their intent was clear. They reminded the assembled listeners, especially the dignitaries, that promises had been broken and obligations had not been fulfilled. Jane Stewart told an audience at Eskasoni the following day that she had received "holy heck."

Much to the surprise of the Eskasoni gathering, Stewart did not respond with defensive statements, perhaps a first in the history of an Indian Affairs minister. One could almost be fooled into thinking that the federal Liberals were actually on the side of the First Nations were it not for the spectre of the notorious *White Paper*, which Prime Minister Jean Chrétien had authored when he was Minister of Indian Affairs. Erosion of Aboriginal rights with no compensation for past inequities was at the heart of the paper and only constant vigilance on the part of First Nations has prevented the hated document from being implemented through the "back door" over the years. It was known, though, that Stewart was appalled and saddened by the devastation created by residential schools, and that a compensation package, and hopefully an apology, would be forthcoming in the near future.

Sister Dorothy Moore had been intensely involved in organizing the two-day celebration and believes such celebrations are important. Except for the elected officials, however, they are largely ignored by non-Aboriginals in Nova Scotia. She believes that celebrations, such as this one, help Aboriginal people take a step toward regaining a rightful place in society. She also knows that they are only surface gestures and that much work remains to be done. As a consultant for Mi'kmaq Education for the Nova Scotia Department of Education and Culture she is willing to utilize her considerable leadership talents and do more than her share of the work to ensure there is progress.

How did Dorothy Moore, Mi'kmaq child from the reserve at Membertou, Nova Scotia, become Sister Dorothy Moore? What directions has her path taken to bring her to the point where she was to play such a prominent role in education of Mi'kmaq children in Nova Scotia?

The first question is easily answered. The stereotype of nuns in residential schools is usually one of harsh, unfeeling, or even cruel women. Sister Dorothy is quick to point out that those nuns were the Sisters of Charity and she is a member of the Sisters of St. Martha, who were never connected with the residential school debacle. And she says simply that she had learned early in her life that she had a calling to become a nun. She put her complete trust in God and has never wavered in her early decision to enter religious life.

The second question has a more complicated answer, and the child Dorothy was to have many, many painful experiences on her road to success. Some of this pain still haunts her to this day.

Dorothy was born at Membertou into a stable family, but, like most Mi'kmaq at that time, they suffered from extreme poverty. Her mother had received an education at the reserve school and could read and write well. Her father had received what he called a "three-day education," but he could also read and write. They loved and respected the reserve teacher who was an Irish Catholic and had spent forty-nine years teaching the children of Membertou.

The Mi'kmaq language was the language of the home; their father insisted that it be spoken at all times. It was not until after he died that Sister Dorothy fully realized his commitment to keeping his culture, language, and history alive. It was then that she wanted to continue to promote how her father had lived, and for this reason she calls herself a "born again Mi'kmaq." Life was very difficult for the family because of the extreme poverty the First Nations of the Maritimes suffered in the face of encroaching European settlement. Her father worked off the reserve sanding floors and gradually adopted non-Aboriginal methods of childrearing. He expected the children to follow rules and adopt behaviours he found in non-Aboriginal homes, and he disciplined the children severely. Dorothy was often beaten at home, though her siblings seemed to escape such extreme punishment. At all times, however, the girls were more severely disciplined than the boys.

Sister Dorothy's parents were very active in the little on-reserve church, which was run by local leaders. Rituals were conducted at special times, with prayers and singing done in Mi'kmaq, led by Mi'kmaq

Elders. The prayers were based on Catholic prayers. In 1610, Membertou, chief *sagamore* (leader) of the Mi'kmaq, had converted to Catholicism, and most Mi'kmaq followed his lead. Sister Dorothy's parents were strongly committed to the Catholic Church and instilled in their children the value of going to church and living devout Catholic lives, even though they experienced discrimination within the church. Sister Dorothy recalls that when they attended church off the reserve in Sydney, they sat at the back of the church on a little bench because they had no right to pews. White people sat in the pews because they had paid for the privilege.

When Dorothy was nine years old she and three other girls from Membertou were taken to the Shubenacadie Residential School by her mother. There were no explanations, no preparation for going, and she remembers little of that fateful day. She believes she has blocked out many memories. She remembers being warned that she had to be good or she would be punished. She stayed there for two years and during that time there was no contact with her parents except that her mother did write occasionally. Dorothy also remembers care packages from home and getting a doll for Christmas. Isabelle Knockwood, in the book *Out of the Depths,* wrote about the Shubenacadie School and described how the children were allowed to play with their Christmas gifts for a few days. Then they were confiscated and, at best, put on display, but often they just disappeared never to be seen again. [34] Dorothy was never allowed to play with her doll.

At age eleven, Dorothy was taken back home because her parents said she had learned English and it was time for two of her other sisters to have a turn at the school. She does not think her parents encouraged their educational endeavours since they strongly discouraged anyone from leaving the reserve, but they did recognize the need to learn English in order to function in a changing society. One of Sister Dorothy's sisters had a mostly positive experience at Shubenacadie, but, of her own experience, Dorothy says that she was never touched in an affirmative way by anything that happened at the school. She believes that every interaction she had with staff at the school was meant to be hurtful.

She remembers a very cross-looking woman teaching an arithmetic class on division the first day she was there. The majority knew some English, and Dorothy had difficulty keeping up. By the time she was whacked on the head and poked in the back she was incapable of learning anything. Her hands were soon bruised and swollen from being hit with a ruler. Finally she was sent to the blackboard to draw a picture of a jackass. She did not know what a jackass was but drew a stick animal anyway. The teacher told her to stand aside and then said to the class, "See? She has drawn a picture of herself. Laugh at her." And the whole class obliged with a hearty laugh.

The teachers could be very inconsistent in their attitudes toward the children, which continually kept them off balance. The same person who tormented Dorothy in the classroom could be super-nice during recreation time. This perhaps indicates that they did not have the patience to teach the children, yet they did harbour some guilty feelings about their own behaviours, which they attempted to assuage with friendliness at recess time. Dorothy tried very hard to please her teachers but felt that she was never successful.

Punishment was the only avenue of communication between staff and students, and, out of fear, Dorothy learned to be proficient in English very quickly. When she went home at the end of June she would not speak Mi'kmaq for fear of losing her English. She was so proud of her ability to speak English that she spoke loudly that first summer, so white people could hear that she knew their language. Her father, however, would threaten her with punishment for not speaking in Mi'kmaq, so her confusion and fear increased. Today she speaks Mi'kmaq but feels she is not as proficient as she would like to be.

At the school she was forever being strapped for minor infractions. For example, she ran up the stairs instead of walking. In her book Knockwood described one particularly sadistic staff member, Sister M., whom all the students hated and feared. She would put a bucket over the water fountain so the thirsty children could not get a drink. She would place a tempting bowl of apples on the table in the recreation room, and sometimes a hungry child could not resist taking one. Then the child would be punished for "stealing in the recreation room." Dorothy often felt the brunt of this Sister's meanness.

Dorothy was always sick and suffered stomach pains the whole time she was at the school. If she complained about the stomachs pains she was given a whole bottle of castor oil. She also knows how it feels to have her face pushed into her own vomit. Any type of illness had to be repressed; the fearful children even stifled their coughs for fear of being punished. A great deal of energy was used to avoid punishment, or lessen its severity. The children would automatically lie down on their beds, waiting to be strapped, when they had wet their beds.

Dorothy became such a fearful child and was abused so often, especially in the classroom, that it inhibited her learning. She would have revelled in learning new things had she been given half a chance. She developed a nervous habit of rubbing her hand on her thigh when she was agitated, and she rubbed a hole right through her skirt. The one activity she might have excelled in, singing in the choir, was forbidden her. She feels it was out of sheer perversity because the nuns recognized how much she loved to sing. Likely they justified their decision as rightful punishment for all her other misdemeanours.

She never spoke to her parents about her experiences at the school. If she had, she would simply have received another beating for having been such a bad child. She had been raised in a home where there was no physical contact, no closeness between parents and children. If she ever felt anger at the school or at her parents she would have repressed it because she and her siblings had been raised not daring to cry or express anger in the home. They did not ever question their parents and did not even dare to feel anger. On the other hand, the children did feel secure and protected in the home, and a consequence of their upbringing was that they grew to be very self-directed people. At the school, Dorothy consoled herself in her loneliness and despair by drawing her home in great detail with a stick in the ground. She persevered in her studies because she never gave up trying to prove that she was not what the nuns said she was—dumb. At age eleven, when her parents removed her from Shubenacadie, she returned to school at Membertou. She had finished grade four at the residential school, and she feels today that if she had not left there her academic learning would have foundered as it did for so many residential school students. When asked by the teacher at Membertou what grade she was in, Dorothy said she was in grade four. It was normal for students who left the residential school to have to repeat a grade. Lack of skills and ability should not have held Dorothy back, and today she exclaims, "Wasn't I dumb? I was afraid of being punished if I said I was in grade five. My life was so filled with fear—at home, at school, off-reserve."

She stayed at the Membertou School until she was in grade seven, but by Christmastime she was doing nothing because the school had never had a student in grade seven before. When she reached grade eight her parents told her she would have to quit school and support herself. They felt her desire for further education meant she was turning her back on her culture. She began to take whatever jobs she could, like scrubbing non-Aboriginal people's floors.

A turning point in her life came when she went to stay with an aunt and uncle in Eskasoni. She was able to take grade seven there. The teachers at the Eskasoni School were also nuns, and though Dorothy approached the experience with trepidation, she was determined to get an education. Much to her relief, the Sisters of St. Martha were loved by the community and were friends with the students. They laughed. They visited with community members and participated in the life of the reserve. It was when she was in grade eight that Dorothy understood that she was called to be a nun.

She attended St. Joseph's School in Sydney in order to complete grade nine, the first Mi'kmaq student to ever attend a public school. Her stay, however, was short-lived because she was expelled for failing to do her homework. The assignment was to paraphrase a poem she did not understand, and her teacher told her, "Go back to the backwoods where you belong." At age sixteen she was back at home. Her parents said, "We told you so! You do not belong there," and she took a job in a laundry.

However, not all was lost. A former grade-eight teacher recognized Dorothy's thirst for knowledge and had some connections. She facilitated her acceptance into a school run by the Sisters of Notre Dame at Mabou. The school was austere and the work was hard, but Dorothy persevered. After grade ten she returned home and attended the Holy Angels High School in Sydney. She was the first Mi'kmaq to ever enter that high school and it was a very difficult experience for her. At twenty years of age she was older than the other students. Her life at home was hard and it was equally hard at school.

At the end of the year she was forbidden, by the school, to write the provincial exams. Though not said openly, the school implied that she did not have the ability to pass the exams, and striving for a high-school education was futile. She was frustrated and acutely embarrassed, fearing that she was destined to forever be a failure.

Ultimately she was able to write and pass the provincial exam because of the assistance of another girl in the class who became her friend and tutor. At this time Dorothy also was beginning to feel a pride in her heritage that for many years she had viewed only as negative and detrimental to her success. A small measure of confidence began to return. In retrospect, she says, she had to struggle all her life, against great odds, just to learn, an activity that was her inherent right as a child.

When Dorothy announced her intention to pursue a religious life there was strong opposition from her parents in spite of their devotion to the Catholic Church. They interpreted her move as rejecting her Mi'kmaq culture and turning her back on everything they valued. For a Mi'kmaq to become a religious was simply unknown in Nova Scotia.

Dorothy was undeterred, knowing what was right for her. Even after her residential school experience her faith was unshaken. To be a religious is a call from God, and there was never a question in her mind about the fact that she had been called. In a dream she had seen a statue of Our Lady who said to her, "You will be alright." Though it pained her greatly that her parents did not understand or sanction her decision, her great love of God sustained her. She had always turned to God in her struggles and received the strength and love that helped her grow into what she is today.

She needed permission from her family to join the Order of the Sisters of St. Martha. Finally she told her father, "I'll soon be 21. I would rather have your blessing than go on my own." So her father relented and signed the necessary document.

There were further complications, however. She needed a dowry of fifty dollars and she needed some personal items for entry into the order. Her father could have provided the dowry, since they no longer were as poverty stricken as when Dorothy was a child, but he refused to do so, on matters of principle. She worked all summer, hoarding every penny, and had enough money for her personal items. Her brother gave her a trunk for the trousseau, and her parents did drive her to the Mother House in Antigonish, but her father refused to enter the building with her.

She spent two years in the novitiate of the Sisters of St. Martha, but the question of the dowry had not been settled. She found her own solution. She knew she could receive money if she became disenfranchised under the terms of the Indian Act. She would renounce her Mi'kmaq status and in return she would receive a portion of the reserve revenues, the amount ascertained by the Department of Indian Affairs. By renouncing her status she became a full-fledged "Canadian," with the right to vote and to drink alcoholic beverages. She also renounced her treaty rights and the right to live on a reserve. When she got the money, it was a cheque for thirty-three dollars and thirty-three cents. She took it to the treasurer, hoping the amount might be accepted since, as a member of the order, she had no other way to make money. The treasurer informed her that she would not have had to concern herself with the dowry because a deceased Sister's dowry had been signed over to her. No one had informed her. She was grief stricken because she had sold her birthright for such a small sum. She never told her father about the renunciation of her status, and today, thanks to Bill C-31, which restored status to all who had lost it under the terms of the Indian Act, she is once more legally a Mi'kmaq.

Sister Dorothy went through times when she harboured bitter feelings because her life had been such a struggle in residential and public school simply because she was an Indian. She went through a period when she felt she did not want to be Indian anymore. She felt that her religious habit and her fair skin would make that possible. She soon discovered, however, that she could not hide behind a religious habit, and she also came to realize that she did not want to either.

Her many struggles to get an education came to fruition when she enrolled in Teachers' College for one year of training. She began her career as a teacher in various Nova Scotia schools in 1958—Lakeside School, Park Street School, Captain Allan School, and the Tracadie Consolidated School. She taught at Picture Butte in Alberta for three years and then went back to Nova Scotia where she accepted a teaching assignment in Eskasoni, first as a classroom teacher and then as principal. When she returned home to her own people in 1974, they merely said, "You're back with us." Her father died of a heart attack on her first day of teaching at Eskasoni.

Sister Dorothy's religious and educational commitments have combined with her work experiences to provide a varied and interesting career. She spent twenty-two years as a classroom teacher and two years as principal at Eskasoni. In 1974 she received bachelor of arts and bachelor of education degrees from St. Francis Xavier University. Illness struck, and after some months of recovery from cancer, she returned to full-time study at Mount St. Vincent University, earning a master's degree in educational psychology in 1984.

In 1984 the University of Cape Breton asked for her assistance to help alleviate the high drop-out rate of the Mi'kmaq students who were attending that institution. She accepted the challenge and never looked back. She established the Mi'kmaq Student Support Service and was a counsellor and advisor. Besides developing a Mi'kmaq course, she also invited other qualified Mi'kmaq to teach courses relating to Aboriginal and Mi'kmaq issues. Between 1984 and 1995, the Mi'kmaq student registration and retention went from 9 students to over 150. As the director of Mi'kmaq student services, she also lectured, teaching the Native Studies courses she had developed. She also did a part-time teaching stint at St. Francis Xavier University in Antigonish in 1994 and 1995. In 1995 she became the Mi'kmaq education consultant for the Nova Scotia Department of Education and, in 1997, became the acting director of the same department, a position she held until her retirement.

Recognition of her innate abilities was slow in coming because her elementary and high-school education was fraught with such great difficulties. However, after she found peace and security in her religious order and acceptance by her home community she can be said to have "blossomed." She did so well in her religious and academic endeavours and her career that her outstanding qualities have been recognized in many different ways: by her congregation, by the Aboriginal community, and by Canadian society at large.

From 1975 to 1980 she fulfilled the role of Sister Superior of the Teachers' Residence at Eskasoni and from 1986 to 1991 was Sister Superior of the Martha Community in Sydney. She served as chairperson and manager of the General Chapter of the Sisters of St. Martha, Bethany Mother House in Antigonish, and coordinator of communications for chapter affairs, as well as serving as a member of the admissions board for the Congregation of the Sisters of St. Martha. In 1998 she was appointed to the board of directors of the Nova Scotia Canadian Bible Society.

Her artistic abilities were recognized when she was invited to be the director of costumes for the National Film Board movie *Thecla's Choice*; she had an acting role as well. When the movie *Justice Denied* was made, it was Sister Dorothy who was the solo singer. It is the story of Donald Marshall Jr., a seventeen-year-old Mi'kmaq youth who was wrongfully charged with murder and imprisoned for eleven years.

As awareness of Aboriginal issues increased and concern arose regarding the inequitable treatment of Aboriginal people in Canadian education systems, Sister Dorothy was ready and enthusiastic, participating in finding solutions through her involvement in various organizations. She became a member of the board of directors of University College of Cape Breton in Sydney, and was on the advisory board for the Micmac Teacher Education Program at the University of New Brunswick in Fredericton. She was a member of the curriculum committee of the Micmac School of Social Work at Dalhousie University in Halifax from 1986 to 1989, as well as a member of the Advisory Network of Native Peoples for the Department of Educational Multicultural Services from 1989 to 1991. For four years she served on the board of directors of St. Rita's Hospital in Sydney. She was on the advisory board of the Native Urbanization Transitional Program in Halifax. She was appointed to the Literacy Nova Scotia Board and to the Advisory Committee for Access to University for Minority Students at Dalhousie, to the board of directors for Learning for a Sustainable Future, and was on the advisory board of the Education Department at Mount St. Vincent University. Most recently she was appointed to the board of governors of the Institute of Early Childhood Education and Development and to the Nova Scotia Human Rights Commission.

In the judicial field, she has been commissioner of Nova Scotia Human Rights, the body that hears human-rights complaints, and for five years was a member of the Nova Scotia Judicial Advisory Committee, the body that makes recommendations to the government when there are vacancies on the bench. She has indeed proven, again and again, that the Sisters at the residential school were wrong. She is not "dumb!" She is in great demand as a public speaker and summarizes her presentations as "numerous talks on Education, Racism, Residential Schools, Native Spirituality, Native Education, etc."

Her work has been recognized with numerous awards, tangible evidence that she is a beloved and appreciated human being. In 1981 the Eskasoni community gave her a Public Service Award for the services she had rendered the community in both church and school. Ten years later she was similarly honoured by the Membertou community at Sydney. In 1989 she received the Stephen Hamilton Outstanding Achievement Award in Education for her contributions and efforts in pursuing higher education for Mi'kmaq youth. In 1990 she was named the Atlantic Innovator of the Year, education category. In 1991 she received the Canadian Citation for Citizenship Award in recognition of efforts and accomplishments in the field of education and, in particular, for her work with Native students in Cape Breton. In 1993 she received one of Canada's Commemorative Awards on the occasion of the country's 125th anniversary. In 2002 she received a honourary doctorate degree from Mount St. Vincent University.

Today, Sister Dorothy remembers the residential school and how negative the experience was for her, but she also puts the experience in context. The role of the school was to integrate and assimilate Mi'kmaq children; the schools were expected to remake them into something they were not meant to be. In western Canada events moved very quickly after Confederation and treaties set the course for Indian/government/settler relationships. In the Maritimes there had been sustained interactions between the three groups for three centuries, and the extreme poverty of the First Nations was as effective in forcing parents to send their children to school as coercion or force might have been. Indeed, there were many who sent their children to the school to ensure that they would not go hungry. The Mi'kmaq culture, however, was not as greatly damaged as many others because the school was not built until 1930 and it was closed in 1968. It was open for "only" thirty-eight years, and so a relatively small percentage of Mi'kmaq children of school age attended the residential school. Though individuals may not have appreciated this advantage when they were in the school, the damage to the culture as a whole was not as severe as it was in those areas where three or four generations of students attended the residential schools.

Though the school was open for only thirty-eight years, it did almost succeed in destroying the Mi'kmaq language. Today only about fifteen per cent of the Mi'kmaq people are fluent speakers, but, as in many other areas, every effort is being made by Mi'kmaq educators to support language revitalization.

Sister Dorothy attempts to focus on the positive experiences in her school years. She learned to speak English; she learned to read, to make a bed, to darn socks. She fondly recalls the many friends she made, and she still values these friendships today. She believes the school regimen prepared her for the life of a religious, and the experience has made her a much more empathetic human being.

She was never encouraged to believe in herself; no one ever encouraged her in her educational endeavours in any way, neither in her home nor in the schools she attended. She was hurt again and again when teachers called her dumb, and her only survival technique was to prove that she was not dumb. She accepted every challenge that came her way, and though her successes were never acknowledged at either the residential school or at the provincial schools she attended later, she knew that she was intelligent. She had a profound faith in God that sustained her over the years.

She recognizes that she was one of the lucky ones. Her two years at the school were devastating but she was removed before permanent damage could be done. Had she spent as many years as some children did, she, too, would likely have become a casualty. There were some, the orphans or the ones who came from severely dysfunctional homes, who were confined to the school from the age of five until they reached sixteen. These children had no family, no Elders to help them, no one they could relate to, no nurture, no love. Today they have no language and no culture. No one in the community knows them; they know no one and are largely illiterate. Yet, even these children considered the school better than the dysfunctional homes from which they had come, or the lack of a home because no other social services were available.

Sister Dorothy recalls those at the school who received preferential treatment from staff, the ones who are referred to as the "pets." The price these students paid, like any spoiled child, was high. They suffered loss of freedom to develop in their own ways. They learned no decision-making skills. Compared to some of her schoolmates, Sister Dorothy considers herself lucky that she never lost her personal integrity or her ability to at least attempt to chart her own course. When asked what her position today is regarding residential schools, her response is quick and decisive: "Right up to my neck in correcting past harms."

When Isabelle Knockwood wrote her book about the Shubenacadie

School she corresponded with the Sisters and was dismayed to find that they were concerned only with the unfairness of the statements made by the "complainers" and seemed quite unaware of any damage the schools had done. Residential school survivors deal with many painful memories by repressing them, and perhaps the Sisters are equally adept at selective memory and repression. Male abusers from the residential school system have been tried by Canadian courts and found guilty; no female has been charged. Likely the type of abuse that was more common among the female staff is more difficult to describe and prove. Canada has no specific laws that make it easy to prosecute people for psychological and spiritual abuse of children.

Though she had forgiven, as best she could, the wrongs that were done to her, Sister Dorothy still had some unfinished business she needed to attend to. She felt that she had to meet with the Sisters in their retirement and speak with them one more time. In part, she wished to show them all that their mean-spirited predictions about her were wrong; in part she wanted to see, through adult eyes, not through the eyes of a frightened lonely child, what kind of people they were. When she visited them she did her best to ignore Sister M., the meanest of the group. But Sister M. was not about to be ignored and called out, "I knew that some day you would do it." Sister Dorothy responded with, "No you didn't," and walked away.

The continual negative reaction she received from the Sisters at the residential school and the positive reinforcement she got from the Sisters of St. Martha at Eskasoni have had a major influence on Sister Dorothy's life. It has influenced her actions in not only educational situations, but in her daily life as well. She says, "My life now is to see the positive things in everyone."

As Sister Dorothy concluded her comments at the treaty day celebrations in 1998 she quoted an old proverb: "It is not where we are that counts; it is where we are going that matters." She went on to say:

I have a great sense that we are entering a new era of the 3-R's—an era of *Re-awakening* and *Revival* as the Mi'kmaq take over their rightful *Responsibility* in their own educational affairs. In doing so, we are empowering ourselves in all that relates to making the school curriculum more relevant in relation to the history, language, and culture. The prime goal has to be the provision of quality education to all students.

She pointed out the many reasons that the Mi'kmaq have to celebrate—more qualified Mi'kmaq teachers, Mi'kmaq representation on all regional school boards, specific Mi'kmaq Studies programs, Bill C-30, which gives educational jurisdiction to the Mi'kmaq, and the establishment of the Mi'kmaq Services Division of the Department of Education and Culture. She concluded her speech with buoyant optimism and considerable charm:

> Let us go forward knowing that we are not the Ki'Kli' Kuejk (chickens), indeed, we are the Kitpu'k (eagles) and like the kitpu (eagle), we too will soar into the future filled with hope, pride, and gratitude to our Creator Spirit.

Shirley Sterling (Seepeetza)

Shirley Sterling, a Nlakapamux (Thompson) Indian, was born on the Joeyaska Indian Reserve #2. Joeyaska Ranch, as it is commonly called, is nestled between the Coquihalla Highway and the town of Merritt in central British Columbia. The ranch and a second reserve at the opposite end of the valley make up the Lower Nicola Band. Shirley's ancestors lived there, spending the severe winters in underground houses. There are still pit sites on the ranch, though they are not readily apparent to the untrained eye. The houses were made by digging holes approximately 13 to 20 metres in diameter to a depth of approximately 2 to 4 metres. The roofs for the pits were made of logs covered with dirt, with a smoke hole in the centre. A notched pole was inserted through the smoke hole to act as a ladder. The houses were warm, but smoky. The remains of these *keekwillie* houses gave Shirley and her siblings a sense of connection with the distant past. As children they found tiny horseshoes from donkeys belonging to Mexican traders who had stopped at Joeyaska on their way to the Yukon gold fields. The Mexicans exchanged corn and vegetable seeds for fresh meat.

Shirley was born to Sophie Voght and Albert Sterling, the fifth of seven children. This gave her a unique position in the family. Though she was also a younger sibling she played the role of "older sister" to the younger ones.

Albert Sterling was a hunter, rancher, hay contractor, court interpreter, storyteller, and veteran of the First and Second World Wars. He was of Nlakapamux, Okanagan, and Celtic ancestry. Shirley points out that she was born in a time of merging worlds. Her Nlakapamux heritage, which she refers to as the "old" tradition, merged with the "new" Celtic traditions of her mixed-blood father. Just as many Canadians who belong to minority cultures find their place in the Canadian mosaic, this merging of Nlakapamux and Celtic traditions also eventually led to a unique niche in Canada's cultural landscape.

Sophie Voght's parents, Shirley Sterling's maternal grandparents, were William Voght Jr. and Shannie Antoine Voght. William's father was William Voght Sr., originally from Germany, and his mother was Theresa Klama, a Nlakapamux from Boston Bar in British Columbia. Shannie's father was Chief Yapskin Antoine, and her mother was Quaslametko, a master basket maker. Sophie Voght described her grandmother, Quaslametko, as very strict and hard working; she and her husband had embraced the teachings of the Catholic Church and adhered to the church's strict disciplinary approaches in raising children. Furthermore, as the Spanish flu was decimating the First Peoples of the Nicola Valley, Quaslametko was strict in order to maintain a clean home environment to spare her family. She objected vehemently to white people's education systems and urged strongly that the children not be sent to school because they would lose the skills they needed as Indian people. Though her daughter, Shannie, was married to a mixed-blood, Quaslametko had little use for white or mixed-blood people in general. Shannie was often bearing children and was not well, so the grandmothers stepped in and helped raise the family of twelve children. Sophie remembers her great aunt, Yetko, Quaslametko's sister, as very child-oriented, happy, laughing, and a great storyteller.

Shirley is a second-generation residential school survivor. Her mother, Sophie, attended the Kamloops Residential School before her. Shirley remembers Sophie's beautiful wavy black hair, which she braided and then wrapped around her head like a little crown. When she went to town she always wore a little hat. Sophie was soft spoken, smiling, singing softly as she did the household chores. She passed away in September 2001. Like her mother and grandmother, she was a herbalist and a gatherer of medicinal teas and remedies in her younger years. Her herbal remedies cured headaches, woman troubles, rashes, and wounds. She was knowledgeable about methods of birth control. She was a gentle, kind-hearted woman who, in her younger years, laughed a lot and loved to go into the mountains with her children and, later, her grandchildren.

Shirley can trace her heritage back for seven generations on her mother's side. It was her parents' generation that was the most influenced by European contact. She recalls that in her early years:

> My parents took us to Coquihalla or Tulameen Summit to pick huckleberries at the end of summer. The Coquihalla highway now cuts through the little mountain valley where we used to pick berries and a rest stop and toll booth bring tourist traffic to our old campgrounds forcing our family to camp further up the mountain.[35]

Both of Shirley's parents were great storytellers. Her father believed strongly that the creation stories are sacred and not to be passed on lightly. In common with many Aboriginal people, he believed they should not be written down and above all felt they should not be collected by white people or be sold for money. However, he had a great store of non-creation stories that he told freely.

Shirley was taken to the Kamloops Residential School when she was five and a half years old and spent eleven years there. She took grade thirteen in Kamloops and then went to Vancouver to study classical ballet. There she married, had three children, then moved on to live with the Wet'suwet'en in Moricetown. When her marriage broke up she moved back to the Nicola Valley with her children.

When her children left home after high school she fulfilled a lifelong dream of going to university. She enrolled in the Native Indian Teacher Education Program (NITEP) at the University of British Columbia (UBC) and eventually went on to earn a Ph.D. degree through the Ts'kel Program at UBC. Over the years she took a sixty-credit-hour business administration program from the University College of the

Cariboo and received a certificate in fashion design from Fraser Valley College. In her Ph.D. dissertation Shirley wrote that she has been a childcare worker, daycare supervisor, home and school coordinator, recreation coordinator, adult basic education instructor, curriculum developer, author, and a college and university instructor in creative writing and education courses.

She spent two and a half years as student services coordinator of the Ts'kel Program at UBC. This is a graduate program offering both master's and Ph.D. programs to Aboriginal scholars from across Canada. Shirley gave back manifold contributions to the educational institution that helped her overcome the miseducation that burdened her so much of her life. In 2002 she was invited to move back home and take over the role of principal at the Lower Nicola Indian Band School, a position she holds today. Ill health forced a change of pace for a period of time but as she regained her strength she devoted her time to developing curriculum materials. "Finally I am able to put to use what I learned in all those art courses I took," she exclaimed happily when she described her interim job. At Lower Nicola School cultural teachings are incorporated into the school program so children no longer need to live in two distinct and separate worlds.

Besides her academic accomplishments she has also received the Native Teacher Education Alumni Award twice, and she was awarded the Professional Women's Association Scholarship and three graduate scholarships that enabled her to complete her Ph.D. work. She has published an award-winning book, *My Name is SEEPEETZA*, as well as articles in *The Canadian Journal of Native Studies* and in *Guidance and Counselling*. She contributed a chapter to *First Nations Education in Canada: The Circle Unfolds*.[36]

Much of Sterling's residential school experience is described in her autobiographical children's novel, *My Name is SEEPEETZA*. The book is the result of a creative writing course she took from a Jewish instructor who encouraged her to tell her story. The novel fictionalizes the names of people and places, but the experiences in the book are real. Some happened to Shirley herself, some happened to other people around her but might as well have happened to her. The book is in the form of a clandestine journal kept by a lonely, frightened child. One entry, which was also chosen for the cover of the book, states:

Last year Father Sloane took some pictures of us when we were in our dancing costumes at the Irish Concert. It was funny because I was smiling in those pictures. I looked happy. How can I look happy when I'm scared all the time? [37]

A most effective technique Sterling uses in the book is the juxtaposition of events in the school and associated memories of her home. Seepeetza tells how the girls are quietly sitting and shucking corn. Then they secretly start taking bites of the raw vegetable until the cob is bare and they have to hide it under a pile of husks. She relates how the girls "start to get happy" and they begin a rare interlude of laughing and joking. Abruptly, Seepeetza is transported back to Joeyaska Ranch and she remembers:

They tell stories and laugh all day while they are working. Sometimes they have to work all night when the fish are running, and still they stay jolly and happy. [38]

Twelve-year-old Seepeetza is determined, heartsick, confused, frightened, lonely, powerless, and funny. She refuses to give up her identity, though at school she is forced to respond to the name, Martha. She resists all the indignities heaped upon her, but her resistance is so covert that the oppressors never suspect the strength of the child that is in their midst. She never, for even one moment, forgets that her name is Seepeetza.

Seepeetza tells a poignant incident about the lonely children who, above all else, missed the love and nurturing they would have received from their parents at home. She tells how one girl had pushed her blanket off the bed in her sleep. The supervising Sister noticed it as she was passing by and covered her up. The other children noticed the casual gesture and were so overwhelmed by yearning for their parents that some dropped their blankets deliberately, hoping for even this absent-minded expression of concern for their well-being. The ruse did not work. "Sister just got mad at them," Seepeetza recalls succinctly.

Equally poignant are Seepeetza's memories of summers at home. The school never left the students' consciousness, and it loomed as a threat all year round. When they were at the school they day-dreamed about being home and did their best to put their drab surroundings out of their minds. During the summer they did their best not to let thoughts of the school encroach on their happiness. They began to get stomach aches in late August and fearfully watched the trees to see if the leaves were changing colour. Seepeetza and her sister would "look at each other with sick eyes. Then we walk home so we can be near Mum." No written record exists of the feelings of the parents, as they, too, must have fearfully watched the changing season. Seepeetza recalls that when the fateful day of returning to school arrived she felt numb all over her body and would hide away down inside herself once the doors of the school closed behind her.

Shirley was a mediocre student and took solace in reading novels and daydreaming. She showed remarkable writing ability early and was encouraged to write by one teacher, though she found the school's assigned topics stilted and uninteresting. She loved to write if she was allowed to choose her own topics. Horses were a favourite topic because Shirley was a passionate horseback rider. When she was home she was free to gallop across the fields, unencumbered by any restrictions.

Shirley also belonged to the dance troupe. Seepeetza tells about the dance experience in a relatively positive way, and in her adulthood Shirley did move to Vancouver to study classical ballet. At school, life for the children in the troupe was not particularly pleasurable. They derived satisfaction from performing well, and dance competitions were a break in the monotony of school life. Sometimes the dancers even received special privileges but then had to face the resentment of the other students. The training was rigorous. The dancers were expected to follow an extremely strict regimen, and they gave up every second weekend to perform. When other children went out to play after school or after supper the dancers practised or made costumes. They were not allowed to participate in sports because they might hurt themselves. Their own Native dances were strictly forbidden so they learned the dances of other cultures—reels, jigs, and Swedish masquerades. They were popular performers and won top marks at music festivals. Seepeetza says:

We hardly ever made a mistake when we were performing. It's not just because we know we'll be punished, it's also because we practice every day after school. [39]

Celia Haig-Brown, in her book on the Kamloops Residential School, collected first-person stories from numerous informers. One dancer, Linda, recalls:

My toenails are permanently damaged from [having] to stand on your toes. If you didn't stand on your toes, you were whacked with a ... shillelagh and she'd whack you damn hard on your legs. [40]

Another informant stated:

If you were dancing she'd come up and she'd hit you on the legs, "Lift them legs up!" Geez them poor girls would be just ... you know. [41]

The dance troupe, like the school bands and hockey teams, was largely used as a showpiece to be displayed in public and create support for the school. Haig-Brown questions the value of the "savage" training and one of her informants stated:

After a while, it's not fun anymore; it's a chore because you're never any good ... They never swore at you but they called you dumb and stupid ... and so then the fun was out of it. And after a while you kind of didn't want to do it but ... They didn't want to retrain somebody so they'd keep making you do it. You won prizes and wondered why the hell you even bothered to go because when you got back it was still the same way.[42]

One informant from the school near Lestock in Saskatchewan tells of a similar experience. They won all the hockey games against the surrounding residential schools and made the provincial playoffs in Estevan. They lost the final game—the first loss of the season. They returned to the school for a celebration, "baloney sandwiches and cocoa. What a feast!" At least, the informant thought it was a feast until he walked past the staff dining room and noticed that the staff was having "a king's feast—steak and chicken!"[43]

Though Shirley felt trapped at the school she did have her moments of rebellion, and she did win. In *SEEPEETZA* she tells of an incident in the tub room, which was based on her actual experience. A nun told Shirley to take her clothes off and get into the water; the nun did not leave the room. Shirley refused because she would not let anyone see her naked. The nun yelled at her to take her bloomers off and get into the tub. Seepeetza says:

> I looked at the DANGER sign up where the electricity switches are. She saw it too. I was thinking if she made me do it I would wait till she left, climb up on the pipes, touch the switch and get electrocuted. We stared at each other. Then she opened the door and went out. I took my bloomers off and climbed in the tub. My hands were shaking for a long time. We're not supposed to look at sisters like that.[44]

In another instance, the Sister was haranguing Shirley's younger sister. Shirley confronted the nun and demanded, "What kind of people *are* you?" The Sister yelled back at her, but the constant humiliation of her sister stopped. Shirley believes these were very meaningful moments in her life. They were moments in which she recognized that she did have choices and that she had reached the limit of her endurance. She realized, quaking as she was, that she could stand up to the bullies in the world without drastic consequences, and that the bullies likely would back down in the face of her determination.

In retrospect, Shirley views her life at the school as the life of an incarcerated person. She recalls being bullied and how the children would form gangs and beat each other up when the Sisters were not around. When the lookout would yell, "Sister's coming," they would all pretend that nothing had happened. Seepeetza explains, "The worst thing you can be in the school is a snitch. You don't ever tell on anyone here." Shirley believes that she still carries this prison inside her to a certain extent. Even today her first reaction to an authority figure is fear. She grew up with the feeling that she was a person with no rights and no freedoms; this mindset has been difficult to overcome.

She feels that once she started school she no longer had any rights as a child. They were punished, not because they were bad, but because they were children. She still mourns the loss of a normal childhood. The dedication page of *SEEPEETZA* states:

> To all who went to residential schools, and those who
> tried to help, may you weep and be free. May you laugh
> and find your child again.

Great spiritual damage was done to the children in residential schools because all the spirituality taught to them was on the side of darkness. Shirley now views the Christian creed as an attempt to keep people under control. She feels strongly that the purpose of the schools was to destroy Aboriginal family life and to remove the children from the land and resources coveted by church and state. In that way, Native cultures would ultimately disappear through lack of cultural transmission. She is convinced that the government did not deal with Indians honestly or honourably. This is especially pertinent to most areas of British Columbia where no treaties were ever signed but Aboriginals still were dispossessed with no compensation or protection. Today, she goes to church for funerals and weddings, where she sings and plays her guitar or drum for her own people in her own way.

Attitudes about residential schools are diverse. One of Shirley's relatives actually got high marks and seemed to enjoy the residential school. Shirley speculates that she may have enjoyed her experience at the school because she had so many childcare responsibilities at home. Many residential school girls do claim to have found some reprieve at the schools, especially those who had found their responsibilities at home too onerous, and most especially if they were the only girls in families of boys. When Shirley set out to write *SEEPEETZA*, nobody talked about the residential schools. In writing the book, Shirley was "really scared," an emotion found among many Aboriginal people when they first disclose the abuse they have suffered. They fear censure from non-Aboriginals and from their own people. Shirley feared there would be considerable outcry because she was dealing with a topic that had been shrouded in silence for many years.

In spite of her fears, Shirley proceeded with the book as a personal memoir for herself. She had come to understand that people cannot live their lives motivated by fear, especially the kind of fear instilled in the children at residential schools. The book was first published in 1992, a time when there was little public awareness of the damage residential schools had done to the children involved. There were still many Canadians who were almost totally ignorant of the history and the inequitable treatment of First Nations. Many did not understand the issues, and most preferred not to really think about the residential schools. There were many who reacted emotionally to any negative comments and would not tolerate any criticism of the churches. In spite of her fears, writing the book was cathartic for Shirley. She was able to write about her experiences in a way she had never been able to talk about them before.

When Shirley was nominated for an award for the book, she had no expectation of winning. At the last minute, her mother decided to accompany Shirley to the awards ceremony. She witnessed, with considerable pride, the honours bestowed upon her daughter. The book won the Laura Steinman Award for Children's Literature as well as the Sheila A. Egoff Children's Book Prize. It was shortlisted for the Governor General's Literary Award. According to the *London Free Press*, the book "is destined to be a classic." It is well on its way. In 1997 it was reissued in hardcover and is also available on the World Wide Web.

Now a grandmother, Shirley feels she has come full circle and is embarking on a new phase of her life. She has settled in at the "home place" so carefully remembered and diagrammed in *SEEPEETZA*. The charm of the Joeyaska Ranch is immediately apparent to visitors. Shirley is renovating the house in which she grew up. When I met with her we sat beside a cosy wood fire in the late autumn while construction on a new living room was halted for the night. Shirley's grandson Keiran, who was visiting for the weekend, played quietly at our feet with his cars and trucks. Keiran's mother, Haike, is a lawyer in Vancouver. Shirley's son, Eric, works in forest technology. A second son, Bobby Wayne, died in a boating accident in 1991. Shirley's books and research materials are scattered throughout the house, but the bedroom in which I slept demonstrated her skill as a seamstress. The room was littered with brightly coloured fabrics, patterns, and quilts, the sewing machine open and ready for odd moments of relaxation. Later she brought out more "projects," lovingly caressing the soft material as she described the creations she had in mind.

Her older sister Sarah and her husband live a stone's throw away. Sarah was a health worker for the Upper Nicola Band and gave up a promising career as a health administrator in the city in order to raise a young grandson. Her house was delightfully permeated with the odour of simmering soup and fresh apple pie her husband had bought at a bake sale. Down a winding trail, but still on the ranch, lives Deanna, another older sister. Deanna is a teacher but was working as caregiver to Sophie, mother and anchor of the family, in Sophie's old age. Deanna lives in a picturesque wooden house under tall shade trees. When I visited Sophie in 1999 she was not as spry as she once was. Sometimes her mind had a tendency to wander, but when she understood that I had come to talk about residential schools, her eyes flashed indignantly. Over herb tea and smoked salmon she repeated with great agitation, "They punished us for speaking our language! Just for speaking our language!"

Shirley points out that though members of her family were traditionally hunters and gatherers, today her extended family includes ranchers, ranch hands, trappers, loggers, teachers, computer experts, firefighters, administrators, carpenters, plumbers, backhoe operators, members of the armed forces, band council members, community health workers, and lawyers. But she also emphasized, "We continue to be hunters and gatherers."

In the summer of 1996 the Nicola Valley Band, who are Okanagan, made national media when they set up a road block. Many of the Okanagans believe that while non-Aboriginals, such as ranchers, hold title to the land, they themselves maintain the right to exercise their traditional ownership by going onto these properties to hunt, fish, gather berries and medicinal plants, and hold their annual spiritual ceremonies in the same places they were held in the time of their ancestors. They certainly never ceded the land to anyone and were simply displaced by white immigrants and settled on reserves by the federal government. As a result, there has been trouble for years between title holders and some Okanagans, but in the summer of 1996 the friction escalated.

The Douglas Lake Ranch, in operation for many years in the valley, put up fences to keep their cattle in and tried to deny the First Peoples access to their traditional ceremonial grounds. The ranch hands put locks on the gates. Shirley's brother, Austin, was stopped by the Douglas Lake cowboys on traditional Thompson hunting territory and was told he was trespassing. He replied that he was exercising his Aboriginal right to traditional territory. The Upper Nicola Band countered the Douglas Ranch move with a roadblock in order to draw attention to the situation. This move rapidly dominated nation-wide media attention. The issues were not clarified by the media, who sensationalized the roadblock instead of providing Canadians with accurate information.

Instead of facilitating the negotiation of a peaceful settlement, governments called in police and tensions escalated. The incident was triggered by a misunderstanding about land use, but, as at Oka in 1990, it was presented by the media as Indian "lawlessness" and has never been resolved to anyone's satisfaction.

Shirley's life is a melding of the old ways with the new. She sees her current life as consisting of two roles. On the one hand she has earned the status of "educator" with her Ph.D. degree. She has worked as a researcher, lecturer, and administrator in the formal university community. On the other hand, she is an apprentice storyteller in her own culture. She is engaged in the process of learning her culture, a process that was denied her by the residential school.

Shirley was not allowed to speak her first language at the residential school, and Sophie did not teach the language to her children because of the trauma she herself had experienced. The main language of Shirley's childhood home was English, but Sophie was still what Shirley terms "a cultural professor" who passed on information about language, stories, place names, material cultures, history, genealogy, and plant medicine. In adulthood, Shirley formally studied the Thompson language for two years.

Shirley is also engaged in the process of learning her culture's stories and is taking her role as grandmother very seriously. She is teaching not only her grandson but her "world family" and is always cognizant of the fact that she is "older sister" to the younger generation. When she made the decision to work on a Ph.D., she chose as her dissertation topic *The Grandmother Stories: Oral Tradition and the Transmission of*

Culture. Her dissertation is a ground-breaking document that combines current non-Aboriginal educational theory with traditional stories.

In her work she challenges the university rationale that stems from the conventions of the Western world at the time of European contact. The European monopoly on truth, manifested in a Eurocentric world view founded on Greek, Roman, and Biblical traditions, has long been jealously guarded by institutions of higher learning. The main source of Western information has been books and written materials interpreted through the writers' own paradigm. The institution has not validated oral transmission of knowledge unless it is filtered through some academic discipline's screen. This is too narrow a definition of what body of knowledge informs our society today. Shirley has mastered everything the institution has asked of her, but in her dissertation she proves that university-sanctioned knowledge is not the only foundation for truth. This basic premise that there are other ways in which to access knowledge and truth is becoming more and more relevant in Canada's increasingly multicultural society.

Shirley believes that nothing can ever give her back the stolen years at the residential school. She has sought to rehumanize the dehumanized existence that she led for eleven years. The grandmother stories have brought joy and a sense of inclusion back to her life. The stories show First Nations learners their unique place in their nations' history, Canada's history, and that of the world.

From her early childhood Shirley was taught to value education; however, she came to believe that it meant denying and cutting herself off from her Native heritage because education was provided only in Western institutions. She was taught to believe that the education she received from her family and culture was worthless. Today she is immersed in bridging the gap between the two and explains her dual roles:

> In my traditional role I am an apprentice storyteller engaged in the process of learning the stories, interpreting the meanings of the stories, applying the meanings to my life and transmitting them in song, dance, drama, and storytelling. The meanings of the stories are personal in my role as apprentice story teller.

> As a researcher I analyse the stories for what they can tell us about being better educators of First Nations and other learners in terms of pedagogy, philosophy, history, and healing. My roles of researcher and apprentice storyteller are similar because they serve the same purpose, the acquisition of traditional Native stories and the interpretation of their meanings in terms of cultural transmission. [45]

She considers herself to be an informal storyteller, rather than a historian or recorder.

Though she had known the grandmother stories all her life she had never had the opportunity to really consider their implications. As she began to research, she began to understand how the stories had the power to take her back to a time and place she had lost because of her years in the residential school. She began to explore the knowledge that had been denied her, and she came to understand who she was in relation to other culture groups. She could recover a cultural identity, and an emancipating process took place as she wrote. She was able to overcome the indoctrination she had experienced, which had led her to believe that Native culture was something evil and despicable.

For many years she believed that education consisted only of getting a degree in a Western institution; this was, in fact, the only way she could achieve any credibility in the wider academic and educational community. Yet, for herself, she needed to answer the questions: Who am I? Where do I come from? Where am I going? Because of the cultural discontinuity in her childhood she did not know who she was in relation to her family, her culture group, or her nation. Where she came from had to do with her ancestry, the traditional knowledge, and the traditional history of her people. She knew only bits and pieces of information about herself. Before she could determine where she was going, she had to find answers to the first two questions.

Shirley explains that in her culture there are five seasons. The fifth is the late fall when the seasons and the moon merge. She sees herself in the same way, merging traditional and contemporary society, merging her Native identity with the Celtic part of her heritage, and living successfully in contemporary mainstream society. She has come to the

Marjorie Gould

point where today she can comfortably be both Seepeetza and Shirley.
Marjorie Gould was a curious nine-year-old when her father took her,
along with her three sisters, to the Shubenacadie Residential School in
1947. Marjorie was born at Whycocomagh, Cape Breton, Nova Scotia,
but her parents moved to Eskasoni in 1943, when she was five years old.
Her paternal grandfather was a carpenter and farmer who had moved
around a great deal, so her father, Roddy Gould, had only gone to
school for short periods of time. Her grandfather had no understanding of English so "white-man" style education meant nothing to him,
and he saw little need for his children to go to school. Consequently
Roddy's education had been brief and sporadic.

Marjorie's mother, Caroline, was the daughter of an illiterate
Irish serving girl but was raised by Mi'kmaq and French foster parents
as their own child. It was not an uncommon practice at that time for
poor non-Aboriginal women to give their illegitimate children to
Mi'kmaq parents, where they would receive love and nurture, rather
than have them grow up in poverty, hopelessly stigmatized by their
birth. Caroline attended the Indian Affairs day school at Chapel Island.
She showed particular promise in art and penmanship but the academic

expectations of the children were low. At age twelve, Caroline had reached grade four and could read and write English proficiently. She left school in order to help at home. Caroline quickly became a master basket maker. The unique Mi'kmaq baskets, woven so tightly that they could be used to transport water, were essential to the survival of the family since there was always a good market for them. From an early age, Caroline's baskets were favoured and brought a good price. Over time she added embellishments, which are her personal trademark.

Caroline married Roddy Gould at an early age and they raised a family of four girls. Eventually Marjorie's parents moved into a tidy little retirement home on the #105 highway in Whycocomagh. Her mother, well into her eighties, still lives there today. Caroline and Roddy were well known and dearly beloved Elders who had to build additional cabinet space in their home to display the many honours and gifts they received over the years. Their fiftieth wedding anniversary was a community event that brought guests from far and wide. Roddy, a carpenter like his father, was recognized for his dedicated community service and his devotion to the Catholic Church.

Caroline grew to be a world-class basket maker; much of her work is found in museums today. The home is a mixture of traditional Mi'kmaq artefacts and Roman Catholic icons indicating the strong religious beliefs held by both Roddy and Caroline.

The demand for Caroline's baskets far surpasses the work she can do. She has a marked preference for making little baskets for members of the younger generations in her large extended family and the families of her friends. She finds that catering to the tourist market can be stressful and unfulfilling. Caroline did not bring out her baskets until she felt that I had no intention of badgering her into selling me one. Their home is a place that welcomes one and all. When I was interviewing Marjorie she often said, "Go see my mother, she can answer that question better than I can." The subsequent interview was all, and more, than what Marjorie had promised. Her parents extended gracious hospitality and shared their great wealth of information generously. Caroline's spritely manner and involvement in community affairs belie her advanced years. She regrets she can no longer climb the hills to pick the blackberries for her special jams and jellies. She told of the unfortunate death of an acquaintance and concluded, "He was still a young man; he could not have been more than seventy-eight." It is evident that Marjorie has inherited the same energy and zest for life that characterizes her remarkable mother.

Marjorie and her sisters grew up in a very close, loving family. They lived an orderly, highly disciplined life with strict but reasonable rules that the girls were expected to obey. English was not used in the home, though it is used now that the children are adults. Their parents took great pride in their Mi'kmaq heritage, and the reasons for passing on the language were basic: You have to understand Mi'kmaq so you will know how to behave. Valuable lessons about deportment and interactions with others simply could not be transmitted in the language of foreigners.

The family attended the Catholic Church every Sunday. They observed all rituals strictly and were active in the small church on the reserve. This attachment to the Catholic Church has stayed with Marjorie all her life.

In Eskasoni Marjorie's father operated a store and did construction work. When she was nine years old their happy family life was disrupted drastically; their mother was diagnosed with tuberculosis. There was no option for Caroline but to leave her young family and go into a sanatorium for a cure. Roddy did his best to look after the girls but the difficulties of his job—the store, the construction work, and pulpwood cutting to make ends meet—made childcare almost impossible. He tried several unsuccessful solutions. He put the girls in homes and paid others to look after them but he could not find a home that could accommodate all four of them. Marjorie remembers the disarray this caused because they were "all over the place" and family cohesiveness was broken. He experimented with hiring housekeepers but that did not work out either. Canada had not yet developed the safety nets, such as welfare, that we take for granted today; had he opted to stay home and look after the girls himself there would have been no income to sustain them. Finally he resorted to the only solution left to him—the residential school at Shubenacadie.

The Shubenacadie School, often referred to as "Shubie," was not built until 1930 and had a relatively short history. It was the only residential school in the Maritime provinces and could only accommodate a small minority of the First Nations children in that region at a time. As a result, many children were spared the residential school experience entirely, and consequently the Maritimes were also spared much of the devastation that successive generations of residential school attendance created. When the Shubenacadie School was in the planning stages, the viability of residential schools was already being questioned by many, and they were being severely criticized by some. Duncan Campbell Scott, deputy superintendent of Indian Affairs, decided that the school should be built in full view of the railway and highway so that "passing people will see it as an indication that our country is not unmindful of the interest of these Indian children." [46] Consequently, the school stood on top of a hill with no trees for shelter. A playground surrounded the school where students sought shelter from the wind in protected corners. Isabelle Knockwood, who has recorded her experiences and perspectives on the school, stated, "We huddled in the corner like cattle trying to get a little warmth from the other body." [47] When the school was demolished, the bricks were found to be of such poor quality that they could not be salvaged.

Numerous examples of outrageous abuse, both physical and sexual, have been documented by Knockwood and other survivors. The documentation that exists seems to point to the fact that treatment of students was unequal and that the abuse was directed at certain students, especially those who were too timid to defend themselves. Those who did not have older relatives at the school to protect them, those who were orphans, or those whose parents did not visit the school received much harsher treatment. On the other hand, privileged students fared reasonably well.

Marjorie recalls her time at the school—two school terms—as generally positive. Home was not home anyway because their mother was not there. The Sisters of Charity, who ran the school, were harsh and did not relate to the children on a personal level. However, Marjorie believes the rules and strict discipline in her home, as well as the role the Catholic Church had played in her and her siblings' upbringing, helped them adjust to the ways of the school more easily. The Mi'kmaq language had been their primary language, and because English was not the language of their home, there was a considerable degree of excitement at the prospect of learning to communicate in English. An older cousin was already in the school and provided some of the comfort and nurturing that the girls craved because they no longer had the close family ties to which they were accustomed.

The girls did not feel abandoned by their parents. They understood and shared the anguish that the turn of events had inflicted on the family. They were told that they had to go to school in order to be looked after and that their cousin was there and would look out for them. They were not prepared in advance for the academic aspects of the school because their parents placed little importance on academic learning. Their parents' chief concern was that the children be looked after adequately until the family could return to a normal home life. The children felt they were going to an orphanage; that it happened to be a school was simply incidental. They were reassured that they would not be there forever and they would be back home as soon as their mother was well. Their father visited the children once or twice when they were in school but it was a very painful experience for everyone.

Though the school experience was generally good for Marjorie, there were aspects that caused her considerable unease, even as a child. She does not always join the harsh critics today, pointing out instead that the times were what they were and Aboriginal people were surviving as best they could. She points out that there were children, such as herself, who were placed in the school by their parents because they had no choice. They were caught in a web of colonialism that had led to extreme poverty in the Maritimes; the treaty obligations of the federal government were never formalized for the Mi'kmaq the way they were in the west. This may, however, also have had some benefits. The draconian manner of forcibly removing children from their homes or kidnapping them to take them to school, as was done in some western schools, did not take place in the Maritimes. Unreasonable punishments and abuse, however, were just as rampant.

Marjorie knew the situation at the school was temporary and had the advantage of having spent her early years in a family setting. She does not recall being lonesome because she was with her siblings and her cousin. She recalls being really bothered by some aspects of the experience, the most vivid being the poor food. Even today she shudders as she recalls being forced to eat spoiled food and laughs at all the conniving ways they developed to avoid eating it—unless, of course, they were so hungry they ate it in desperation. Even with this memory, how-

105

ever, she does not judge the school too harshly since many Mi'kmaq were on the verge of starvation. But she says, "I knew even then, at that young age, that forcing us to eat rotten food simply was not *right*."

She also recalls thinking that the severe punishments were not right. She was not punished because she was a bright, outgoing, cooperative student. She did not fear punishment for herself and believes she was favoured by staff, but she does not think that she took advantage of her privileged position. Instead, she was grateful for the kinder treatment she received, and she responded by applying herself industriously. She worked hard to meet all expectations. But she was aware of the unfair treatment of other students and was affected by the grief and suffering she saw. She was unable to do anything to help the students around her. All she could do was concentrate on her own good behaviour so she would not become one of them. She saw students whose hair was shorn off, and she trembled at the thought of impending punishment when someone ran away. Especially she was afraid for the little children when they wet their beds. She looked after younger children as much as she could and tried to help them before they were caught and punished.

She excelled in academics. She describes herself as very curious, so any new knowledge that came her way was exciting and challenging. She especially loved the choir and felt it was an honour to learn Latin. She took great pride in being able to respond in Latin in the chapel. In retrospect she feels that she was successful in the school because she was a curious, confident, highly motivated person, characteristics that have stood her in good stead all her life.

She was a highly developed social being when she entered the school, already having learned many of the skills and practices that were expected by mainstream society. Her parents, extended family, and community had taught her and her sisters many functional survival skills. Many of the behaviour expectations that the school had of them were already familiar to her so it was easy to fall in line. Most important to her then—and it is readily evident that this is still the major influence in her life—was the loving, close-knit family unit that has always sustained her.

The family was reunited when their mother's health improved. After almost two years, the longed-for day arrived. Their parents arrived at the school to announce that they were taking the ecstatic children back home.

The children went to the day school at Eskasoni, which was run by the Sisters of St. Martha. The Sisters loved their work and the community people and were loved in return. The natural beauty of the reserve on the shores of Bras D'Or Lake and the gracious, outgoing nature of the people made it an ideal place to work. The students responded enthusiastically to the teaching of the Sisters, and Marjorie finished grade eight at age thirteen.

Marjorie had to leave home to continue her education. This was not traumatic for her, since she had already experienced life away from home at the residential school. She understood the necessity of leaving home and had a great thirst for knowledge and life experiences beyond the reserve. The family unit had stabilized, so the move to advance her education was a normal part of growing up.

She was financed by the Department of Indian Affairs and attended a convent boarding school—Our Lady of the Assumption convent at Arichat, Nova Scotia—along with some other Mi'kmaq girls. The school was designed for well-to-do, non-Aboriginal girls. However, Marjorie and the other Mi'kmaq girls quickly made friends and established lasting relationships with their classmates. Academic standards were very high and rules were as strict as they had been at Schubenacadie. Marjorie stayed at that school for grades nine and ten and excelled academically; in fact, she took grade eleven history as well as her grade ten subjects. Then she went to St. Joseph's High School in Mabou, Nova Scotia, for grade eleven and took a university preparation program in her last year. At the age of seventeen she began university at St. Francis Xavier in Antigonish.

In high school the Sisters had counselled her to go into teaching and facilitated her acceptance in the Sisters of the Congregation of Notre Dame at St. Francis Xavier University. Here she received much nurturing and support from the Sisters and in 1960 was the first Aboriginal woman to ever graduate from a university in Nova Scotia.

She graduated with a bachelor of arts degree with a major in English, then she obtained a bachelor of education degree in 1961, qualifying her to teach high-school English. St. Francis Xavier was a Roman Catholic college, and the instructors were predominantly nuns and priests. Marjorie was one of only five women in the bachelor of education program in 1961.

Roman Catholic school boards in Alberta were actively recruiting graduates from St. Francis Xavier University so Marjorie moved west after graduation. Better salary levels in the west were an added incentive. She began her teaching career in a small southern Alberta town as a high-school English, history, and typing teacher but then moved to the elementary level. From there she ventured to McBride, British Columbia, again recruited by a Roman Catholic school board. She was twenty-four years old when she went to McBride, and some of the students were only a few years younger than she was. Students attended a boarding school at McBride since outlying areas did not have schools of their own. Marjorie's task was to teach them to pass provincial exams, which was a challenge as she attempted to teach Shakespeare to students who came from a largely "frontier" culture. She learned much from this experience as she organized cooperative learning and study groups. Out of this experience she developed a philosophy of education regarding relevant teaching and learning materials, a philosophy that has had a great impact on her decisions as an education professional for the rest of her life.

In 1964 she moved back to the Maritimes and began a career with Indian Affairs. She taught elementary school for two years at Burnt Church, New Brunswick, and then spent a year as language arts specialist for the Atlantic region of Indian Affairs. She believes her services were desperately needed. She had come to understand that there was something terribly wrong with the way Indian children were being taught, so she developed grade one programs that were more respectful of the way the children had been raised in their preschool years.

In 1967 she was hired by Indian Affairs to open district education offices to provide services to educators. She worked as an education counsellor as well. She worked out of Antigonish, covering both Nova Scotia and Prince Edward Island. A part of her job was to be education counsellor for the Boarding Home Program, which was composed of young people who left their home reserves to continue high-school education.

In 1970 Marjorie began a master's degree in education at the University of Maine. She did not graduate until 1979, however, because her career path took unexpected turns. She had an opportunity to work in Quebec to learn French and to work on a research project in the northern part of the province for two years. When she completed that job she filled in as principal at Whycocomagh for six months and worked for Indian Affairs during the summers as holiday replacement staff. In 1973 she took specialized training in teaching English as a second language and then worked as a classroom consultant in New Brunswick until 1978. She eventually became superintendent of Continuing Education for the Indian Affairs Department and in 1981 was appointed to the position of acting superintendent of Education.

Dramatic changes took place in Mi'kmaq education in 1982. The federal government began to fund the bands directly so they were able to achieve some control over the education of their children. Marjorie accepted the position of Director of Education for the Burnt Church Indian Nation in New Brunswick. After seven years as director she returned to the Department of Indian Affairs as manager of education policy and planning.

In 1993 she accepted a new position with the Province of Nova Scotia as Mi'kmaq education consultant; however, in 1994 she had the opportunity to move to a position with the *Mi'kmaw Kina'matneywey*. This is a Nova Scotia organization representing the First Nations communities with a board of directors made up of the representative chiefs.

A highlight of her career has been her involvement in the Mi'kmaq Education Jurisdictional Initiative. After two years of intensive negotiations with the federal government the Mi'kmaq of Nova Scotia achieved autonomy over their own education programs. In June 1998 Bill C-30, *An Act Respecting the Powers of the Mi'kmaq of Nova Scotia in Relation to Education,* was passed. *Maclean's* magazine called it a "milestone for First Nations."[48] As a result of the bill, Nova Scotia Mi'kmaq became the first Aboriginal group in Canada to gain direct control over education on reserves. Chief Lindsay Marshall, chairman of the body that oversees Mi'kmaq education in Nova Scotia, was quoted as saying, "For once, we are masters of our own house when it comes to education."[49]

The final agreement stipulated that a body would be established to assist the participating communities in the delivery of education services. This body, known as *Mi'kmaw Kina'matneywey,* serves as an advocate for the Mi'kmaq of Nova Scotia and addresses education-related issues. Chief Lindsay Marshall is the chairman of this body; Marjorie Gould was the first executive director. There is a staff of seven people who assist with the exciting task of charting new and unprecedented directions in Aboriginal education. Marshall told a *Maclean's* reporter that First Nations from across Canada have asked for advice on how to achieve similar status.[50]

The task of assuming responsibility for education began with Bill C-30; the task ahead required a proposed work plan consisting of fifty-four discreet steps toward implementing the operation of the new system. The implementation phase took a full year.

Separate from the work plan, but highly significant, is the fact that the Mi'kmaw Language Advisory Group was established, demonstrating the high priority that language revitalization will play in this historic move. The importance of language revitalization is emphasized by most educators who experienced language loss in residential schools.

Marjorie Gould came to her job as executive director with a bewildering array of qualifications and educational experiences. Besides her three university degrees, Marjorie's curriculum vitae shows many specialized training courses that she completed throughout her educational career. She has specialized training in teaching English as a second language, in human resource management, in clinical supervision, in employment equity and race relations, and in developing effective schools. Though Marjorie had worked predominantly as an administrator in her career, she also had first hand experience as a classroom teacher, a counsellor, and a consultant. She had been a researcher and a policy analyst for the Department of Indian Affairs.

Marjorie is often asked to sit on boards and task forces, and her activities show a wide variety of interests. She has served on the advisory board of the Mi'kmaq Maliseet Institute at the University of New Brunswick; she was a member of the advisory board for Inmate Employment with Corrections Canada; has served on a task force on Mi'kmaq education for the Nova Scotia Department of Education; is a member of the Assembly of First Nations National Indian Education Council; has been a member of the Race Relations Committee of the Nova Scotia Barristers Society, as well as other human rights committees. She is on the board of governors of the University College of Cape Breton.

The tremendous energy Marjorie has invested in her work has led to effective influences in education that have not only had an impact on the Atlantic provinces but also across the country. Her name is well known in Canadian Aboriginal education circles. She was a board member of the Mokakit Education Research Association, a Canada-wide organization that fostered research on Aboriginal educational issues.

She loves to entertain people at her "country house" on Cape Breton Island, though her pace is such that her guests often have difficulty keeping up with her. She is a gregarious, outgoing person who entertains people wherever she goes, from the sales clerks in a ladies' wear shop who are waiting on her to the gas jockey who is filling up her car. She has an irresistible jovial approach to life. She can be a non-stop talker and her listeners are well advised to pay close attention since they might miss some memorable gems of wisdom she introduces into even the most casual story, or they might miss a turn of phrase or veiled comment that will bring a chuckle long after the conversation is over.

Marjorie exemplifies the qualities that had made the Mi'kmaq Nation strong and self-sufficient before the impact of European influences on their way of life. Her commitment to her people and her dedication to restoring what has been lost over years of colonization have gone a long way toward establishing a solid foundation for *Mi'kmaw Kina'matneywey*. It is well on its way to building a promising future for the Mi'kmaq of Nova Scotia.

In 2002 Marjorie opted for early retirement in order to help her mother cope with her father's declining health. He suffered from Alzheimer's disease, and in December 2003 he passed away peacefully. Marjorie's years of dedication to educational issues are not forgotten. In May of 2002 she was awarded a lifetime achievement award by the Atlantic Native Teachers Education Conference (ANTEC), an honour she values above all others. In December of the same year her contributions to education were recognized by her alma mater, St. Francis Xavier, with a honourary doctorate degree.

Doris Pratt

The year was 1862. The Dakota, often referred to as the Sioux, who had traditionally hunted in the area now known as Minnesota, were starving. Buffalo herds had been systematically destroyed as a result of government policies destined to undermine the major food supply of Plains Indians and bring them to their knees. Treaties had been signed but the terms of the treaties were not being fulfilled by the American government and were subject to the whims of the Indian agents. There was a storehouse full of food for Little Crow's band, but the Indian agent refused to release the rations. After repeated requests Little Crow sent an intermediary to beg on their behalf. The agent responded, "Let them eat grass."

Little Crow's band had hunted all day, finding nothing, since the prairies had been stripped of all wildlife by the starving Dakota. They came upon a small group of buildings and gestured that they were hungry. Fearfully, a woman gave them some food. As they were leaving the men passed a small chicken house and, peering inside, saw a hen sitting on a nest of eggs. Thinking of the hungry children back in camp, they attempted to take some eggs, but the outraged hen created a great uproar. Seeing her precious hen in jeopardy the woman rushed out and

112

began to hit the men with her broom. To be hit on the body by anyone was an outrage for a Dakota warrior. To be hit by a woman was the ultimate humiliation, so they killed her. Recognizing the enormous consequences their actions would have, they killed the five other people on the settlement, as well.

Even today the Dakota refer to this incident as *Witka nakhugha*, literally meaning "breaking the egg by stepping on it." Historians call it the Minnesota Massacre of 1862. The Dakota prepared for war. Federal troops with state-of-the-art rifles were sent to quell the uprising but not before the Dakota had killed the hated Indian agent, leaving him on the ground with grass protruding from every body orifice. The Dakota knew they were no match for the army since they were armed with only bows and arrows. Women, children, and old people were hidden in Birch Coulee, but the army sought them out and massacred them all. Ultimately thousands of Dakota lost their lives in the massacre. Today a cairn has been erected at Birch Coulee, near Mankato, Minnesota, to commemorate this loss of life.

Small groups of Dakota escaped the carnage, hotly pursued by the military. Doris Pratt's great-grandfather, later given the name of Charlie Dowan by government officials, escaped with his family group of about fifteen members. When they came to the Red River, the army in hot pursuit, they hastily tied bunches of willow branches together, which they then tied to the horses' tails for the women and children to cling to as the horses swam across the river. The army arrived in time to fire shots across the river, but it was too late for the bullets to do any harm. The Dakota melted into the bushes, and the army gave up its pursuit.

The Dakota did have a destination, the land to the north, which was British territory. Dakota adventurers had long travelled far and wide, even assisting the British in what is now eastern Canada. They had been personally thanked for their support by an emissary for King George III. The emissary passed on the message that they would always have sanctuary in British territory. Long before the establishment of any "Medicine Line" the Dakota had roamed the prairies, often moving into Canada for the summer as the heat became more intense in the south.

As they were resting after their fearful flight, the shaman dreamed a dream, telling them to go north until they found a cross. Other straggling groups followed the same familiar routes to the

Pembina Hills that they had often used in the past and eventually found sanctuary in what is now southern Manitoba. Their reputation as a war-like tribe, hostile to white people, preceded them, so when they reached the cross at St. Boniface they were met with fear. Many of their members had died of starvation and exhaustion along the way. The priests at St. Boniface hastily gave them some food on condition that they would leave but recognized that the children had reached the end of their physical strength. The mission agreed to provide sanctuary for the sick and starving children. The Jesuit priests interpreted this to mean that the Dakota were selling their children in return for food and had given up their rights to their children. In later years, however, the Dakota families all reclaimed their children and found they had been looked after well. Some of the children had learned to speak English fluently.

The Dakota adults were equally anxious to leave the Red River settlement, since its proximity to the widely used trade routes to the US made them nervous. Twenty-six of their fellow tribesmen had been captured by the American military and eventually were hanged. Many who had escaped were fugitives, actively sought by the American government. They travelled west from the Red River, and when they reached what is now Portage la Prairie, a small group felt it was safe to settle down. The Dakota Tipi Reserve is located in this spot today. Charlie Dowan continued west and settled in the Assiniboine Valley in what is now western Manitoba. Other groups continued to Saskatchewan. Standing Buffalo Reserve in the Qu'Appelle Valley and Whitecap Reserve at Dundurn provided other new homes. Little Crow's band, however, did not feel it was safe to settle until they reached Prince Albert, where the descendants live today on the Wahpeton Reserve.

As Charlie Dowan's group travelled westward from the Red River they were surprised by a river boat travelling east on the Assiniboine River. Rightly speculating that there would be food on the boat they attacked it, killed the owners, and took the supplies. This act not only provided food for their famished bodies, it also provided guns and ammunition. Some items were unfamiliar to them, but they took them along, not wishing to leave any evidence of their passing. They soon happened on an isolated settler's cabin. He treated them kindly and so they confided in him that they had bags of supplies for which they had no use. Examining the supplies, he advised them to leave them with him so no suspicion would ever fall on them. Little did they know that they were giving over bags containing a considerable amount of gold, nor did they understand that gold was the most highly valued commodity among the settlers. The settler promised to guard the supplies for them, lest they be linked to the death of the boatmen. One day when they went to see him, he was gone. They did not see him again until the railroad was being built through southern Manitoba. He was the most affluent contractor with the best horses and equipment and the biggest work crew on the scene!

Charlie Dowan saw the whole Assiniboine Valley as his domain, and his family formed the nucleus of what today is the Sioux Valley Reserve. The land was unpopulated; in fact, the 1900 census counted only 102 people. Other families joined him and eventually spread out to establish the Pipestone and Birdtail Sioux Reserves. The Ojibway, who largely lived north of the Assiniboine River, feared the Dakota at first, but it was not long before peaceful relations were established. This was especially important for the Dakota because very few of their women had survived the massacre and the trek north.

In 1874 the Government of Canada granted the Dakota status as Indian people and designated reserve land for their use. Charlie Dowan wanted no part of negotiations with the government, remembering how this kind of arrangement had devastated the Sioux Nations in the United States. The land he had settled on and farmed for ten years fell outside the reserve boundary and he would not relinquish it. Nor did he have to, because an obscure Indian Affairs regulation stated that an Indian who lived and farmed land like the white settlers could not be removed from his land. Eventually the land passed on to Doris's grandfather. The small parcel of land was adjacent to the main settlement on the reserve, and the Dowan family was granted membership in the Sioux Valley Band by the federal government. Charlie Dowan's gravesite can still be identified on this piece of land.

Unfortunately, Charlie Dowan was not allowed to live peacefully on this land. The Indian agent was irked by his independence and white settlers in the surrounding area coveted the land. One spring the agent announced that in order to retain ownership Dowan had to farm the land as efficiently as the surrounding farmers were farming theirs. Spring plowing had not yet begun but the agent said that if the land was not plowed by the following day it would be confiscated. The agent did not know how determined Dowan was to keep what was rightfully his. He elicited help from the men on the reserve, and they brought their single-share walking plows and horses. By the time daybreak came, the land was plowed, much to the agent's chagrin. Thereafter the land was always plowed by the men of the reserve as soon as the frost left the soil.

After Charlie Dowan died the land was sold to an area farmer. Doris's grandfather and his brother had struggled valiantly to keep the land and even moved into the log house in their attempt to assert ownership. Times were hard, however, and they had to resort to supplemental work to support their families. They were no match for the Indian agent, either, or the pressure from the settlers. It became increasingly difficult to live on the farm. They had received their allotment of eighty acres of reserve land, so they moved into Indian Affairs houses on the reserve and went to work for area farmers. The 160 acres of excellent farm land in the valley was lost to the family. Even the log house was dismantled and removed from the land because settlers had other uses for the logs.

In later years Doris Pratt researched the title to the land under a Treaty Land Claims Initiative and found that, indeed, Charlie Dowan had title to the land and his rights had never been extinguished. The land was sold to an area settler by the government even though it was not Crown land. Dowan's descendants have never received the proceeds of the sale. Doris was advised to pursue the matter but most of the people who remembered the land when it belonged to the Dowan family had passed away; the few who were still alive were not interested in the problems and hard feelings that would arise if they chose to claim it.

Charlie Dowan's grandson, Doris's father, went to work for a homesteader when he was fourteen. They treated him well. The homesteader's wife gathered children from the surrounding area into her kitchen to provide rudimentary schooling since schools had not yet been established. Doris's father was able to participate at times, and he became a proficient, largely self-taught reader and writer.

Doris's mother came from the Dakota Tipi Reserve. She was a two-year-old infant, still crawling, when she was taken to the Portage Residential School where she stayed until she was old enough to marry. She did, however, go home every summer and so became a highly proficient Dakota speaker, a skill she passed on to her children. All her life she saw the residential school method as a normal and natural way to raise her children.

Doris was the youngest of nine children, and when she was six she went to the missionary day school on the reserve. She was the only child in the class who could speak English, which was not a happy experience for her. Other children beat her and pinched her because she was different. When she was seven she was sent to the Elkhorn Residential School, eighty-five kilometres from home. Her older siblings had already returned from the school. Two of them died at the age of fifteen, shortly after they returned home in poor health, but the causes of their deaths are unknown. Her older siblings never talked about their school experiences, so Doris did not know what to expect.

Her memories of the school contain no happy vignettes. She had a great sense of acceptance of the inevitable, assigning no blame and never questioning the system. Her mother approved of the residential school since she knew no other way. Asked about her childhood, Doris exclaims, "What a lonely childhood that was. No one knows the tears we cried!" Her husband, who attended the same school, was separated from his mother when he was three because she had contracted tuberculosis and was sent to a sanatorium. He was raised by his grandparents and was reunited with his mother at age six, only to be forcibly removed again to go to residential school at age seven. He cried without reprieve for a whole month, and the emotional scars this early experience left have had an impact on him, that has lasted all his life.

The saddest part of the experience, according to Doris, was the emotional void in which they lived. There was no nurture, no understanding of their condition as children. She recalls frequently just standing still, inwardly crying out to herself, "Where is my mother? Where is my father?" Outwardly, she was the stolid Indian child who appeared to be adjusting well.

Several memories are seared into her brain. Her bed was next to the hot water pipe that heated the dormitory. One night she was curled up against the pipe, fast asleep, when she awoke to being beaten with a rubber-soled running shoe. Finally the supervisor demanded, "Now are you going to go to sleep?" Doris answered "Yes," because there could be no other response, and the supervisor left. To this day Doris wonders what all that was about.

She was often strapped because she says even at that time she was a "loud mouth" and questioned what was happening around her. That got her into trouble with staff. She tried running away once but was apprehended after fourteen kilometres and taken back to school. The strapping and blacklisting that followed were so severe that she never contemplated running away again. In spite of the harshness of the staff, Doris believes that for her the most distressing aspect of the school was the abuse she suffered at the hands of the older girls. This hurt more than the actions of the capricious staff because it came from people who could have helped and protected her. One fellow student, in particular, she still refers to as "Hitler's daughter."

In 1989 survivors of the Elkhorn School met for a reunion, organized largely by Doris, her sister Kathleen, and the late Ina Whitecloud. The school had been demolished but the small, neglected cemetery plot remained. With help from the provincial government they cleaned up the plot and planted flowers. Many members of the community had not even known that bodies of children who had died at the school were buried in the forgotten plot. As the survivors recalled and shared painful memories, it soon became evident that one incident, above all others, stood out in their minds. The principal had brought Adam, one of the bigger boys, into the dining room because he had stolen some bread. To make an example of him he was to receive the strap. The horrified students watched as Adam was given one hundred blows to each hand by the principal who towered over him. No one could withstand such severe abuse, but as Adam lay writhing on the floor, the blows continued. The next evening he was brought in again, and the process was repeated. Doris was seven when she was forced to witness such brutality.

Another unforgettable incident happened when she was nine. The girl who occupied the bed beside her had swung too high on the playground swing. She fell and broke her neck on the concrete pad below. She made her way to the dormitory, shrieking with the excruciating pain, but she was merely sent to the dormitory to lie down. Eventually a doctor was called in but it was too late. The principal stormed into the dining room at noon, yelling at the children, "What did I tell you? I tell you not to do this and then you do it anyway. See what happened? She is dead." The afternoon dragged on; at dusk the ambulance came and the children watched as their playmate was carried out in a body bag. Then the children were fed their supper and sent to bed. Doris will always remember the terror of the empty bed next to hers where the girl had died. The next day in chapel they sang dismal Anglican hymns about death and that, as far as staff was concerned, was the end of the episode.

In spite of the horror of some of her experiences, Doris feels that the greatest devastation the school system wrought was that they could never feel good about themselves. They were continually called "trash." She did not know what trash meant but she knew that it was not good. She was no good and there was no way out. This feeling lasted until she was well into adulthood and still haunts her. Since the school had been her mother's life it was normal for the school to determine the lives of her children as well. They simply accepted that that was the way it was. They assigned no blame because they knew no better.

At the age of thirteen Doris transferred to the Portage la Prairie Residential School, while her future husband went to Birtle. At age fourteen their education was finished. Doris's parents were eking out a meagre existence by working for area farmers, and Doris, too, began to work at whatever jobs were available. She was strong and healthy so pitched sheaves, cut cordwood, and picked potatoes. She took great pleasure in riding horseback and became an expert horsewoman, earning the nickname "Cowgirl." She was an oddball, the only girl on the reserve who enjoyed outdoor activities more than the constraints of the house.

In early spring she and her sister went out on the trapline with their father. Her sister did the cooking but Doris aspired to become as expert a muskrat skinner as her father was. In time she could equal his record of skinning a rat in three minutes flat.

At the age of seventeen she decided to strike out on her own. With a gift of thirty-five cents from her father, she hitchhiked to the nearby town of Virden. Discrimination was commonplace in those days, so she was not surprised when café owners turned down her inquiries for jobs in rude and humiliating ways. But she had been raised to be strong both physically and mentally; her father was a strict disciplinarian. She was determined to make the job search work. She soon got work cleaning houses, and today her hands show the effects of the many, many floors she scrubbed and the toilet bowls she cleaned.

The experience had positive aspects. People, by and large, were kind, and many of the people she worked for became friends. She was a voracious reader, and she had the opportunity to get reading material where she worked. Her father had already set an example by bringing home magazines and other reading material from the places where he worked, and he always subscribed to the *Free Press Prairie Farmer*. People often told Doris that she was not meant for menial labour and that she should do something better with her life, but Doris could not even imagine any other possibilities. The idea that "trash" could do anything other than menial work was just too preposterous.

When she was twenty-five Doris married Walter Pratt. Walter came from a prominent family of hereditary chiefs, but by the time he married Doris his honoured position was recognized by few. Walter worked as a farm labourer, and they barely got by on his niggardly wages. When their children were too small for Doris to go out to work they lived on relief, though she added to their income by doing as much housework as she could. She gratefully remembers the kindness of a Mennonite missionary and his wife who became close friends. They provided assistance in the form of used clothing but, above all, they became a source of moral support, which was particularly valuable to Doris.

When Doris was thirty-four the kindergarten teacher on the reserve heard that Brandon University was beginning special teacher-training programs for Aboriginal people. She suggested that Doris apply, and though Doris was very sceptical she accepted a ride to Brandon to make inquiries. Doris got an application form for the Indian and Métis Program for Careers Through Teacher Education (IMPACTE). Dutifully, she filled it out and all but forgot about it when she was not accepted into the first group of students. Then, to her surprise, the next year she was asked to report for tests and was elated when she was accepted.

The students were enrolled in a bachelor of teaching program, which normally took three years. Because of their mature student status they were given three and a half years to finish. Doris did not see any point in dragging her heels. Some of the students needed more time to improve their reading and writing skills, but this was not Doris's case. She enrolled as a regular student, and by the fall of 1974 she was finished except for some incomplete course-related work, which kept her from graduating until 1975.

Doris enjoyed the rigours of university work. There were all those new ideas to explore! She learned that she was as capable as non-Aboriginal students and had the pressing desire to prove that Aboriginals did have brains and could do academic work as well as anyone. Because many of the reserve children at this time were being labelled as "special education cases," Doris chose to focus on special education. She felt she could be of greatest service to her people in this capacity.

Part of her training was spent in schools in a practicum setting and was very productive for Doris. She worked in a provincial school that had many Dakota children. Because she had had a great deal of experience working with non-Aboriginal people she had learned how to fit into any situation. She received a lot of positive feedback from both staff and supervisors.

When she graduated in the spring of 1975 she could hardly believe it. She could not accept her success, and, though she knew she was as capable as her classmates, she could not really believe she was their equal. When her community put on a celebration to honour education graduates she felt like a hypocrite. She did not attend, nor did she accept the gift the community gave her. She did not believe that "trash" really deserved these accolades and felt her accomplishments were a hoax.

Her first job was a five-month on-campus position as coordinator for IMPACTE. This was a happy time for her. She slowly began to believe that she really had proven herself as an equal. When the five months were up she took a position as a special education teacher in the same school where she had done her practicum. She was looking forward to being a full-fledged, equal staff member. Her disillusionment was swift and severe. As a student teacher the treatment had been supportive and sharing. As a staff member she felt the brunt of systemic and personal racism. Her credentials were not accepted, her status as a beginning teacher was not respected. If the issues could have been discussed openly Doris would have done so, but she could not deal with the subtle innuendo and pregnant silences. Every case that could possibly be designated as "special education" was channelled her way, and it was expected that she would have the expertise to handle every one of them. Many were not even special education cases; they were simply children who had not yet learned to speak English. If she faltered even a minute there was suspicion that she was not really up to the job. If her supervisors ever made an attempt to help her she cannot remember it today.

Her self-concept plummeted, and though there were supportive people in the school they were complicit in what was going on because they never challenged the racism. Doris soon experienced self-doubt and began to accept that white people can always do everything better than Aboriginal people can, even teaching impressionable Dakota children.

Further disaster struck when Doris's father passed away in a particularly awful traffic accident, and shortly thereafter her mother died, as well. Doris had lived through a parentless childhood. Being reunited with her parents had given her life joy and security such as she had never known before. She was not able to cope with the loss of her parents a second time, and her whole world crashed.

After she recovered from this profoundly sad period in her life she was asked to take a job as principal on the Dakota Tipi Reserve. Success on this job bolstered her morale so she applied for a job on her home reserve of Sioux Valley. This too was fraught with difficulty. The community did not understand higher education and discredited the time and energy Doris had put into acquiring a university degree. They did not understand the concept of special education and believed the small numbers of students she worked with made her a loafer who saw herself as a "big shot."

She persevered and eventually was appointed to an administrative position, then the principalship of the reserve school. After five years in that position she was summarily dismissed without prior warning or explanation. Doris believes her dismissal arose from a misunderstanding, but she was not given the opportunity to defend herself so she challenged the decision. Eventually she won her case. She believes that whether, in their opinion, they had reasons for the dismissal was not the point. The point was that due processes were not followed and they made her feel that as a human being she had no value. The unexplained dismissal was especially devastating because it had come from her own people.

She moved into university work, becoming a centre coordinator for the Brandon University Northern Teacher Education Program (BUNTEP). The students were being trained as Native language teachers and Doris's particular expertise in the Dakota language was utilized. After three years with the program she returned to Brandon University and completed a master of education program.

After completion of her master's program she returned to Sioux Valley as director of education. One of the particular delights of this position was that she was instrumental in establishing a BUNTEP centre on the reserve with an enrolment of thirty students. From there she moved on to help establish a high school on the Birdtail Sioux Reserve, accepting the job of director of education for the Birdtail Sioux Band, as well as performing the principal's duties, a position she holds today. She enrolled in a Ph.D. program at the University of Arizona to continue her work on languages. In 2003 she was awarded a specialist degree in language, reading, and culture. Her Ph.D. is pending, requiring the completion of some ongoing projects. She is the official Dakota translator for the Government of Canada.

She feels it is important for Aboriginal people to talk about their experiences in the work force. She believes that her qualifications have always been suspect. Often she is tempted to agree that she is not a capable person. She knows, however, that hers is not an isolated case. Many Aboriginal university graduates face similar struggles in both their home communities and in non-Aboriginal institutions. Few are able to speak about it openly for fear of reprisals or without raising further doubts about their proficiencies. Doris believes it is vitally important for Aboriginal people to support rather than undermine each other, because if they do not respect each other they cannot expect the outer world to recognize and respect them.

Like many residential school survivors, Doris's personal life has also been difficult. Many could not sustain marriage relationships; many chose never to marry at all. Doris looks back upon her marriage and declares that if they had lived in modern times the marriage would not have lasted. At the time, however, they saw no alternatives. Both came from families where marriage was sacrosanct and long lasting. Doris's mother's advice was very practical: If you terminate one marriage, what guarantee do you have that the next one will not be as bad or worse? The question of terminating the marriage never really arose, though both Doris and her husband carried around so much residential school baggage it often engulfed them both in despair. Perhaps a strong bond between them was that they had both attended the same school at the same time; they understood that they both carried the same dreadful memories around with them. Though they had no words to communicate with each other, they did understand each other in ways that no one who had not been in the school could.

She says, without hesitation, that they were "horrible" parents. They had no concept of how to parent and resorted to residential school tactics. Her husband did not abuse the children physically, but he had suffered much greater emotional damage, so was especially severe. This led to horrific anxiety among the children. In spite of an imperfect home life, however, all six children completed high school. Today three of the six are in university, one works as an autobody mechanic, and two are raising families.

It was not until the 1980s, when the whole residential school issue became public, that Doris and her husband began to understand and question their life experiences. It was their children who asked questions, forcing them to confront and recall past events. It was their children who said: "What was done to you was not right!" The reunion of the Elkhorn School survivors meant that healing could finally begin. The healing is slow but steady. It was Doris and Walter's children who began to understand and to forgive, and it is they who today are helping their parents forgive themselves and move on with their lives.

Edith Dalla Costa

It was on a late spring day that we drove out to the grounds of what used to be the Edmonton Residential School. The forbidding brick building, surrounded by landscaped grounds, was still intact. Edith pointed out the various boarded-up windows—this side was for the boys, this for the girls. These were offices, the basement windows were the dining area, and this is where the girls played, in this corner where they would be out of sight of the supervisors. This is where the girls held secretive puberty rituals when one of them began to menstruate. They did not know how to conduct the rituals, but they knew rituals were required so they made up their own, desperately clinging to familiar ways. They ran in circles because they knew the circle was an integral part of the culture. But often the rituals were hastily abandoned when a supervisor came into view. This is the bush where they smoked. Not very long after our visit the main building was torched by arsonists.

Behind the brick building stands a smaller one, a replica of many small-town schools of the period. It was built to accommodate senior students when the original school became too small. To the east of the building complex is a field, once used to raise produce for the school, now a powwow ground attended by those who are not too sick at heart to rekindle old memories. Edith has never attended a powwow there.

Beside the school and across the gravel driveway, is a handsome house beautifully nestled among tall shade trees with winding footpaths and flowerbeds. It is well kept and obviously someone is living in it today. "That was the principal's house—we used to see the older, privileged girls going there, and we used to wonder what happened in the house. There was an aura of scary evil about the place. There were rumours that the principal kissed the girls." When Edith was a small child in the school, evil lurked everywhere.

Behind the school complex is the modern Nechi Institute, an addiction treatment centre, mute testimony to the devastation the residential schools wreaked on whole cultures. Maggie Hodgson, the first executive director of the centre, knew of the need for such institutions. She is a Carrier from British Columbia whose mother had attended the Lejac Residential School. Maggie was sent to a Catholic boarding school by her mother who, she says, was a "practising alcoholic." Maggie explains: "Thus I became a victim of residential school through the second generation." There are over 350 Native alcohol prevention and treatment centres across Canada today. Hodgson points out that if you reach into a culture and pull out the values, rituals, and societal norms and attempt to inject new ones, like the residential school system did, you create a society of individuals who suffer from disorientation and confusion about values and identity, at home in neither their original world nor in the world for which they were theoretically being prepared.

We leave the residential school grounds and take the gravel road to St. Albert. "This must be the ditch we crawled along when we ran away," Edith points out with considerable agitation, though the scenery has changed and the trees are much bigger. "And this is where they caught us," she says with finality. Later she tells me the whole story.

We find an idyllic little park and sit at a picnic table to continue the interview. Edith has brought a large box of Kleenex because this is not our first interview, and we both know that many tissues will be required before the afternoon is over. I feel terrible, a voyeur peering into things that I have no right to examine. Edith laughs and cries, exclaiming frequently that she has buried so many things about her past for too long. Finally they are coming out, and even though she is devastated by the memories they evoke she continues to talk.

Today Edith Dalla Costa works as the Native Liaison Services consultant for the Edmonton Public Schools, a lifetime away from her farm home on the Saddle Lake Reserve in northern Alberta. Edith comes from a long line of eminent Aboriginal ancestors. Her grandmother was Louisa Testawich, a Métis. Her grandfather belonged to the Kirkness family and worked at the Hudson's Bay Company stop at Spirit River. His father, Edith's great grandfather, had come from Scotland and had married Sarah Steinhauer, an Ojibway/Cree. The Steinhauer name had been given to the family as a reward for getting an education. Kirkness owned a farm in what is now the heart of Edmonton. From Capilano Drive to Ada Boulevard was all Kirkness farm land. The house still stands on Ada Boulevard today, but when he died her grandfather gave up the land to the city.

Edith's mother was born at Spirit Lake and went to school with the other half-breed children. As an adult she was her aging mother's caregiver and later moved to Edmonton to live with her sister. Here she met Edith's father, Zaccheus Jackson, from Saddle Lake Reserve, whose family was friends with the Steinhauers.

Jackson attended the Red Deer Industrial School and became a very successful farmer on the Saddle Lake Reserve. His industrial school training in basic farming practices had paid off. He was an example of what the school policies were intended to achieve, proficient farmers who could be self-sustaining when they returned home to the reserve. Though his academic successes were unimpressive at the Red Deer school, he did establish a highly successful and productive farm on the reserve.

Zaccheus Jackson was especially proficient in the maintenance of farm machinery and non-Aboriginal farmers sought partnerships with him, especially during threshing time. This successful lifestyle, however, did not last. Sale or barter of farm produce had always been controlled by the Indian Act; no transactions could take place without a permit from the Indian agent. When Indian farmers became too successful, raising the ire and jealousy of surrounding settlers, a quota system was established, effectively keeping Indians on the lowest rungs of the social ladder. Often Jackson was forced to work for area farmers for subsistence wages. Edith's father's successful farming practices became futile because he was not allowed to sell surplus produce. His former friends and partners could have sold it for him but few were willing to take the risk since it was illegal to do so. Heavy fines were levied to ensure the system would not be undermined. A few did help in a very clandestine manner. Her father was very hurt. He was betrayed in every way by the uncaring non-Native society that he had worked so hard to accept and emulate.

Edith started school at the R. B. Steinhauer day school on the reserve and recalls her early years with pride. She was very excited about starting school so she could join her older siblings in their activities. Not only did she learn to read and write quickly, she also had many good teachings from her parents long before she started school. She recalls that along with many other skills, she knew the names of all the wildflowers in the area and had already learned the art of birchbark and leaf biting.

Edith can attest to the fact that abuse of Indian children by their teachers was not confined to residential schools. When she was in grade three an "old man," as she remembers her teacher, Mr. Taylor, kissed her full on the lips in a way that was definitely not a fatherly kiss. She broke free and ran to the safety of the girls' toilet. When he kissed Edith's cousin, the girl did not run for safety; she ran to her grandfather's house and reported the incident. After family meetings and a meeting with Mr. Taylor, all of which is a blur for Edith today, the girls were sent to the Edmonton residential school. Edith felt that it was because of the kiss. What no one understood was that she always felt guilty, certain that the move was made to punish her for what had happened.

Edith was ten years old when she was sent to the Edmonton school, and she stayed there until she was seventeen. For the higher grades the students were bussed to the Guthrie Air Force Base School in Edmonton. For grades eleven and twelve Edith went to the Glen Avon Protestant Separate School in St. Paul, and eventually to Alberta College to complete her social studies credit.

Edith was proficient in English and could read and write when she started residential school, but she never lost the ability to communicate in Cree. She and her siblings spoke nothing but Cree in the summer when they were home, and while at school they worked at retaining it in secretive ways. They always went home for the summer holidays and usually at Christmastime, as well. The parents had to pay the expenses of the Christmas trip, and some years they could not afford it so then the children would have to stay at the school.

The children counted the days until they could go back home. Once at home, their parents, especially their mother, coddled them and gave in to their every whim, so happy was she to have her children at home. In typical Métis fashion, she smothered her children with such love and care that they flourished. On the negative side, Edith recalls tearfully, the children manipulated their mother and took outrageous advantage of her love during the summers. She was a slave to the children, and they made the most of the situation, starved as they were for love the rest of the year. Edith's tears are not so much for the actual actions of the children, which are to be expected; her tears are more for the family torn apart by strangers and the loss the children experienced as they were denied the teachings that come from normal family relationships. And she cries for the pain both parents and children had to accept and cope with as best they could, pain imposed on them by bureaucrats far removed from the humble and loving homes and the families on reserves. But she admits that her father was distant and undemonstrative. He had lost his own boyhood at the school at Red Deer, and many of his childrearing practices stemmed from his own barren childhood. Her mother's love overcompensated for the lack of warmth in the children's father. On the other hand, her father was generous to a fault with material goods, and Edith still remembers a beautiful dress he bought her when she was in high school, a dress that cost eighteen dollars!

Her parents valued education and instilled in their children the importance of acquiring the skills to function in mainstream society. Both parents could read and write in English but it was evident to the children that their father, who had attended school longer, had advantages over their mother. Their parents encouraged the children's school efforts and visited the school as often as they could, though it was approximately two hundred kilometres away. Sometimes they stayed with their mother's sister, Edith Herron, who lived in Edmonton, but more often they would camp by the school until it was time to catch a return train. Eventually they discontinued their visits altogether because the school told them not to come any more.

As Edith reminisces about life in the school no happy memories surface. She was very lonely and was petrified of the regimentation. Upon arrival at the school her hair was treated with coal oil though she had no lice. She came from a very clean home and her Métis mother would have been horrified at the very thought of head lice. The matron was overzealous in her application of the coal oil on one occasion. To this day Edith bears a scar that she has always carefully hidden with her hairdo—even if it meant denying herself the pleasure of the "hip" hairdos of the day—in order to keep what she believed was a shameful secret. After the delousing treatment the children were stripped naked and bathed, four to a tub, in total violation of the standards of modesty with which Edith had been raised.

Today Edith remembers the loneliness, but she also remembers being just plain mad. She hated being in the school, but her anger was not directed specifically at her parents. She knew that they tried to stay connected with their children through letters and messages sent through others. They did what they could. Her anger was perhaps a healthy anger, whereas her younger brother, who internalized his anger, was almost ruined by the residential school experience. Several of her brothers have never come to terms with their experiences, and alcohol has been a serious problem for them.

There is no doubt in Edith's mind that they were psychologically and spiritually abused. She suffered physical abuse from staff but escaped the most vicious sexual abuse that some students experienced. She was terrified at night when she heard the sounds of stealthy male footsteps in the dorm. Even the little girls knew they should not be there. The girls never spoke to each other about those nocturnal visits, and they might be attributed to frightened children's overactive imaginations if it were not for the numerous sexual abuse convictions of dorm supervisors in recent years.

The most humiliating experience happened to Edith when she was eight years old and still sleeping in the little girls' dorm. She fell out of bed and in doing so scratched herself in the genital area though she cannot remember how. It was a minor scratch, but it did draw blood. It was treated as a major incident by the dorm supervisor, who made a great public display of concern. A minor scratch was usually ignored, but in this case the dorm supervisor called her supervisor who called the male principal. All three examined her as though she had a major injury while she lay, fully exposed, in the dorm full of girls. Nothing came of the incident but Edith has never been able to come to terms with the humiliation she felt.

Another incident that still troubles her deeply was when she was put into a single bed with another girl. The dormitories were always overcrowded, and it was not an uncommon practice to double up students in narrow beds, with heads at opposite ends. Edith was paired with a girl who obviously was having problems since she was a bed wetter. The girls were forced to strip completely and then put on their nightgowns; panties were not allowed even in this crowded situation. Her partner took out her frustrations on Edith by kicking her genital area over and over again. For Edith to complain to the dorm supervisor was unthinkable. "That," Edith says today, "was sexual abuse."

She recalls an incident of physical abuse by a supervisor when she was in grade ten, still very naive for her age, still small and skinny, and unable to protect herself. She made a practice of drawing as little attention to herself as possible. Some students from BC were brought to the school, and, as was often the case with newcomers, the new girls were given a rough time by the Edmonton students. One girl in particular was taunted mercilessly as they accused her of being a lesbian. Edith did not know what the term meant and did not take part in the taunting. She was, however, an easy target and the enraged girl took out her frustration on her. During one skirmish the supervisor (today Edith understands that the supervisor was a lesbian) also targeted Edith for punishment. She shoved Edith into the hallway, slammed the door to the dormitory, threw her into a corner, and beat her mercilessly. As she kicked and slapped her, the other girls in the dormitory heard the commotion, but nobody dared to come to Edith's assistance, even though they knew she was innocent. Residential school students learned early not to become involved in other people's pain for fear of reprisal. The supervisor screamed at Edith that she had said "good-night" with a "k," as in "good-knight." Edith was so ashamed of herself and so traumatized by both the beating and the fact that no one came to her rescue that even today she sometimes has a strong physical reaction when she hears the term "good-night" unexpectedly.

Memories of some experiences can stir instant feelings of anger, as when she remembers how they were put to bed early with no drinking water, and they were forced to drink out of the toilet tank. Or when she recalls a visit to the nurse's office. She had a painful boil on her back, not an unusual ailment in the undernourished children who had been cooped up in the school for months. When she showed the nurse her boil, the nurse hissed, "Dirty Indian." Edith thought, even through her despair, that if she was dirty it was the school's fault. She had not been home for months. She never voluntarily visited a nurse again.

As an intermediate student she became anaemic and fainted frequently, but she did not receive any medical treatment for her condition. One day she fainted while serving breakfast in the student dining room, cracking her head against a concrete wall. She was in extreme pain and felt as though her head had cracked open. Staff made light of her fall telling her it did not hurt "that much." They told her to go upstairs and lie down. She slowly pulled herself up the stairs. No one checked on her for the rest of the day, though another student brought her lunch and supper. On another occasion she fainted while she was in the choir during a church service. She awakened, confused, thinking she was home because she was seeing the trunks of trees. As she regained her orientation she was deeply disappointed when she realized it was only the legs of the pews that she was seeing.

In some ways, Edith believes, she received preferential treatment. She was careful to follow all rules and not give anybody any trouble, and she was a good student academically. One privilege she received frequently was to work in the staff dining room, a position all the girls coveted. It was a privilege to be in the hallway, to be close to the front door and see people come and go. Polishing the silver and just the act of handling dainty china brought a small glimpse of aesthetic beauty into their otherwise barren lives. They did not particularly like waiting on staff, but the job brought some variety to their humdrum lives, as well as access to more and better-quality food. The girls were allowed to eat the food staff had left on their plates and could often sneak tastes. Edith never stole in the broader sense of the term, as many residential school students did, but instead she believes she honed the art of manipulation and achieved the same ends in more acceptable ways.

Heavy in Edith's memory is a harrowing experience, though some of the details are hazy. She was quite small when she and some others decided to run away. She has no recollection about why they made this decision but believes it was likely made out of loneliness. Crawling through ditches, bushes, and fields they made it almost to St. Albert, four or five kilometres away, before they were picked up by staff. What she does remember, and feels she will never forget, is the sound of gunshots and bullets whizzing over their heads. It was common practice for people to report runaways to the school. Sometimes hunger drove the children to ask for help, and at times they were given food. These small kindnesses have left indelible imprints on the minds of the desperate children, even if the farmers took them back to the school later. Edith is still puzzled by the gunshots. Was it perhaps hunting season, she wonders, or were there human beings so unfeeling that they would terrorize small children in this fashion?

As she grew older, Edith, like many other residential school students, experienced feelings of superiority as she learned to cope with the outside world while her parents continued in their familiar patterns. This, too, brings her a great deal of pain today. "I thought I was better than they were," she recalls in anguish as she realizes the pain she must have caused them. Her pain and shame deepened when she began to understand how insidious the systemic brainwashing of the school had been. These feelings of superiority were the product of policies aimed at relentless cultural genocide. The very purpose of the schools was to create a schism between the generations, and today Edith sees this as calculated, cruel, and unChristian.

Edith had grown up in a Christian home. Red Deer Industrial School was a Methodist institution and both of Edith's parents were active in the United Church on the reserve. The church was also the centre of social events like ball games, socials, and quilting bees. Christianity was a part of their daily lives; rituals such as grace at mealtime and bedtime prayers were observed. At the same time her parents participated in traditional Aboriginal ceremonies, as well. Then life changed dramatically as the Pentecostal church moved onto the reserve. The easygoing social aspect of the United Church was replaced by the more intense practices of the Pentecostal Church.

With the arrival of the Pentecostal Church, sweats and powwows, which had existed side-by-side with the United Church teachings, became unacceptable. Though the government had sought to outlaw the traditional practices they were not nearly as successful as the Pentecostal Church was in forbidding them. Edith's parents joined the Pentecostal Church and traditional and social activities were replaced with prayer meetings and summer Bible camps. Though Edith recalls liking the gatherings, and she did bow to pressure and was baptized into the faith, she never really accepted any of the teachings. The new religion created many deep schisms in the Jackson family and many other reserve families as well, which are still there today. Today Edith attends church only for weddings, wakes, and funerals.

Once, when she was in high school, Edith decided to quit school. Her parents did not argue, they simply observed that if she was around home to do the chores they would be free to do other things. They got into the wagon and drove away for the day. Edith milked the eight cows, separated the milk, put the cream in the well, washed the separator, and was barely finished in time to start all over again. She lasted three days before she returned to school.

After high school Edith went into nursing. She did earn her cap, however she never became a registered nurse because pharmacology was her downfall. When the students from the Edmonton School were sent to Guthrie High School, many were demoted to grade seven. Some, like Edith, were allowed to continue, skipping grade eight and moving into grade nine on the basis of their high academic standing. She experienced considerable difficulty because there were serious gaps in her knowledge but instructors did not seem to be aware of this. One of these gaps was that she had no knowledge of the metric system. During nurses' training no attempts were made to analyse where the students' weaknesses lay, let alone provide remedial work. Consequently, Edith experienced great difficulty in pharmacology, and it was not until later, once it was much too late, that Edith realized what it was that had created the stumbling block. When her children were in grade eight she began to understand that the metric system was a different system of measurement. Trying to fit what she was learning into the imperial system had led to her confusion.

Despite the metric stumbling block, Edith was an eager and highly proficient practical nurse. One day, as she was assisting in the operating room, she accidentally touched the doctor. He not only reprimanded her, he screamed at her, shouting that she had contaminated him, and he banished her from the operating room. Shocked, she continued to work in the post-operating room, which was full of patients. She noticed a change in a patient's condition and recognized distress signals. Keeping calm, she called the doctor, and he immediately performed open heart surgery while she watched. She still feels today that she likely saved the man's life, though she was but a lowly chastised student. However, this was never acknowledged by the institution. In fact, because of her mistake in the operating room, coupled with her difficulty in pharmacology, the hospital informed her that her nursing career was over. In a highly patronizing move, they offered her a position as a nurse's aide, which she declined.

In retrospect, Edith realizes that she likely was ahead of the times. Racism and ethnocentrism on the part of all institutions was the norm during the years Edith was struggling to become a professional. For her to become a registered nurse at that time would simply have been too threatening to the established system. "Failure" at nursing was a bitter pill for Edith to swallow because she was not familiar with failure. It was not so much that she wanted to be a hospital nurse. Her ambition in life was to be an airline stewardess, and in order to be accepted at that time, candidates had to have nurses' training.

To cope with her disappointment and anger Edith walked and walked and walked the streets of Edmonton. The planes taking off and landing overhead reminded her that her life's ambition had been thwarted. Finally she accepted what she could not change and instead decided on a change in direction. She applied for clerical work at Indian Affairs. She got training as a clerk typist, and in office management and speed writing. Her first job was temporary work with the Association of Registered Nurses of Alberta where she worked as a filing clerk. They soon offered her a full-time position, which she held for eight years. She advanced from Clerk I to Clerk IV and was given a supervisory position. She really enjoyed her work. She found she had an affinity for working with the various machines and was challenged by changing technology.

At age twenty-two Edith married an Italian-Canadian welder. She tried to convert to the Catholic religion but was not successful since organized religion had lost all meaning for her. Before they were married Edith had become pregnant and had given birth to a daughter. She made the painful decision to give the baby up for adoption because she was afraid she would lose her boyfriend. Neither one of them was mature enough to make the commitment to parenting. The next year she was pregnant again, and they got married. A third daughter was born the next year, followed by a miscarriage.

For five years Edith stayed home to look after her family, but the miscarriage and other events led to extreme depression. She was overwhelmed, believing she was a failure as a wife and mother. She felt she had degraded her husband because she was an Indian. She had to work hard at making friends. As her children grew she overcompensated by doing volunteer work—block parent, volunteer teacher aide in the school, figure skating, soccer, baseball—and by keeping a superneat house.

She sought help from a mainstream counsellor. The counsellor informed her that she was a "word fucker." She recalls this slap in the face with an involuntary shudder, still asking in bewilderment, "What is a word fucker?" Something terrible, judging by the negative connotations of the term. What fragile confidence she had was shattered, and she left the psychologist's office never to return. She felt that everything sad and negative in her life was her fault, and that every negative thing in her life was exacerbated because she was an evil person. It did not occur to her that the federal government and church-sanctioned policies and practices had begun the destruction of her self-concept long before she was capable of charting her own course in life.

It also did not occur to her at the time that university-trained people like the psychologist were pathetically ignorant and totally incapable of helping people with Edith's history. Today she understands that a mainstream psychologist would have had no insights into what it is to be a residential school survivor or a member of a generally despised minority group. The psychologist would not have understood that there was something lacking in her own credentials, and that her incompetence and arrogance were devastating for people like Edith, whom she was supposed to be helping. Or worse still, perhaps she thought that the coarse language she used was the appropriate way to approach an Aboriginal client because that was the kind of language "they" understand. The coarse language jars years later, particularly when contrasted with Edith's gracious, soft-spoken manner.

Throughout this difficult time, Edith's marriage remained intact and today she has a happy, accepting relationship with her extended family in Italy, whom they visit regularly. Her husband refers to her as a "True Canadian" and has always been proud of the fact that he is married to a Canadian Indian. She, in turn, calls him her "Christopher Columbus."

After five years as a fulltime homemaker Edith felt she wanted to do more with her life. She especially wanted to work with her own people. She enrolled in a correctional justice course. She was the oldest person in the class, a woman, and was one of only three Aboriginal people. She "flew" through the course and graduated at the top of the class.

She took a job at the Fort Saskatchewan penitentiary where she felt she would have the opportunity to work with Aboriginal people. Though it was difficult work, she stayed for three years. She had been a rarity in the training course, and she was a rarity on the job. She was the first female to ever drive the prison van and the first female in charge of work crews doing community work.

There were several reasons why she decided to leave. She had initially entered the field because she wanted to help Aboriginal people. During the three years she was there she had worked her way through the correctional officer I (CO I) position and was promoted to CO II. However, she was given an acting CO III position, and she was responsible for supervising the other levels. In this capacity she had little time to work with inmates. Also, the shift work took too great a toll on her and on her young family.

They decided to move to Edmonton, but finding a house in Edmonton was no small feat. She was an Indian and no one would sell to them for fear of lowering real estate values in the neighbourhood. Finally they bought a dilapidated old house, which they remodelled, in an area populated largely by recent immigrants who accepted Edith as one of them. One dreadful night when her husband was out of town a Peeping Tom appeared at her window. She felt it was only natural that it happened at her window because she was the only Indian in the neighbourhood.

Edith took a job at the Edmonton Remand Centre, as an acting CO III, and worked her way up to a probation officer (PO) position. As a PO, she again hoped that she would have an Aboriginal caseload. Her life on the job, however, was very difficult. She suffered outright prejudice and cruelty from her fellow POs. They had university degrees, which she did not have. The added dimension of cultural understanding and her years of prison experience did not, in their minds, compensate for her lack of "proper" qualifications. She dismisses this period of her life as "a story in itself" but when pressed for more specific detail she recalled examples of treatment that she still finds galling.

She was not assigned what her supervisors deemed to be "difficult" cases because of her lack of education. These "hard" cases were invariably Aboriginal, so she was again effectively prevented from working with her own people. She had no problems with home visits, a task other POs often dreaded, and she was able to work effectively with whole families. Today Edith understands that the ease with which she handled these cases and the high regard the clients had for her were likely a threat to Probation Services that they could not tolerate. She felt "put down" by her co-workers on many occasions, especially when she did such uncharacteristic things, for an uneducated Indian, as go to Europe with her husband and family for summer holidays.

When a new career opportunity as a Native facilitator for the Edmonton Catholic School Board presented itself, Edith did not hesitate. Her job was to go into classrooms and act as a resource person for the teachers. She was to teach about Aboriginal culture, educating both teachers and students. She took the job because it was an opportunity to work with Native youth. She often worked as a referral agency though formally she was not a counsellor. In 1988 she transferred to the Edmonton Public School System, where she works today.

The Native Services Branch of the Edmonton system is part of the Sacred Circle Project, a Native education project established by the Alberta government. Though the project, per se, lasted for only three years, the services still exist. Its mandate was to develop programs for teachers who wished to learn more about teaching Aboriginal students. The teachers were taught how Aboriginal students learn and were given information on the sweat lodge and other ceremonies by Elders. Those involved in the project assisted with curriculum development, acted as liaisons between the two worlds, and provided general teacher inservicing.

Until she took this job Edith had always preferred to work in institutions because that was what she had been trained to do. She was quite accustomed to doing mundane things without questioning them for long periods of time. She had, however, acquired many coping skills over the years and found the educational work challenging.

When questioned about why she has never gone to university, Edith says she was told so often, by different teachers and especially counsellors, "Edith, you are not university material," that she came to believe it. She has proven over and over again that she can master any training she attempts, as long as adequate instruction takes place. She knows today that she has the ability and work habits that would have guaranteed university success, but too many other responsibilities and interests have made university training irrelevant in her life. She has, however, placed great emphasis on university education for her children.

In 1994 a miracle happened. Edith found the daughter she had given up before she was married. Her daughter's friend, quite by accident, met Edith's brother and was so struck by the family resemblance that she approached him. The same day that Edith learned that her oldest daughter existed and lived in Calgary she made contact. Today her daughter has become an integral part of the family while still maintaining equal contact with her adoptive parents. She is a brilliant woman with a master's degree in business administration and works as Senior Policy Analyst for Saskatchewan Intergovernmental Affairs. Edith's second daughter is an announcer on an Aboriginal radio station, the third is enrolled in a master's program in architecture at the University of Calgary.

All three girls are vocal, articulate Canadians who consciously maintain their Aboriginal identities. English was their first language but two are studying Cree. All three react emphatically to the slightest suggestion that their Cree heritage is somehow less valuable than their Italian roots, and will not tolerate negative comments about First Nations people. Edith is a grandmother three times over and delights in the fact that her youngest daughter and her grandson live with Edith and her husband.

Today Edith recalls her residential school experiences as negative though she believes there were some good, helpful people at the schools. For many years she would have described herself as unscarred by the experience, believing her feelings were neutral. Yet she knew there were many unhappy thoughts deeply buried in her subconscious.

It was not until she became a grandmother that she began to think honestly about her experiences.

Edith's older siblings did not benefit from education the way she did. When it became evident that the residential schools were too expensive to operate and had few successes to show for their efforts, Indian Affairs unilaterally decided to send Indian children to provincial schools. The Indian agent made the decision that Edith's two older brothers would walk many kilometres to a provincial school because that particular school needed more students to remain open. Her brothers suffered greatly from discrimination at the provincial school and eventually returned to residential school. They garnered very few benefits from any of their school experiences.

Edith has come to realize how dramatically the residential school has impacted on her family. Her siblings never talked about the school in their home or even to each other. The greatest damage the school did—damage Edith finds hard to forgive—was that she never really got to know her parents. The precious times in summer were not long enough to establish normal family relationships even though they had good parenting from their mother who "loved them to pieces." Edith also speaks with pride of her father and his ability to farm successfully and regrets that she never told him that she was proud of him. This, however, is in retrospect. As they were growing up their father was distant, though he was a lax disciplinarian. They were home only during the busy summer season when their father was out in the fields most of the time so they rarely saw him.

Alcoholism is a problem for some of Edith's siblings but Edith herself does not drink. "I think I would be a mean drunk," she says, indirectly alluding to all the unresolved issues in her life. This is an amazing statement from the vivacious, soft-spoken, loving person she has become. The statement offers the tiniest of glimpses into the dark chambers of despair that have affected her all her life.

She believes that one reason she survived the school experience was because of her ancestry. The residential school students attended McDougall United Church in Edmonton. This was the church of Edith's Steinhauer ancestors; in fact, Steinhauers had been ministers at that church. However undervalued she felt as an Aboriginal person, the church provided a comfort zone for her and answered the important questions of who she was and where she had come from.

Edith still feels her father could have kept them out of residential school if he had chosen to do so and this continues to stir feelings of anger. On the other hand she does recognize the quandary he was in. His success as a farmer depended on the goodwill of the Indian agent. If the agent wished the children to be sent to a residential school or to be sent to an integrated school far from home, parents took considerable risks in defying him. Uncharacteristically, Edith says, "You had to kiss ass to be successful; Indian agents had so much control."

Her father died in 1971, her mother in 1996. With the death of her mother, family cohesiveness, tenuous at best, died as well. None of her siblings have ever dealt with their residential school experiences, and her youngest brother, especially, is hiding his past. The relationships among the siblings are very distant. As Edith begins her long journey of healing the hurts of the past, she hopes that her relationships with her siblings will improve and that if she speaks about her feelings it may help them as well.

The rifts and frustrations created by the catastrophic events in the lives of Indian people make Edith angry but she has found a niche in life with which she is comfortable and happy. Today, thanks to Bill C-31, Edith has her status back, which she lost when she married a non-Indian. She has travelled widely with her husband and children both in North America and Europe. She felt a burning need to find out about other countries, countries not bedevilled by historic dichotomies between a conquering and a conquered race. She understands the disintegration of Native cultures brought about by the residential school era and the further damage done by the early integration of Indian students into provincial schools. In her role as Native liaison consultant she can work with students and teachers to clarify the past and hopefully build a better future. With her engaging personality and optimistic outlook on life she is well suited to the position. She looks forward to her retirement in 2004 and a well-earned rest.

Bernice Touchie

About twelve years after leaving the residential school, Bernice (Joseph) Touchie and a friend were examining a picture taken when they were both students at the Port Alberni Residential School. As they reminisced, they sadly realized that there is only a handful of them who have "made it." Some have passed away, often dying violent deaths; others suffer from substance-abuse problems; most are divorced, many have lost their children, and some are in jail.

Today Bernice has a B.A. in linguistics and a teaching certificate from the University of Victoria, a master of education degree from the University of British Columbia, and is currently working on a doctoral program. She is strongly committed to restoring Aboriginal languages to their rightful place in Canadian society. For her publications she uses her "little girl name," Nalthna Touchie. She belongs to the Nuu-chah-nulth culture. Her home band is Ditidaht, once located on the west coast of Vancouver Island. After cajoling and coercion from the Parks Department, the reserve was moved inland to make way for the renowned West Coast Trail. With the move, the once-isolated and self-contained community had more opportunity to participate in the job market, and it gained road access for education, but it was also subjected to the detrimental effects of living near Port Alberni. The residents still fish and collect seafoods, once a viable economic lifestyle that had sustained them since time immemorial, but today they are relying more and more on the forestry industry for their livelihood.

In spite of her excellent academic record Bernice is not at all sure she has really "made it." She too is divorced and has suffered from substance abuse. She has gone through a treatment program and gained considerable insight into her own behaviour, but she does not feel that the treatment really dealt with the hurt and devastation the residential school caused in her life and in the lives of her siblings. She suffers from anxiety and occasional bouts of depression that often result in severe insomnia. She wishes that the Port Alberni School had not been demolished—the site unrecognizable today—because she feels that revisiting the premises might have been helpful for her in coming to terms with the past. When asked why she has survived when so many others did not, she simply says, "I don't know."

Bernice spent twelve years at the United Church residential school at Port Alberni on Vancouver Island, as did her ten siblings. The school took a dreadful toll on the family. Suicide, substance abuse, violent accidental deaths, spousal abuse, marriage disintegration, multiple marriages, and temporary apprehension of children have all dogged their footsteps. Only six of the ten siblings are alive today. Bernice fears that violence may take the lives of still more family members. Particularly she fears that accidents during social drinking may cause more deaths.

Only Bernice and one younger brother continued with their education after residential school. Her brother has a law degree and a master's degree in urban planning. He is married with two children. He too was vulnerable to the use of alcohol—likely because of emotional frustrations—but with a supportive spouse and family has successfully focussed on his work.

Bernice feels that her ability to express concerns with her siblings is limited. The residential school experience made family bonding and cohesiveness difficult. Their mother, also a residential school victim, has difficulty in following the achievements of her children. Bernice's siblings appear to be proud of her achievements, though there was one instance when a brother seemed to resent her success and accused her of being a snob. If others also feel she is snobbish, Bernice is saddened, but feels that in the past it was her extreme shyness, not snobbery, which prevented her from reaching out to people.

Bernice has a good relationship with her children and grandchildren, though she wonders sometimes whether she distanced herself from them too much. She was so devastated by the death of her father, who died of a ruptured appendix after having been released from the hospital, and the violent deaths of so many siblings that she became preoccupied with some dreadful catastrophe befalling her too. She wanted to prepare her children for any eventual trauma so they would be able to survive on their own. Today she feels she likely drove them into premature relationships since she was not providing the support they needed.

Her daughter works as a waitress in Port Alberni, and one son has a business degree from Malaspina College in Nanaimo. Her second son was a provincial firefighter until he quit because of the racism he encountered on the job. She has five grandchildren whom she loves unreservedly. Bernice believes that on the whole she has been a fairly good mother. When the children were small she had the opportunity to take night classes in early childhood education and she believes these courses were invaluable in reinforcing the basics of family living that had been denied her in residential school.

Bernice was seven when she first went to the Port Alberni Residential School. The trip to the school was long and arduous since the reserve could only be accessed by water. Sometimes their father took them in his own fishing boat to the point where they could catch the train or travel by car on logging roads. The year Bernice started they travelled on the supply ship, which had a regular route around the island.

Usually the children stayed at the school from September to June. Their parents rarely visited them at the school, and all too often, when they did get to Port Alberni, the pubs claimed them before they got to see the children. Though Bernice's younger brother interprets the rare visits as parental neglect, Bernice has kinder feelings towards her parents. She is more inclined to blame the infrequent visits on the difficulty and expense of the journey as well as the pain of seeing unhappy children in the school when there was absolutely nothing they could have done about it. Especially, there was the pain of saying good-bye after a short, unsatisfactory visit, and her parents' drinking was a way of avoiding the pain.

In some aspects Bernice was well prepared for the school experience. Both her parents could read and write, and English was the language of the home and the community. Her parents communicated with each other in Ditidaht, as did all the older people, so the children could understand it. Bernice's mother had attended the Coqualeetza Residential School on the mainland until she was sixteen, and her grandmother had attended day school on the reserve. Bernice remembers learning the alphabet orally from her mother when she was a preschooler.

Since Bernice's older siblings were already at the Port Alberni School she looked forward to a great adventure, anxious to join them when they left in the fall. Her older siblings had told her nothing about the school, but her parents admonished her to be obedient or she would be punished. In later years she made a point of providing information to her younger siblings when they started school so they would be better prepared for the rules and the structured existence in store for them.

Bernice's first day at the residential school is etched indelibly on her mind and still brings grief and tears. She had naturally assumed that she would be in the company of her siblings, and she screamed mightily when staff attempted to separate her from them. They had to take her forcibly. It was with considerable difficulty that she was finally subdued and taken to the little girls' dormitory where she was told to strip and put on an uncomfortably stiff nightgown. After they were all in bed the supervisor left the room. In a few minutes Bernice felt the need to go to the bathroom and thought nothing of going, not knowing she was forbidden to leave the bed after "lights out." She was just climbing back into bed when the supervisor returned. Before she knew what was happening to her, the supervisor flipped up her nightgown and strapped her over and over again on her legs and bare buttocks. Bernice, who had never received physical punishment before, was left stunned by the shock of it all.

That was the beginning of a life of terror for Bernice. Though she never received another strapping as severe as the first one, it was largely because it was never necessary. She became one of the many acquiescent students at the school, too afraid to test any rules. She set her own limits, and those limits were always well within the school's parameters in an effort to avoid ever giving offence to anyone. In later years, when her fear was not so intense, she was still too cautious to test any boundaries. When other students jumped over the schoolyard fence to pick wild apples they taunted Bernice for not joining them. She found the taunting preferable to the potential consequences of disobeying any rule, however insignificant. This attitude of fear of giving offence was so ingrained in her that it has impacted strongly on her behaviour for the rest of her life.

As she grew older Bernice became braver, and at times she was punished for her misdeeds. She remembers that once she was strapped on her hands for eating cookies her friend had given her, unaware that they were stolen. She believes there may have been more strappings, but she does not recall them clearly. There were, however, many other punishments, like lost privileges and scrubbing floors and stairs on her knees, resulting from minor misdemeanours.

Bernice did well academically, but her later years were disrupted so she did not complete grade twelve until she was nineteen. By that time the students were attending the town high school and using the school only as a residence. She had a good relationship with an older brother and often looked after his daughter, developing a very close bond with the child. When Bernice was in grade eleven her brother's marriage broke up, and he moved away with his daughter. Bernice was devastated by the loss of her niece.

Bernice believes she had the maturity of no more than a naive fourteen-year-old when she was eighteen. She had a boyfriend, and though she knew about babies and pregnancy, she succumbed, first to her boyfriend's insistence that she drink with him and then to sexual relations, which led to pregnancy. She believed she could not become pregnant if she indulged him only once but she was mistaken. She was devastated. She considered herself a model student and here she was, having committed the most unspeakable crime. Most of all she feared the wrath of her father who was always overly concerned about the family's reputation. Her fear was not misplaced, and she seriously considered suicide. Her father took over and made arrangements for an uncle to adopt the baby. What helped Bernice through the whole ordeal was a friend who also was pregnant but planned to continue with her education. Together they finished high school.

The support of this friend was invaluable to Bernice. Unmarried women from her reserve who became pregnant were socially ostracized. They were viewed as loose, sexual creatures, but there was no particular censure of the men who had impregnated them. Often the pregnant women simply disappeared into urban centres and were never heard from again. This surely would have been Bernice's fate if it had not been for the support of her friend.

The baby was born in Victoria, and Bernice stayed on with her aunt and uncle, helping with the baby and supporting herself by working as a kitchen aide. She was very hurt by her father's rejection of her and her child and could not understand why the child could not simply be incorporated into the family. To care for all children was a time-honoured cultural tradition. Sadly, many changes had taken place on the reserve because of the morality taught by missionaries and the detrimental effects of alcohol. On the other hand, she did not object to her uncle's adoption of the baby because she did want her daughter to have responsible parents. Today her daughter knows Bernice as her birth mother and they keep in contact as extended family.

Bernice met the man who would become her husband while she was waiting for her parents in a bar. When she found herself pregnant again she did not divulge the name of her boyfriend or her situation because she feared her father's reaction. She still harboured resentment and wanted the right to decide what she would do with her life. They left for her boyfriend's home reserve at Ucluelet. During this time she wrote to her mother saying she had grave doubts about him as a marriage partner but had no other way of getting to know him. They were married and ultimately had three children; the marriage lasted for twenty-two years.

Bernice's husband was a logger, and during the early years of their marriage they lived at Campbell River while her husband worked at the Gold River logging camp. Bernice adapted to a life where her husband was away at the logging camp for ten days followed by four days of drinking with his friends and abusive behaviour when he did come home. At times Bernice joined him in his drinking, and then she would have the courage to defend herself, at least verbally, but that would merely enrage him and the abuse would escalate. Mostly she retreated into her residential school behaviour of making herself as inconspicuous and unobtrusive as possible, doing everything in her power to keep the peace.

It was in Campbell River that Bernice had the opportunity to take early childhood courses. She became involved in a preschool program run by Kwakiutl Elders from the Cape Mudge reserve. Bernice had never given her future much thought, accepting that marriage and child rearing were all that women of her society expected from life. When it became apparent that her marriage was not working she began to consider what she herself might do with her life.

She enrolled in a diploma program for languages at the University of Victoria, a program that trained Aboriginal language teachers. She had lost most of her ability to speak Ditidaht, and knowledge of her own culture had not been included in her education. Further study in this area seemed to be an appropriate move.

She entered the university as a mature student, though she had a complete high-school education. She does not know why she entered as a mature student, perhaps because it was expected of her and she was too shy to speak up. She found the first year very difficult. The openness of the university contrasted strongly with the controlled environment she had been accustomed to, and she had great difficulty making the required adjustments. She was with a group of ten Aboriginal students so had moral support. All were highly motivated and excited about the prospect of their own languages actually being recorded. They presented a proposal to the university to extend the program for a second year, which was accepted. The second year of study was considerably easier for Bernice, and she was strongly encouraged to continue her studies. She continued and earned a B.A. in linguistics. Bernice's Tribal Council funded her from September to April, and she was able to secure steady summer employment at the Royal Museum of British Columbia throughout her undergraduate years. She and a friend taught language courses at Port Alberni, as well.

However, when they presented a plan to include language teaching in the public school system, which all the Aboriginal children of her Tribal Council attended, they were met with resistance from educators. It was true that few curriculum materials existed but Bernice felt that a start needed to be made somewhere if the languages were to be reclaimed. She felt she had the skills and creativity to teach language classes even without good curriculum supports. More materials could be developed along the way. Support from the public school system would have been invaluable but was not forthcoming.

Realizing that her B.A. in linguistics gave her no credibility in the education community, she enrolled in a one-year education program to get her teaching diploma. Upon graduation she found that in Port Alberni, only one independent school run by the Tribal Council was teaching language courses and that program was run by Elders. There was no employment for Bernice at that school nor was there a job for her in the public school system.

An organization called the Indian Education Awareness Society operated out of Port Alberni and ultimately provided employment for Bernice. The society applied for funding and received a two-year grant; the Port Alberni School Board provided office space and clerical help. A non-Aboriginal educator was hired to develop curriculum for kindergarten to grade eight and Bernice was given the task of developing a high-school curriculum. She planned to do legend-based learning units, as well as compile histories of the various bands in the Tribal Council. The high-school component was eventually shelved because Bernice could not finish it in the allotted time. Her work was forever being interrupted as she was called upon to assist with the elementary program. Today the elementary units are published and used in schools in that area. Bernice would have liked to have been acknowledged as interpreter, cultural consultant, and community liaison, a role similar to what the Elders play, but her name does not appear on the materials.

With the move toward local control of education, the Tribal Council today has more control over hiring practices. Funding goes directly to the bands and the numbers of Aboriginal teachers have increased slightly. However, in the year 2000, the British Columbia Teachers' Association estimated that there were still fewer than four hundred Aboriginal teachers in the whole province, not even twenty per cent of the number required if the needs are estimated by the number of Aboriginal children in the school system. Bernice's units of high-school work have been unearthed and are being used by the few Aboriginal teachers in the district even though they have never been finalized.

When funding for the curriculum program was discontinued Bernice took a job managing a Makah language program in the state of Washington. The Makah and Ditidaht languages have similar structures since they both belong to the Wakashan linguistic family. Bernice enjoyed the work but she reluctantly resigned after six months because the travel logistics were too difficult. She felt her children and marriage were suffering because she only got four days off out of every ten and two of those were taken up with travel.

Bernice applied for a job with the Port Alberni School Board and was offered a principal's position in a small isolated school. She did not think much of the idea of being a principal before being a classroom teacher, nor did she want to work away from home again. At Ucluelet she had a chance to obtain band housing, and she hoped that settling down on the reserve would improve her marriage. She had applied for the teacher/librarian position at Ucluelet, but that was not to be. She was given a half-time position, team teaching grade two with another teacher who had been in the classroom for ten years. The non-Aboriginal teacher she was teamed with was not very focused on teaching, spending more time and energy on running a business on the side. Bernice still feels that as a first-year teacher she was left to fend for herself too much of the time. In retrospect, she realizes that she had been given a class largely composed of special needs students. She still shakes her head over how impossible the situation was. She had never been in a classroom with non-Native children, let alone children who were out of control. She found the noise level intolerable and the children's manners shocking. Over and over again she asked them to lower their voices, but out-shouting each other seemed to be the means of communication. Bernice's voice is naturally very soft, and she had great difficulty making herself heard.

Bernice had no training or experience with special needs children. One child had Fetal Alcohol Syndrome, though that term had not yet gained currency. She feels the classroom was a dumping ground for children other teachers did not want; consequently they had four reading levels to contend with, ranging from nonreaders to children in grade two. One child spoke only French but Bernice had learned some French in high school so was able to work with him. Her teaching approach was to provide the children with seatwork, which served the purpose of keeping them busy because she spent all her time on class control instead of on teaching and learning. There were four Aboriginal children in the class, and she could see how irrelevant most of what was happening in the classroom was to them, but she had little time to do much about it.

Though it was only a half-time position, Bernice worked long hours. Many problems that arose with Aboriginal children in the school were referred to her whether the children were in her classroom or not. The principal seemed very reluctant to contact parents, either Aboriginal or non-Aboriginal, so expected Bernice to deal with discipline problems arising among the children from the reserve. When Bernice wanted to contact the parents of a non-Aboriginal child who had stolen money from her, the principal forbade it. Instead a child psychologist was called in. The child's academic performance was assessed, but no action was taken on the theft.

The only feedback Bernice received all year happened one day when she kept several students in over the noon hour to help them with some math problems. The principal watched her teach and told her she was doing very well. At the end of the year a supervisor was scheduled to visit the classroom. Though Bernice's teaching partner had been told about the impending visit, no one passed the information on to Bernice. Her partner prepared accordingly and Bernice vaguely wondered at her increased activity. Bernice was caught completely by surprise when the supervisor arrived. The children did not behave well, and when the supervisor attempted to model what Bernice should be doing she was not successful either. This supervisor did not have administrative responsibility for Bernice but informed her at the end of the day that her contract would not be renewed because her teaching was inadequate.

Bernice feels to this day that even if she was a totally inadequate teacher she was treated unjustly. She readily admits that her teaching left much to be desired, but she was little different from the other first-year teachers in the school. She knew then, demoralized as she was, that given half a chance she could have done a much better job of teaching the Aboriginal children of Ucluelet than the non-Native teachers were doing. She considered grieving her case but knew that she could expect little support from the teachers' union since they were all non-Aboriginal.

Petty politics played a role in everything that took place in the school, with great emphasis on the seniority system and job security. She was too tired, too inexperienced, and too insecure to fight her own battles. Her early socialization, which had taught her to be accepting, unobtrusive, and above all guilty of anything she was accused of without recourse to justice, prevented her from defending herself. There was no one to point out that there could be a different way or to help her.

The next term Bernice was hired for a half-time position as a preschool/kindergarten teacher on the reserve, a position she held for five years. She recognized the desperate need for enhanced experiences for the children and the need for daycare for working parents. She tried to compensate for these shortcomings and often took in children who were too young to be in the program.

She joined the life of the community with enthusiasm and became involved in band council activities. She was part of each and every education committee that was established on the reserve as well as the Economic Development Committee, which was developing tourism as an industry. Her involvement included travel to attend meetings and conferences on behalf of the band, which she found interesting and challenging.

It was a productive time for Bernice, but at home her husband's abuse escalated and the marriage was going from bad to worse. She was too proud to admit that she was a battered woman, and in common with many other women like her, accepted the blame for having caused her husband's outbursts. In her case the guilt went even deeper because she understood and empathized with the unresolved issues in his life stemming from his early childhood and residential school experiences.

Her husband was an illegitimate child whose mother, a product of a residential school, had given him up for adoption. Later she got him back, but she was very young and found adequate parenting difficult. He recalls that the affection he did receive from her always came after she had given him a beating, when she would be remorseful. Bernice suspects that he may have learned to be deliberately disobedient in order to receive the crumbs of affection that followed punishment.

His residential school experience had been traumatic. How much and what kind of abuse he suffered is unknown because he steadfastly refused to talk about it, drowning his memories in alcohol instead.

He had excelled in sports, especially soccer, and showed considerable promise in other areas. He exhibited much self-confidence and enjoyed public accolades as lead singer in a rock band. He was innovative, creative, and daring, but, on the other hand, he was a tough street fighter. In his early childhood he had received many traditional teachings within his extended family, but he grew up to be a harsh, authoritarian husband and father with a sadistic streak. The marriage was characterized by his total disrespect for Bernice and by his continual womanizing. Bernice did her best to protect the children from his abusive behaviour.

For Bernice, life became worse when her husband became part of the reserve police force. She felt she had nowhere to turn. Once, when they were still living in Campbell River, she had covered her own battered face with a scarf to hide the bruises when she took one of the children to the doctor. The doctor expressed a wish to examine her too, and then advised her to lay charges. She complied, hoping something might change but believing that likely it would not. She was right. The case did go to court, however, and he was found guilty. He was fined forty dollars and told that if he ever abused her again the fine would go up to five hundred dollars. In common with other abused women at that time, Bernice knew there was little hope of help from the justice system.

Her husband did not last long in the position of special band constable, and matters came to a head one night when their daughter inadvertently broke a rule. It appeared that he was about to strike the child when Bernice found the strength and courage to intervene. She stormed at him, "That's it. Get out!" He left without an argument. Bernice had ample proof of his infidelity and began divorce proceedings immediately. He did not contest the divorce, but it was still a big hassle for Bernice because he resisted passively. The legalities were dealt with rapidly because his reputation was well known, but Bernice personally had to drive him to the courthouse to sign the final divorce papers. Today the children have a good understanding of the abuse that took place in their home but still have occasional contact with their father. Although divorce severely stunts one's tribal identity and sense of belonging, Bernice retains communication with the Ucluelet Band, and she has retained her band membership there.

Bernice's next career move was back to Port Alberni where she and another person worked as Language Development Coordinators for the Tribal Council. They worked with fourteen different bands on a variety of tasks—fund raising, writing reports, conducting professional development days for teachers, and examining how language programs could mesh with regular school programs. Bernice felt she was not doing what she really wanted to do, that is, working directly on language programs. Although they had been promised long-term employment, her job was terminated after a year and a half because the bands made the decision to run language programs individually.

Faced with unemployment again, Bernice made the decision to go back to what she loved to do and knew she could do well. She enrolled in a master of education program at UBC, receiving funding from the Tribal Council to do so. She returned to her first love, the field of language learning and wrote a major thesis on language immersion as a means of learning a new language. In many ways she found her studies very depressing because few references pertinent to Aboriginal languages exist. She was given colonial references written by non-Aboriginal scholars to peruse, and often she wondered what she was doing in the world of academe. Everything she read was totally removed from the realities of the children she was hoping to teach. Above all, she longed to teach them the languages of their ancestors.

She came to realize, however, that the experience of doing a master's degree had some specific benefits. She improved her reading skills and became proficient at doing research. She had done well academically in the residential school, but she is very critical of the way the children were never taught to read for either content or pleasure. Unsupervised reading was a rare privilege bestowed on the more proficient students, and libraries were out of bounds except during structured library periods. Her university undergraduate studies were much more difficult than they needed to have been because she did not have the requisite reading skills. She feels it was not until she was in a master's program that she really learned how to read.

After she completed her master's degree her emotional health took a slump, which overwhelmed her. She was very tired after the stresses of many years of struggle. Accepting her condition, she applied for welfare, thereby exposing herself to further judgement for taking what some saw as the easy way out. But she knew she had no options. During this time she did, however, do some work with several bands on language programs, as well as work as a short-term substitute teacher.

After a year of respite she applied for and received funding to pursue a Ph.D. program. She continues to work on language learning and learning styles, identifying the oral component of traditional cultural transmission as a vital key to language learning. Oral narratives and traditional songs have always been integral components of the culture's vitality. She is no longer willing to accept the universities' practices of acknowledging only written sources of information that have usually been compiled by non-Aboriginal scholars. Particularly she recognizes that these written sources largely follow the specific protocols the universities have validated for all situations, while ignoring other sources of perhaps more accurate information from within a culture. She does not accept the focus on the written word as the only, or even the best, way of learning for everyone.

In reflecting on her residential school experiences, Bernice can recall few positive memories. The school did provide social contact with people from outside their community, and it did broaden the students' horizons. Their home community was small, boring, and restrictive, and Bernice knew from an early age that she wanted more from life. However, she believes that whatever benefits she derived from the residential school were destroyed by the many hurtful aspects of the experience.

Bernice does not seem to have suffered personally from the most severe excesses that occurred in the schools, yet she feels the school has had a very detrimental impact on her life. Many students had language difficulties, but speaking English was never a problem for her. The loss of her own language, however, had a profound impact on her life. She had spent most of her childhood with her grandparents and spoke Ditidaht in her early years. After a year in school she ran to greet her grandmother, and did so in English, which had become her language of communication. This did not seem right. Her grandmother scolded Bernice when she came home for the summers because each year her Ditidaht speaking skills became worse. Bernice remembers being confused and frightened, not knowing what language she was supposed to use. Silence became the safest avenue.

The school's focus on religion did not represent a personal conflict for Bernice either. Her home on the reserve was the house with the biggest living room, so in the absence of a church building on the reserve, the itinerant United Church ministers held their services there. All social activities were also held there, so the spiritual aspect of Bernice's upbringing became a confusion of traditional and United Church teachings.

A major change occurred when Pentecostal missionaries moved onto the reserve. Services, again, were held in Bernice's home; United Church services were held during the day and Pentecostal services in the evenings. For Bernice, there was no escaping the fire and brimstone theology of the Pentecostals, and she was frightened by their demeanour and their theology. As the Pentecostal teachings gained a foothold on the reserve almost everything in Bernice's life became a "sin." Reserve members grasped at the promise of eternal salvation and respite from earthly woes as the only solution to their sinful lives. Bernice's brothers adopted the beliefs and occasionally played their guitars at the Pentecostal services. The Pentecostal Church, however, never gained a foothold in the residential school, so Bernice continued to be indoctrinated with United Church teachings there.

Today Bernice has no contact with organized religion or any church. She feels she was deceived as a child by both the United Church and the Pentecostal Church. The Pentecostal Church terrified her and caused her great frenzy in her formative years; the United Church, she feels, was purely hypocritical. Religious services at the school were coerced, formal motions. The preacher who purported to be a loving father figure for the captive children preached about the love of Christ and forgiveness of transgressions. He was same person, however, who would turn into the terrifying principal figure who would strap children unmercifully and condone the actions of others who also handed out unreasonable punishments. As the students grew older they did not accept the hypocrisy, and hated church services with a passion. Today Bernice feels that she can, perhaps, forgive misplaced religious zeal, but what she cannot forgive is how the United Church sought to destroy a whole culture, far overstepping its mandate to teach people about Christ. They did so from a position of white superiority, and for Bernice, it is this blatant racism that still rankles today.

Bullies were common in all schools among both boys and girls, and at Port Alberni gangs were formed along community lines. Bernice never suffered at the hands of bullies personally. She has the perception that the girls from the northern reserves were tougher and more aggressive, more prone to fighting and violence than southern girls. Only on one occasion, when she was mixing powdered milk, was she involved in aggressive violence. One of the bullies made a snide remark about lumps in the milk as she passed by, and Bernice, uncharacteristically, answered back. She was about to receive a beating when her older cousin came to her rescue. A hair-pulling, punching, and kicking fight ensued, but Bernice was spared.

Bernice will never forget the physical abuse on her first night at the school and even today cannot talk about it without tears. On the other hand, she was not victimized the way some students were at the schools. When residential school abuse was exposed in mainstream media in the 1980s, the Port Alberni School at first appeared to have been less abusive than some of the others. Then a former student, Willie Blackwell, found the courage to press charges against Arthur Plint, one of the male supervisors. Other survivors from the school supported Blackwell's allegations, and it became evident that Plint had practised some of the worst sexual excesses recorded in residential school history. He was sentenced to eleven years in prison for sexually assaulting fifteen boys over a twenty-year period. The presiding judge called him a "sexual terrorist" and described the residential school system as "nothing but a form of institutionalized paedophilia." Blackwell was the first residential school survivor to win a medical claim for Post-Traumatic Stress Disorder. When I asked Bernice if she knew Arthur Plint a look of horror crossed her face and she could scarcely answer. Staff members may not have known of the abuse, but the question remains about the general ambience of the school where so many children could have been abused for so long with no place to turn to for help. Thirty former students have filed claims against the United Church for abuse at the Port Alberni School. Bernice believes that these disclosures shed some light on why her brother committed suicide and at least partly explain her husband's abusive behaviour. The Royal Commission on Aboriginal Peoples (1996) gained access to previously unavailable documents that reveal enough correspondence between school principals and the Department of Indian Affairs on the subject of sexual abuse that it ought to have been a matter of grave concern.

Bernice herself had little awareness of sexual abuse. She does recall one supervisor, the person who was in charge of the canteen, harassing one of the girls. He was forever leaving notes for her to meet him in the canteen but she steadfastly refused. He deliberately masturbated where the girls could see him. Bernice says she herself was so dumb and naive about sex that she did not really understand what was going on.

In spite of being spared the worst excesses of the school Bernice was still traumatized, and she suffered severe psychological damage, surrounded as she was by violence and indifference. A sense of abandonment and total helplessness led to deep depression and since there was no escaping the situation, apathy set in. She is still haunted by the memory of her youngest sister crying for a whole week when she started school while Bernice could only stand by helplessly. The inability to help or comfort younger siblings is cited by many residential school survivors as the most painful part of their educational experience.

Bernice points out that she has been struck by how much of the literature on residential schools comments on loss of identity and negative self-concepts of the students. She admits to a personal loss of self-confidence. She has always felt that negative events happen in her life because of her personal shortcomings, but she does not accept that her identity as a proud member of the Nuu-chah-nulth culture has been compromised. Rather than accepting the superiority of white cultures, she simply rejected the whole notion because she saw no evidence that white people were superior in any way. Parental teachings were strong and no amount of punishment, coercion, or proselytizing could destroy her identity as a proud member of a First Nation.

Bernice was supported by her grandfather in her resistance to the relentless brainwashing she received. He clearly understood the "them and us" mentality of the missionaries, which was highly evident even as they preached brotherly love. He was openly critical and fearless in his resistance. He played a major role in teaching Bernice to be a critical thinker, whatever her life situation might be. Her grandmothers also played a major role in Bernice's life. One was a respected historian of the culture and was the "mentor" for doing potlatches and other ceremonies. No amount of outside pressure or proselytizing could sway her from her task of passing on the cultural history of her people. Perhaps the Nuu-chah-nulth people were more fortunate than some other culture groups because they lived in isolated enclaves where they could continue to be self-sufficient long after European contact. They were home-bound people whose economies remained intact until relatively recent times. Their cultural identity was strong and was not severely impacted by contact until families and economies were disrupted.

Bernice would call herself a survivor, however tenuous her self-confidence is from time to time. Her focus on restoring Aboriginal languages to their rightful place in West Coast cultures is clearly defined and executed. She believes that the cultures had everything they needed to live happy, productive lives, and they have never accepted a colonized status, regardless of what the colonizers believe. She believes confidence in their own cultures and spirituality will be restored, but basic to this process are not only the artefacts and the historical and cultural knowledge, but also the underpinning of language. The language was stolen from them as surely as were the artefacts. She recognizes in herself the ability to do research both at the academic and community level. She can do the writing to put it all together, and she has the ability to develop programs in order to pass on the information. She is tackling the task with considerable energy and enthusiasm. Bernice is positive that the Nuu-chah-nulth culture will adapt to changing circumstances as it has adapted over the millennia, and she is determined that never again will people from outside the culture be given the opportunity to destroy what the people themselves value.

Mary Cardinal Collins

From 1989 to 1999 Mary Cardinal Collins was Supervisor of Native Programs for the Northland School Division in Alberta. The division serves the people of the forested region, particularly the area between the Peace River and the Athabasca River north of Lac La Biche. Though federal schools were in existence in the 1950s, they were no longer able to accommodate all the students. Infant mortality rates in the Aboriginal population had dropped significantly with improved health services, and non-Aboriginal populations were increasing partly because of resource development. Consequently, four school districts were established to provide education for the Métis and non-Aboriginal children in the 1950s. Mission schools that had been operating in the area were experiencing financial difficulties because of the rising costs of education, and they, too, appealed to the government for help, so eight more school districts were subsequently established.

By the fall of 1960 over twenty northern school districts were in operation. It soon became evident that some structural organization was required. A model existed in Saskatchewan where the Department of Education had established a Northern Schools Branch with its own professional and support staff. Alberta recognized the need to streamline administrative structures in a similar manner, and so the Northland School Division came into existence in December 1960, with its own act under provincial legislation.

When the division was first established the buildings were structurally substandard, student attendance was poor, achievement was below grade norms, many teachers lacked Alberta qualifications, and books and supplies were inadequate. Since the 1960s the situation has changed dramatically. New buildings with the latest technological equipment have been provided, and all teachers are certified professionals supported by qualified paraprofessionals. Students follow the provincial curriculum, and there has been a significant increase in the number of students who receive high-school diplomas.

The division is sufficiently unique that it requires the services of a supervisor of Native programs. Mary Cardinal Collins' job as Supervisor of Native Programs for the Northland School Division was multifaceted. The "Employee Orientation Package" that is given to all who are hired to teach in the division has a section entitled, "The Language and Culture of Northland School Division Communities," which was authored by Mary Cardinal Collins. Unlike the provinces of Saskatchewan and Manitoba, which have made concentrated efforts to train Aboriginal teachers, Alberta has not undertaken such initiatives. Expectations are that the majority of new staff hired each year will be non-Aboriginal with little or no knowledge about Aboriginal students, their cultures, and the communities.

Though there are other ethnic groups in the division, such as small settlements of Mennonites and Ukrainians, the majority of the students are Aboriginal; both Métis and First Nations are included. In the orientation package Mary states: "The goal of this paper is to give the fundamentals of history and language, hence culture, of the Northland School Division communities." The orientation package represents a significant change from past educational philosophies where Aboriginal children's history and language were, at best, ignored, but more often discredited. Teachers were not expected to have any knowledge about the structures of the children's original languages and so had no understanding of how to help those with language difficulties by applying English as a second language teaching principles. Educational philosophy, though perhaps unstated, generally was that teachers were expected to teach their own values to the children while disregarding, and hopefully replacing, the values they had learned in their homes. Frequently, the values taught in the classroom were based on white, middle-class, predominantly urban cultures portrayed in the teaching materials approved by the Department of Education.

In the orientation material Mary also discusses the kinship systems and the impact they may have on teaching. She warns prospective teachers about unprofessional behaviour in this regard. This is an aspect of education that has usually been totally ignored. Because kinship systems are often not understood, they may be violated unintentionally by teachers from outside the culture, thereby further widening the gap between the school and the community. She also talks briefly about the effects residential schools may have had on today's parents.

A cartoon of a teacher and child enhances the objectives of the orientation package and gets right to the crux of improving education for Aboriginal children. The child in the cartoon has added 2+2 to get the answer 756793. He explains to the teacher: "In an increasingly complex world, sometimes old questions require new answers." [51] The success of the Northland School Division depends on providing new answers to old problems, answers that will recognize the children's life experiences and provide them with a realistic education. Mary is instrumental in providing some of these new answers.

Mary Cardinal was born when her mother, Theresa Batoche, was only fourteen years old and her father, Peter Cardinal, was seventeen. Although married, they lived with Theresa's mother, Mary's *nohkom*, who had adopted Theresa late in life. Theresa applied for family allowance for Mary at the same time as *Nohkom* was receiving Theresa's.

Mary's grandmother was Métis and had a Métis cultural perspective even though she lived on the Saddle Lake Reserve because she had married a First Nation band member. She had attended a mission school at Lac La Biche in the late 1800s, and her memories dated back to the Riel Rebellion in Saskatchewan. She remembered that the nuns at the mission, frightened by rumours of marauding Natives, had taken the children to the safety of a small island in the lake until the crisis was over.

Mary grew up in a home filled with contrasts. Her *nohkom* was very old and spoke French and Cree. Theresa was very young, spoke only Cree, and had never gone to school. At the mere suggestion of sending her to school she had cried and cried, and continued to cry for two days, until the decision was reversed. Peter Cardinal had attended the Blue Quills Residential School at St. Paul for eight or nine years and spoke fluent English, though Mary never once heard him speak anything but Cree. Mary's young parents had an acrimonious relationship in which Mary was often the source of conflict. They simply were too young to be effective parents.

Her grandmother was the most significant person in Mary's life; in fact Mary was a *nohtikwew-ohpikyakan*, meaning a child "raised by an old woman." It was a privileged position in the culture and was usually reserved for first-born daughters. Mary feels she was lucky in that she learned many things before she went to school that would have been lost to her forever. She learned to be comfortable with old people as she travelled and visited with her grandmother. Mary saw first hand an era that was fast disappearing. They travelled with horse and wagon, or sleigh in wintertime, and visited old people who still lived in traditional ways. Many lived in old-style cabins, and a few still had dirt floors, though plank flooring was becoming more common. There was no furniture in these cabins; life was conducted in the ways practised before the coming of modern conveniences, like European-style chairs and beds. These early-childhood experiences left an indelible mark on Mary, firmly rooting her identity in her Cree heritage and language.

Religion played a significant role in the lives of the Saddle Lake people. Mary's *nohkom* was a devout Catholic, but she burned sweet grass during thunderstorms, so religion, too, was as full of contrasts as the other aspects of Mary's life. Peter's family also held traditional beliefs but Mary does not remember any conflicts over traditional practices. She remembers her paternal grandfather travelling to participate in a Sundance every year at Frog Lake. The sweat lodge was a part of the spiritual fabric of the community.

Mary was raised as a Catholic and did not participate in any traditional ceremonies, except round dances, as a child. As an adult she was to have a long journey of spiritual soul-searching and therapy before she was able to find a balance in her life between Catholic and traditional practices. The traditional practices were never discredited when Mary attended the residential school; they simply were rendered irrelevant.

A further contrast in her life developed over the rivalry between the Protestant and Catholic residents of the Saddle Lake Reserve. It was so intense it had effectively split the community into north and south with irreconcilable differences. Catholic children attended the Blue Quills School at St. Paul, whereas Protestant children were sent to the United Church school in Edmonton. They often grew up not even knowing about each other.

Mary was sent to the Blue Quills School in 1953 when she was seven, as dictated by the Indian Act, and she stayed there until she completed grade twelve in 1966. Grades one to eight were offered at the school, but for grades nine to twelve the students attended the school in town while still living in the residence. Mary's language of communication was Cree since that was the common language of the home. The worst epoch of language suppression had occurred at the residential schools before Mary's time. She does not remember being disallowed the use of Cree; it was not encouraged but the students were not punished for speaking it. In fact, Mary remembers that the school offered a Cree course taught by "an old, old priest."

Mary started school with no knowledge of English, but by Christmastime she was quite fluent. She found it very easy to learn languages, and she regrets that the school did not teach French. Because French was the language of her *nohkum*, Mary had an affinity for it and could have learned it effortlessly. French was also the language of the nuns, but they used it as the language of exclusion. They often spoke French to each other in front of the children, and the children were sure the nuns were speaking about them, which may or may not have been the case. There was a further reason, however, why French was excluded from residential school programs. In 1909 Deputy Superintendent of Indian Affairs Duncan Campbell Scott had decreed that only English was to be taught in the schools. There were protests, and the Bishop of St. Boniface, especially, argued that this was too restrictive. He believed that French-speaking non-teaching staff could be employed in the schools. In a letter of protest he stated: "If, in addition [pupils] hear and become in some measure familiar with French, no danger to the commonwealth will thereby be created nor will they be less equipped for the battle of life." [52] In spite of the protests, Campbell's decree was not reversed, as was always the case whenever he had made a decision.

Mary's memories of the residential school are generally positive, and she describes her experience as good. She was an excellent student and a favourite of her teachers. One priest, in fact, gave her a rosary that was over a hundred years old as a reward for her dedication and hard work in grade one catechism, which was taught entirely in Cree.

When Mary was at Blue Quills the meals were better than at some of the other schools. The priest/administrator was himself a diabetic and frequently emphasized that he wished for the children the good health he did not enjoy. Nutrition was his primary concern in meal planning and the food was not unappetizing. Mary comments that she is frequently complimented on her excellent teeth, and she wonders whether the good nutrition at the school established the foundation for the good health she enjoys today. Certainly it was better than what she would have experienced at home on the reserve where poverty was extreme.

Severe physical abuse of both boys and girls has been documented at Blue Quills School, most recently by Linda Bull in "Indian Residential Schooling: The Native Perspective"[53] Mary herself never saw any severe abuse. Her father, on the other hand, sometimes alluded to dark memories, but, in common with most residential school survivors, he rarely talked about them. Bull quotes one survivor as saying: "There may have been some good, but 90 per cent of the students from the 1930's and 1940's later became alcoholics ... We were brought up unloved and unwanted." Alcoholism was definitely a severe problem for Mary's father in his youth, but in his later years he overcame his addiction.

The regimentation at the school was strict, but it soon became routine for Mary. She was strapped once while she was at the school; her crime was that she had smiled in chapel. Punishment often followed some minor lapses in procedure, and Mary, like other students, was frequently punished for minor misdemeanours. Punishment was in the form of slaps, and she remembers missing many, many movies.

There was considerable conflict between students at the school as Cree and Dene students were confined in restricted areas. Historic animosities existed in their home communities, and the children brought these to the school with them. The child who had older siblings for protection was fortunate indeed. Mary recalls an older girl helping her in an Easter egg hunt, though she did not think she needed help.

The girl explained that she was a relative and that Mary's mother had asked her to look after Mary.

The conflict between community groups increased with the formation of gangs. The staff did try to prevent these gangs from forming but were not very successful. The staff was very vigilant, however, in forbidding any display of affection between students both of the opposite sex and of the same sex. Close friendships were strongly discouraged. Maggie Hodgson, past director of the Nechi Centre in Edmonton, explains:

> Some really cared about the young people they were in charge of but had been trained in a system that taught harshness and therefore they treated the students harshly. They were taught to believe that the more they sacrificed and denied their humanity, the closer they would be to God. Their seminaries and postulants' houses were not houses of warmth and love but places of sacrifice to God; places where they were denied human comforts as a sign of commitment. They expected their students to hold the same values. [54]

Mary recalls, "I didn't learn any love or affection—not at home nor at the school."

It was a school practice to assign older students to look after younger ones when they first arrived. They looked forward to this task, and when Mary's younger sister came to school Mary was deeply disappointed when she was not assigned to her. Mary was the oldest of ten or eleven children, but she really did not know her younger siblings. She had hoped to get to know her little sister better. When staff found out they were sisters Mary was ultimately assigned to look after her.

Mary feels that, for her, the academic aspect of the school worked well. She was a curious child, eager to learn, and she had wanted to go to school badly. She believes that during the 1950s and 60s many changes in social policies took place. Residential schools were being scrutinized much more carefully, and, except for a few isolated exceptions, the worst abuses no longer existed. Many schools were being closed permanently.

Mary was a good student and minded her own business as much

as possible. She soon became an avid reader, a habit that persists to this day. Her favourite author is Margaret Laurence, a person she even resembles physically. Her coping mechanism at the school was to disappear into a book. She made maximum use of the residential school library, though the range of reading material was very limited. She recalls that she read many, many biographies of saints. Her parents were very supportive of her educational endeavours because her mother was conscious of the limits that illiteracy placed on a person. Mary was encouraged to do something better with her life.

When Mary, as a seven-year-old, was overanxious to attend school, her *nohkom* warned her about the loneliness in store for her, but Mary promised never to cry when her parents visited. Though the Blue Quills School was only twenty-six kilometres from her home her parents rarely visited during the time she was there. She saw her family only during the summer so it is not surprising that she did not know her younger siblings. When she was older they were allowed to go home for Christmas and Easter, as well as for the summer.

True to her promise, Mary never once cried or made a scene during the parental visits. A certain stubborn streak did not allow her to prove her *nohkom* right. Her promise, however, had not included her *nohkom*, so when *nohkom* visited Mary felt free to cry her heart out. The family visits took place in the "Indian" parlour, where furniture consisted of several wooden benches. The other parlour, the "white" parlour, was furnished with rugs and upholstered furniture in the manner to which priests and other dignitaries were accustomed.

Mary knows she was definitely not a pet at school; she was far too insular as a child and was too frequently accused of minor infractions of the rules. That a system of pets existed was readily evident. There were those who used the pet system to their advantage, and all the children learned to use manipulative behaviours in order to receive favours. "Sucking up for favours," as Mary terms it, was almost mandatory for survival.

Mary believes, though, that the system of having pets was also used in a positive and culturally familiar way. Less-favoured girls would use the pets as intermediaries because the pets could acquire privileges on behalf of the other girls. They could also explain situations with greater hope of being heard, so punishments did not occur or were less

severe. Mary points out that Cree tradition had long utilized the practice of using an intermediary to speak for another. The system of pets
could be damaging, but on the other hand, when it was not used for
destructive purposes, could well have arisen from the nuns' instinctive
responses to the easiest method of managing the girls, whether they
understood Cree cultural practices or not.

Mary knows that the residential school took its toll on her personal life but believes the consequences were not as acute for her as they
were for some. All the students suffered from lack of decision-making
skills when they left the schools. They did not know how to shop or how
to handle money and were painfully shy. Mary was never tempted to
resort to alcohol or other destructive behaviours, but, like many survivors, she struggled with severe bouts of depression.

She dealt with her depression through therapy and various personal development activities. Her healing began when she recognized
that she was on a spiritual search, and she achieved spiritual balance
only after she became involved in traditional spiritual ceremonies.
Today she has what she terms an "uneasy truce" with the churches. She
is a practising Catholic but cannot accept the dogma of sin, hell, and
damnation. She is much more attuned to the contemporary attitudes of
love and acceptance of one's fellow human beings.

She also joined AlAnon, a support group for people affected in
any way by alcohol. Though herself not an alcoholic, her life has been
profoundly influenced by alcohol. AlAnon helped her understand how
she had let the residential school and her alcoholic father determine
her reactions to situations around her and how other people's emotions
controlled her life. She has arrived at the conclusion that people choose
their own directions in life and must take personal responsibility for the
paths they have chosen. She is quick to add, however, that her relatively
benign residential school experience is personal to herself, and she
does not presume to speak for other survivors.

Mary did well in whatever jobs she undertook after she left
school but recognizes in herself an abhorrence of certain residential
school behaviours. She will not line up, preferring instead to go without
whatever service the lineup offers. She will not join clubs or participate
voluntarily in any activity that has rules and regulations. She does not
protest or attempt to make change; she simply withdraws, a behaviour

that kept her personal integrity at the school and helps maintain her personal autonomy today.

Mary does not deny the abuse at the school but believes, in her time, no children who had vocal parents involved in their children's schooling had anything to fear. There were others, however, victims of intergenerational abuse or family breakdown, who were vulnerable and unprotected. These were the children whose parents could not care for them for whatever reason. Some parents had themselves been damaged by the residential school experience; some were damaged because of other factors. The residential schools came to be used as repositories for children from inadequate homes, whereas today childcare agencies with professional workers would be involved. These children, already traumatized by events in their lives, had to stay at the school all year round, and they were the ones who most often suffered further abuse at the schools. These were the children who had absolutely no place to go and often had no adults in their lives who were concerned about or able to look after their welfare. They were betrayed by society, the churches, and the schools in the deepest sense of the word. Mary recognizes that there were children such as these at the school when she was there.

If success or failure of the residential school system is measured in terms of graduation rates, it was a dismal failure. Though various degrees of literacy were acquired by most students, few graduated. When Mary started it was with a group of twenty to thirty students; of those, Mary and three others graduated from grade twelve. Of the ones who did not graduate, large numbers are alcoholics or have passed on because of various causes. Of the women Mary knows who continued with their educations and pursued careers or even other kinds of work, all are divorced. Mary believes this indicates a high degree of problems with intimacy.

In 1966 Mary graduated with a grade twelve diploma. In grades eleven and twelve her work slipped badly, and she chose the easiest courses, seeing that as the simplest way to get out of school. She was still living in residence, but the students were bussed to the provincial school in town. Absenteeism, partying, peer pressure, and lack of experience with making decisions that affected their personal lives all took their toll on the students, and Mary was no exception. After high school she completed senior matriculation at Alberta College in Edmonton, which was a semester school so she was able to get the required courses.

Her first job was as a ward aide in a hospital, and following a summer of this mundane work she enrolled in the Northern Alberta Institute of Technology. Again, she was searching for something easy that would require little effort and application on her part. She rejected a secretarial course that attracted many Aboriginal girls because she did not want to be part of what she recognized as ghettoizing Aboriginal women. Instead she registered for a dental assistant's course.

She did not even commence the course, however, because she became pregnant. She married the child's father, a Métis from Elizabeth Colony. As she reflects on the marriage today, which lasted seventeen years and produced two children, she believes it was the wrong move for her. Residential school students were not prepared for marriage. Marriage was not modelled and sexuality was presented as being wrong and sinful. Except for what she terms "a brief episode of hormones" she believes she had been much better prepared to become a nun though she felt none of the commitment required to become one. She would have been quite comfortable with the regimented life.

Like her father, Mary's husband was a drinker, which exacerbated the already difficult situation of an unfortunate marriage. Since her divorce in 1987 Mary has had no desire to embark on another potentially difficult relationship. She is enjoying a freedom she has never had before in her life.

Her first child, a son, today lives with his father. Mary describes him as a "lost boy" who follows his father's formerly destructive lifestyle. He was in a serious accident and received a head injury, which has further complicated a difficult life of substance abuse. His father, who is diabetic, lost a leg, and the two of them look after each other. Her son lives in anticipation of a generous insurance settlement. Mary has done a great deal of soul searching and eventually benefited from her involvement with AlAnon, which helped her differentiate between helping her son and enabling his destructive behaviours.

Mary's daughter went to university and completed an arts degree in Native Studies. Mary has two grandchildren, and she is able to love them in ways she was never able to love her own children. She believes she was always affectionate with her children, but a great deal of learning had to take place in the process of raising them. She sees her grandchildren as a second chance for her to enjoy the pleasures of having children around and being involved in their development. Her daughter became more knowledgeable about her culture at the university and is slowly coming to terms with the experiences of her parents and grandparents. Mary believes that both children recognize that the residential schools wreaked havoc with a whole culture, but they do not really understand what impact the consequences have on shaping the realities of today's Aboriginal peoples.

After her marriage Mary worked at jobs that were neither interesting nor challenging at the Alberta Native Communication Society and at Alberta Health Care. Mostly she was doing secretarial work. Then, in 1975, a small step toward training Aboriginal teachers was begun in Alberta.

Blue Quills, like many other residential schools, was slated for closure by the Department of Indian Affairs. The students were to be integrated into provincial schools. This was a decision that had been made with virtually no consultation with Aboriginal parents. Twelve communities connected with the school, with the backing of the Alberta Indian Association, blocked the move to close Blue Quills. They forced the government to turn the school over to the Saddle Lake–Athabasca District by means of a contract with the Blue Quills Native Education Council in 1971. It was a hard-fought battle that lasted eight months. The council wanted the school transferred to Indian administration while still remaining under federal jurisdiction. The department stated this could only happen if the council would become a school board under provincial jurisdiction. This was a move consistent with the principles of the *White Paper*, which sought to relieve the federal government of responsibility for First Nations and turn it over to the provinces. The council feared that a transfer from federal to provincial jurisdiction would not protect their rights as First Nations. They also feared that integration would not be beneficial to their children, a position that subsequently was proven to be quite correct.

Finally the school was occupied by tribal members. The old buildings were ringed with tents, hunting parties were sent out for deer, Saskatoon berries, and rhubarb, and children went fishing. Elders moved into the gym. John S. Milloy, in his book *A National Crime*, stated that over a thousand people supported the occupation, not only from

Alberta but from Saskatchewan as well, since the right to self-determination was at stake.[55] There were rarely fewer than two hundred people at the site at any given time. The Elders led prayers and chants. Three Indian-appointed reserve police kept order and committees were set up to organize activities, such as cooking, cleanup, and recreation. Political support for the occupation grew and the National Indian Brotherhood became involved. It was strongly supported by T. C. Douglas and David Lewis of the New Democratic Party, and by some other Members of Parliament as well. Finally, Minister of Indian Affairs Jean Chrétien capitulated.

The Blue Quills occupation was the first step in dramatically changing the relationship between the federal government and Indian bands with regard to education. Twenty-three other residential schools were subsequently turned over to the management of properly constituted Indian groups. More importantly, the government accepted the National Indian Brotherhood document *Indian Control of Indian Education* in 1972, which recognized the concept of parental control of Indian children's education.

Blue Quills was turned into an adult education centre and recently has become an accredited First Nation College. In 1975 a program called Morning Star was established to train Aboriginal teachers. It was part of a move across Canada to make professional training available to Aboriginal people in remote areas and to those who had not been able to finish high school for whatever reason. Courses were delivered at Blue Quills by the University of Alberta, and various support services enabled the students to succeed in their endeavours. Mary joined the program, eager to continue studies in a way she perceived as being challenging, and also enabling her to break out of the stereotyped roles that Native students were continually being expected to follow. After two years she had a teaching certificate, the teaching credential required in all provinces at that time. She taught for one year and then completed a bachelor of education degree at the University of Alberta.

After she got her degree she taught for the High Prairie School Division at Slave Lake for seven years and then went back to university to begin work on a master of education degree. However, she went back to work before she had completed her major thesis, and because of work pressures and other interests, she has never completed the degree.

Instead, she accepted the position of Supervisor of Native Programs for the Northland School Division, a job that she held for ten years. Though she lived in Peace River, her job entailed supervising Native programs in all the communities in the division.

Teacher and Aboriginal language instructor inservicing comprised much of her work. Approximately ninety-five per cent of the students in the Northland Division are Aboriginal, speaking either Cree or Dene. There is a teaching staff of about two hundred, eighty per cent of whom are non-Aboriginal. The teacher turnover rate is very high; hence orientation sessions with new teachers have to be held every year. Mary touched on many different aspects of Aboriginal culture during these orientation sessions but stressed language differences and how they impact literacy. Curriculum development was another major component of her work and she co-authored some of the Cree resource material for Alberta Education.

Mary conducts many cross-cultural workshops. This aspect of her career is stressful for her, but she has learned to take it in stride. She admits that she has become much more tolerant since she has reached the half-century mark, and her sense of humour has seen her through many difficult situations. She has arrived at the conclusion that it is unfair to expect non-Aboriginal people to act like Aboriginal people; in fact, those who try often end up with disastrous results. Her aim is to heighten perceptions and understandings so non-Aboriginal teachers can be sensitive and non-coercive with Aboriginal children, while maintaining their essential integrity as non-Aboriginals.

Mary is an educator who lives in the present and looks to the future to determine what role she can play in improving education for Aboriginals. She reflects on the residential school era frequently, but tries not to allow it to exert too great an influence on her life. The scars are there, and she knows that years of healing are still required, but she has other concerns that are more immediate.

Her greatest educational concern today is the lack of Aboriginal teachers in Alberta and especially the lack of trained Aboriginal language teachers. The high teacher turnover rate in Northland School Division is an ongoing problem that will be alleviated only by more Aboriginal teachers who are willing to make permanent homes in the communities in which they teach. She points out that it is easier to staff the schools closest to Edmonton and ruefully admits that even Aboriginal teachers prefer to teach in the schools in the southern parts of the division.

She worries about the lack of political will to solve Aboriginal teacher shortages in Alberta, pointing out that the Northland School Division is only one area where they are needed. Many Aboriginal teachers are required in cities as well, especially Edmonton, as Aboriginal people become increasingly urbanized. She points to Aboriginal teacher-training programs in other provinces and wishes that Alberta would follow some of the directions found to be so successful there. "We have always looked to Saskatchewan and Manitoba with great envy," she admits.

The Morning Star program at Blue Quills trained only two groups of students before it was discontinued. In Manitoba and Saskatchewan the Aboriginal teacher-training programs began at the same time and still continue today. It was once thought that the programs would have a limited lifespan because the needs of northern communities would be met. This has not proven to be the case as demand always exceeds the supply. Not only has the birth rate increased in Aboriginal communities but the demand for better education with a greater variety of options is as essential in northern communities as it is elsewhere.

Both Saskatchewan and Manitoba have Aboriginal legislators who advance Aboriginal issues, but this representation is lacking in Alberta. The effects of the teacher-training programs have been so profound that the whole face of Aboriginal education is changing in some provinces. All northern schools in the provinces with ongoing Aboriginal teacher-training programs have at least some Aboriginal teachers and administrators. In some communities Aboriginal teachers are in the majority. In Winnipeg two provincial schools administered by the Winnipeg I School Division have been designated as "Aboriginal" schools with Aboriginal administrators and teachers. In Alberta such programs have been perceived as unnecessary frills.

Mary worries especially about teacher shortages predicted for the twenty-first century. A lack of mathematics and science teachers was already impacting on the Northland School Division at the turn of the century. As shortages escalate in the south the northern schools will suffer the most. There is considerable fear that the situation of unqualified teachers that existed prior to 1960 could be repeated.

Mary's particular concern is the lack of trained Aboriginal language teachers. Destruction and devaluation of Aboriginal languages in residential schools was deliberate, so restoration of these languages is a difficult and daunting task. Several generations of Aboriginals not only lost their languages but many also grew up with negative biases against them. These attitudes are changing as the value of the languages is universally recognized today; however remediation is slow, since the pool of proficient speakers has been drastically reduced. Language programs and training of Aboriginal language teachers will go a long way toward rectifying historical injustices. Special programs need to be put in place because only too often both language and culture have to be re-examined by teacher trainees who have been denied this information during their formative years. Alberta's eight Aboriginal languages further complicate the training of teachers, since each language has to be accommodated.

Mary hopes that some form of Aboriginal teacher-training programs for teachers of all subject areas will soon be "taken out of mothballs." Whatever actions are being taken, however, are already too late since an adequate body of educated, experienced Aboriginal teachers in Alberta is far off in the future. But even the tentative discussions about training programs for Aboriginal teachers are a hopeful sign.

In the year 2000 Mary opted for a change in focus and accepted a three-year secondment to Alberta Learning (Department of Education) as a consultant in the Aboriginal Resources Learning and Teaching Resources Branch. In this position she can facilitate Aboriginal language projects as well as the development of Aboriginal resources.

There is a personal benefit to her move to Edmonton. She can now live with her daughter and grandchild. Though she participated in the vibrant cultural life of the north when she lived in Peace River, she was far removed from her family and her own cultural roots. Today it takes her only two hours to reach her parents' home, and she has the opportunity to attend ceremonies and feasts with her own people. She values this connection with her roots and heritage. She is not speculating on what she will do when her three-year secondment expires, content to focus on the tasks at hand. Whatever improvements in education for Aboriginal children of Alberta take place in the future, Mary Cardinal Collins will surely be instrumental and influential in charting their course.

Elizabeth Bear

After years of searching for an identity and a home, Elizabeth Bear finally returned to Pukatawagan as the director of the Nikawiy Health Centre, the Mathias Colomb First Nation Health Authority. The norm for all reserves across Canada is that men hold the power positions. Only on very rare occasions has a woman been elected chief or been given one of the more lucrative community positions. At the turn of the millennium, Pukatawagan had a female chief. The director of education was a local woman, as was the director of the crisis centre. Though a certain degree of political unrest remains, men in the community respect and support these women, restoring the balance to a Cree lifestyle where men and women were considered to be equal and supportive of each other. The Indian Affairs system of patriarchy and misogyny is simply no longer being followed at Pukatawagan.

From the air Pukatawagan, home of the Mathias Colomb Band, is picture-postcard perfect. On a brilliant fall morning the deep green of evergreens interspersed with brilliant autumn foliage is breathtaking. The Churchill River flows south of the little reserve community, while sparkling azure blue bays and coves ring the other three sides. In the middle of the community "Mount Puk" dominates the landscape.

Pukatawagan is about eleven hundred kilometres by air northeast of Winnipeg. It is only after the plane has landed that the first-time visitor realizes that there still are four kilometres of road to cover between the landing strip and the community. All is not as idyllic as it appears from the air. A regular van picks up medical passengers, if there are any on the plane. If that is the case, it is possible to catch a ride in the van. The more common practice is to hitch a ride in any vehicle that happens to be there, if, indeed, there is one there. A payphone has conveniently been placed outside the little terminal, so passengers can phone the community for a pickup since the terminal is not always open. But a pickup is not assured since there are few vehicles in the community, and they may be in use, they may not be working, or the community may be out of gasoline.

The road between the airstrip and the community has been the subject of political debate in far-away southern Manitoba. Its maintenance is a provincial responsibility, and one can only assume that the politicians entrusted with the welfare of all Manitoba's citizens have never been required to travel this road. It is a narrow gravel road, a high grade, with deep ditches on both sides, and curving roller-coaster hills. At its best, it is a white-knuckle ride for the first-time visitor. Few have experienced it at the best of times. Thick clouds of fine limestone dust obscure all oncoming traffic when the weather is dry. If it is raining the dust turns to mud as slick as wagon-wheel grease. In winter it quickly ices over so that even walking is hazardous. The only reassurance is that there have been no fatalities on this road in recent times. The first-time visitor strives to assume a nonchalant air, in keeping with the other passengers in the vehicle.

The final curve of the road brings the community into view. First is a picturesque little church on immaculately kept grounds, white steeple pointing to eternal salvation. Locals are quick to point out that there is an organ in this church, brought at great expense and even greater labour by way of the Churchill River many years ago.

The village is spread along the river, though new development in the "suburbs" is taking place. One can walk from one end of the village to the other in half an hour, or in one hour, or more, depending on the road conditions. High rubber boots are essential much of the time and mud-spattered pants are the norm.

On a sunny day the residents are out, and courtesy is the order of the day. A new visitor is greeted by one and all. One may be welcomed by an Elder ascertaining the purpose of the visit and then passing on some vignette about Pukatawagan's past. Often it is a teenager wired to a Walkman, who nevertheless pauses for a friendly word. Or it is the children who ask your name before they ask for money. The feeling of goodwill that envelops the visitor at the first sight of the community returns quickly.

Pukatawagan has frequently been in the news. It took its turn at being labelled the most violent community in the north. It made newspaper headlines in 1985 when Chief Pascal Bighetty finally forced Manitoba Hydro and Indian Affairs to admit that the school had been built on a PCB disposal site. After years of protracted effort the school was demolished and the children were moved to a temporary cluster of ramshackle buildings and trailers for their education. Today a chain-link fence surrounds the disposal site and signs warn trespassers of danger. A new state-of-the-art school was finally opened in 1999. The incidence of hysterectomies in Pukatawagan is high, but no one seems to have any statistics on whether it is higher than average or whether there is a connection between the victims and the PCB site.

Pukatawagan was also in the news when, in desperation over acute housing shortages, band members camped out on the grounds of the provincial legislature in Winnipeg. There were talks and news cameras and eventually they agreed to move to a less conspicuous site at The Forks. Finally, they went back home, having achieved very little after several months of protest.

It might be said that Elizabeth Bear had, at last, come home, though this was correct only insofar as that her band membership is at Pukatawagan and her parents' domicile is there. It is incorrect in that, for most of her life, Elizabeth has felt that she has never had a home. She has not known who she is, where she comes from, or where she belongs. If it can be said that home is where the heart is, then Elizabeth's heart has been broken, for her mother, herself, and her son were all victimized by a residential school system without a heart.

Elizabeth was five years old the first time she was betrayed by her family and her church. Children were to be six when they were sent to the residential school, and the priest told Elizabeth's mother he had proof she was, indeed, six years old. How was a mother who spent all her formative years in the residential school to argue with the infallibility of a priest? So five-year-old Elizabeth was taken to Guy Hill Residential School near The Pas, Manitoba. It was not until she applied for a driver's licence that she found that she was twenty-four, not twenty-five years old as she had been led to believe. Elizabeth was by no means the only child to be taken to school early; some were taken at the age of three.

The government was constantly being pressured by the clergy to admit children earlier in order to remove them from the "deleterious" influences of parents, but the government never bowed to this pressure. In fact, the age of entry had been raised to seven in 1909. The supervision of schools, however, was lax or non-existent; record keeping was haphazard and school principals, who, with a few exceptions, were clergy, did as they pleased. Government officials did not wish to raise the ire of the clergy on this or on any other matter.

Both Elizabeth's parents had attended the Sturgeon Landing Residential School. Her father left at the age of sixteen after three years of schooling. Her mother left at the age of twenty-one to marry Elizabeth's father. They had nine children and all were sent to residential school.

Both parents spoke highly of their residential school experience pointing out that it had taught them to survive in the working world. They were totally devoted to the Catholic Church, obeying all rules meticulously and never missing mass. They denied themselves many creature comforts during Lent. This devotion to the church has not diminished over the years.

For Elizabeth, the Guy Hill experience was hurtful and distressing. The pain of the residential school, however, was superimposed on a much deeper pain. She lived with emotional neglect from the day she was born. She understands today that the pain and separation inflicted on her by the school system was mild compared to the desolation she felt within her family.

Feelings of anger and deep-rooted hurt at her mother's indifference to her lurk beneath the surface of Elizabeth's usually cheerful and controlled demeanour. Ambivalent feelings about her mother bring tears to her eyes, and she grasps for words. "I will not let her disown me again," she attempts to explain, with reference to her return to Pukatawagan to work. Often she says, "I'll have to talk to my mother about that," as she attempts to sort out some particularly painful memory. That her mother would remember details of Elizabeth's life is likely a forlorn and hopeless wish.

Elizabeth's family lived at Sandy Bay, Saskatchewan, when she was tiny. She does not remember when she could not speak both Cree and English with equal proficiency. The nearby Island Falls community had been established when a dam was built, and Elizabeth and her family interacted with the non-Aboriginal families who managed the dam. Elizabeth has always found moving between the two cultures easy.

Elizabeth has few memories of her early years at the school. She had grown up defiant and tough, hardened as only a child without nurture can be. At Guy Hill she was punished frequently. She was strapped so often she believes today that eventually it did not matter any more. When she was small she cried, even before she was hit, because that often served to make the punishment less severe. When she got older she presented a stoic front, hands unmoving, never flinching or crying out until the person meting out the punishment grew tired. Ten blows per hand were not unusual, and her hair was forever being cut short as punishment. Never once were they able to break her defiance.

The cause of her punishments was frequently over bathroom privileges. Even as a small child she felt it was inhumane to refuse children permission to go to the bathroom when they were in physical distress. Accidents, as they were called, happened frequently and an "accident" meant punishment and ridicule. As she got older, Elizabeth often spoke up on behalf of the more timid students and was doubly punished for her interference.

Another cause of punishment was food. Unfamiliar foods caused the children a great deal of anguish. Food, such as red beets that coloured the soup, horrified the children. There were no explanations or warnings, just platefuls of awful-looking brew. Had they known that beets were a vegetable, it might not have made the meal any more enjoyable, but it would have decreased their repugnance. Even worse was their abhorrence when the food was green. Because spinach was good for them they were forced to eat it or suffer the consequences. The consequences could be brutal. Most disgusting, however, was old vegetable soup that had turned sour, causing the children to vomit in revulsion. They ate it though, and struggled to keep it down, since they were forced to eat what they had regurgitated.

Elizabeth was also punished for speaking Cree. Rules regarding Cree were inconsistent, since some students were allowed to speak it. Elizabeth feels she was singled out for punishment by staff because they feared and sought to break her independent spirit. They were relentless in this task and, though they never succeeded, many other students were cowed as they observed the ferocity of her punishments.

Elizabeth is quick to point out that not all the nuns at Guy Hill were cruel. Sister Joseph, now known as Sister Evelyn, and Sister Pat were not quite twenty when they arrived at Guy Hill. They were neither cruel nor vindictive. When the residential school closed, the two Sisters were hired by the Kelsey School Division in The Pas. There Sister Pat eventually taught Elizabeth's daughter as well as the children of other residential school survivors.

When Sister Pat was her child's teacher, Elizabeth always treated her with the respect and deference which was her due. Elizabeth was raised to treat anyone connected with the church with respect, which she still does willingly, provided they have integrity. Sister Pat had shed her long habit and was a very good teacher. Elizabeth, however, always held herself aloof when she spoke with the Sister, making very careful conversation. The slightest break in her veneer was dangerous, and she did not want Sister Pat to know how desperately the school had been able to hurt her. When asked what she would say to Sister Evelyn today if she were to meet her, Elizabeth reached her arms out in a welcoming gesture and responded without hesitation, "Hey, I made it!" And she is sure Sister Evelyn would be very proud of her.

However, Sisters Pat and Evelyn were the exception. Sister "Porky" and Sister "Ogre," as the students had dubbed them, were cruel and vindictive. When asked how she would respond to them if she met them today, Elizabeth's face darkened and she made a threatening gesture with her clenched fists. It was not a good question to have asked. Then she relaxed with a self-deprecating laugh and said that never once had she imagined anything so dreadful or traumatizing as meeting those two women again. In any event, they were old when Elizabeth was a child and have long since gone to meet their Maker.

At the age of fifteen Elizabeth had spent ten years at the school. She had passed grade eight and was beginning grade nine when she was "kicked out." The incident that precipitated her expulsion occurred in the principal's office where she had gone to take a phone call from her father. He had cut his foot and he called to see if she could come home to help. Father Poirier (now deceased) took the opportunity to grab her chin, puckering up her face. Then he kissed her, forcing his revolting old tongue into her mouth. Elizabeth was a strong, assertive child and struggled mightily. She still shudders as she recalls the feel of his stubby whiskers on her chin and the revolting smell of his cigar as she was gagging and struggling to breath. She broke free of Father Poirier's grasp, picked up a portable typewriter from his desk and flung it at his head. As he ducked, she ran out of the door and across the schoolyard to the safety of the bush where she stayed for two days.

No attempts were made to find her. She believes it was because had she been forced to go back, she would not have gone quietly. She was known for her defiance and her strong, clear voice. The whole school would have known of Father Poirier's actions before they would have been able to subdue her.

The bush held no terror for her. Children ran away every year but were brought back just as regularly. They knew all the hiding places. It was early November when the incident happened so the weather was cold at night. Elizabeth crept back to the school and slept under a shed where there was shelter. The children were adept at breaking into the school and stealing food so she did not go hungry.

After two days, not knowing what else to do, she returned to the school. Before she fully realized what was happening to her she was hustled out, put on the train, and sent back to Pukatawagan. Terror seized her. Her life experiences had consisted of riding the train with other children, getting off at Prospect Point about fourteen kilometres from the school, being herded onto a yellow bus and delivered to the school. She knew the area around the school and the shore of Clearwater Lake, and she knew the area around Pukatawagan. Anything in between was uncharted territory, and she had never been alone before. She was on the train with no food, no companionship, and no contact with any other human being whom she knew. Her parents did not know where she was.

After a ten-hour ride the train stopped at Mile 99, the closest point to the reserve, and she was in familiar territory again. It was approximately eight kilometres to the reserve, and since no one had been notified of her coming there was no one to meet her. She was undismayed as she began the long walk to the community. She recalls that it was a Wednesday evening because, as she rounded the bend, she saw her mother and her aunt coming from a Legion of Mary meeting at the church. To this day her mother still attends Legion of Mary meetings every Wednesday evening. She called out to them, and her mother became frightened.

"Is this a ghost I'm seeing?" her mother stammered. Elizabeth assured her that she was real flesh and blood, and she explained that she had been expelled from school. She tried to tell her mother about Father Poirier's actions. In a fury, her mother grabbed her by the ear and led her along the road shouting, "Don't you make a lie like that. You are just BAD." Once they reached their home Elizabeth sought her father's help and again attempted to tell her parents what had happened when she had answered his phone call. Her father refused to listen and simply limped away.

Elizabeth has finally come to terms with the incident with the priest to the extent that today she can smell a cigar and stay calm, no longer needing to fight revulsion and horror. She tells herself, "It is only a harmless cigar," and firmly pushes associated memories aside. It took maturity and years of intensive healing sessions with other residential school survivors to reach this point. She can now talk openly about her residential school experiences and willingly shares details because she believes that catharsis is the only way to purge the evil from her life. The retelling, however, is still extremely painful and tears flow as she tells of the devastating aftermath of the incident. The beauty of the fall day on the shores of Clearwater Lake and of the pristine environment at Pukatawagan is juxtaposed in her memory with the cruelty deliberately inflicted by adults on the helpless, lonely child she was.

Elizabeth had no recourse but to stay home. She badly wanted to learn but the local school only went to grade eight and had nothing new to teach her. She got a job at the store for lack of anything else to do. She felt isolated and bored. Pukatawagan was where her parents lived but it was not home to Elizabeth. Since she was five she had spent

September to June at Guy Hill and that was where her friends were. During the summers the family had always moved to a fish camp. Pukatawagan was a place she had only visited briefly for a week or two after school closed and again in the fall before it reopened.

After a miserable summer of working in the store Elizabeth ran away again, this time from her home. She knew she would get no empathy or support from her family, so she asked the store manager to drive her to the train stop where she caught the train for The Pas. She was not missed right away but her mother was furious when she found out Elizabeth had gone. She contacted Indian Affairs and instructed them to send Elizabeth to a reform school if she applied for educational assistance.

Elizabeth had absolutely no idea what she was going to do when she got to The Pas. Fortunately her friend, Mary Jane McCallum, was at the station when she arrived. She literally followed Mary Jane to the group home where she was staying. The home was operated by Audrey and Orville Goreau, and they allowed Elizabeth to stay. They knew she was a runaway with no sponsorship, but with the help of an Indian Affairs student counsellor they paved the way for her to continue her education. Elizabeth was placed in grade nine.

This was the time period when many questions were being asked about the viability of residential schools. Even some churches were suggesting that education ought not to be their domain. The government was experimenting with less expensive and more successful alternatives. Guy Hill School was still open but Elizabeth's peer group was boarded with families in The Pas and attended the provincial high school. One of Elizabeth's friends and classmates was Helen Betty Osborne. Later, the name Helen Betty Osbourne became well known across Canada because she was forced into a car by four non-Aboriginal youths and was brutally raped and murdered. Though there were those in The Pas who knew the perpetrators, no proper police investigation took place until sixteen years later. Only one of the four men has been punished for the crime. It was one of the cases the Manitoba Aboriginal Justice Inquiry focussed on in 1991.

Elizabeth's was the first group of residential school students in the community to attend a provincial school, and it was really impressed upon them that they "had to be good" and make the program work.

And they were good. They were highly motivated to learn and broke no rules. The rules in the provincial school were logical and benign after their experiences in the residential school. Inside the classroom, however, life was very difficult for them. The teachers at Guy Hill had taught various subjects, but changing from subject to subject simply meant putting away their books and getting out different ones. In The Pas they had to change classrooms, and the building was big and confusing. They received no orientation and no special help in adjusting. They had never been allowed to make any decisions for themselves at Guy Hill so when they had "spares" they had no idea what that meant. At Guy Hill, a spare was a catechism class. At Guy Hill, silence reigned; in The Pas schools they were bewildered and confused by what, to them, was a very high noise level and the shocking liberties taken by the students.

Not all the students were able to survive the drastic changes, but those who did were highly motivated and intrigued by the knowledge and opportunities that an education could bring. Though many of the students preferred the back seats in the classrooms where they could be quietly invisible, that was not Elizabeth's style. She preferred the front of the classroom and wanted to be part of the action.

She tried her best to participate in class discussions but soon began to notice a disconcerting pattern. She knew the answers to questions and though she raised her hand hopefully she was never called upon, at least not until all the other students were stymied. Then one teacher, especially, would fire at her, unexpectedly and rapidly, "OK Elizabeth. What is the answer?" By then she too was stymied, or her mind had been wandering, since she had little expectation of being called upon and had tuned out the whole process. She would become flustered, particularly because of the teacher's accusatory tone, and would be unable to answer. Soon she ceased to raise her hand, fully realizing that she was falling into the "stupid Indian" stereotype.

Worst was the French class. The residential school students saw no need to take French, and they had no desire to learn it because it was so closely associated with Father Poirier and the nuns. Only Elizabeth, however, voiced her unwillingness to learn it and so was once more branded as uncooperative. She eventually accepted the inevitable and, deep down, she felt that learning something so new and different was challenging. But again, disconcerting patterns emerged. As at Guy Hill,

Elizabeth's assertiveness made her vulnerable, and the teacher paid undue attention to her pronunciation; in fact he embarrassed all the residential school students unnecessarily. Even that might have been tolerable, but the content they learned was not the same as that of non-Aboriginal students. Whereas the other students were learning real life-situation sentences like *Open the window* or *Where is the library?*, the Aboriginal students were infantilized and taught sentences like *I am a little girl*. Never once were they asked to repeat a sentence that did not in some way describe themselves.

A major clash in the French class would have been inevitable had it not been averted by a helpful counsellor who transferred the students into typing and library work. The one good experience Elizabeth had in the school was in grade nine science. The school had an excellent science teacher who did not differentiate between residential school and town students. He expected quality work from all the students, challenging them with his innovative teaching and encouraging them with his supportive manner. Elizabeth enjoyed the course and did excellent work, defying the stereotype that there was something inherently difficult in science for Aboriginal students. Mary Jane McCallum, in fact, went on to become a dentist. Elizabeth knew she was smart but, except for science, her marks in grade nine did not indicate this. She barely passed. Social interactions with non-Aboriginal students were very stressful and the words "dirty Indian" were commonly used.

Elizabeth did not go home for the summer, and by the time school opened again in fall she was pregnant, but she had no idea how it had happened. Starved for affection and physical closeness, she had agreed to her boyfriend's requests without remotely understanding what was happening. She had received no sex education from either her mother or the school. When she began to have morning sickness Audrey suggested she might be pregnant, and she explained how babies happened.

Things began to "click" in Elizabeth's brain and she realized she had done that terrible thing that the nuns had referred to obliquely so many times. She was terrified. She did not know what to do or where to go. Above all, she was mortified that everybody would know what she had done and was certain that she would go to hell. She particularly did not want to go back home.

The baby was born in The Pas hospital, and for a while she lived with her boyfriend's parents. When her son, Vince, was nine months old her mother came looking for her, having heard that she had a child. She announced that she would raise him, and Elizabeth would continue school. Vince grew up believing that Elizabeth was his older sister, and when he was old enough, he, too, was sent to Guy Hill School.

Vince's life has been fraught with difficulty. When he grew older and learned that Elizabeth was his mother, he reacted bitterly saying he was just a mistake and she had never really cared for him. He relented somewhat when he came to understand the circumstances of his birth. His has been a life of anger and aggression, spent in and out of jail because of random acts of violence. There is a missing element in his life. So thoroughly has he been institutionalized that he cannot function outside of prison. Today a tenuous relationship exists between him and his mother.

Elizabeth went back to school when Vince went to live with her mother, and the next summer she went home to Pukatawagan. Before the summer was over she was pregnant again. Back in The Pas, she left the Goreau home but moved into another supportive foster home. When her second son, Victor, was born at The Pas hospital she met with intense pressure to place him for adoption. He had jaundice and she was released from the hospital before he was. She was told he could not be released from the hospital and was almost tricked into signing adoption papers. She persevered and eventually succeeded in claiming her baby.

Her mother phoned to tell Elizabeth to bring the baby home. Elizabeth had known that there was some unexplained tension between her parents regarding another woman. Eventually it was revealed that she had a half-brother, Gilbert. Though her father never acknowledged paternity, he did not deny it either. Gilbert's wife had given birth to a stillborn child so Elizabeth's mother suggested that they raise Victor. Elizabeth took Victor home to Pukatawagan by train when he was only ten days old. They were met at the station by her mother, who was happy and greeted both Elizabeth and the baby with considerable affection. The fact that she was quite inebriated did not mar this very special occasion for Elizabeth.

Gilbert and his wife took Victor to raise as their own in their home at Pelican Rapids. Elizabeth kept in contact and visited often. When he was old enough he was informed of his parentage and eventually he even tried living with Elizabeth and the two other children she had by then. It was readily apparent, however, that he missed his home so he returned to Pelican Rapids. Today he is a well-adjusted person, coping well with life and has a trusting and satisfying relationship with his birth mother.

After Victor's birth Elizabeth returned to The Pas for grade eleven. She met Brian and established a stable relationship; in 1972 her daughter was born. Her formal education was disrupted when she stayed home to raise her daughter, and in 1977 her third son was born. It was a peaceful and relatively happy interlude in her life. The Pas was a good place to finish her education since Keewatin Community College (KCC) was nearby. She finished grade twelve through adult education courses and revelled in the variety of training that was available. She took a stenographic course, a clerk typist course, and a business accounting course. She enjoyed every course she ever took and did very well in each one.

Tired of being channelled into "women's work" courses, she and a group of her friends decided to challenge the non-traditional areas where, as a side benefit, their pay would be considerably better. If anyone suggested an Indian or a woman might not be suited to specific training they set out to prove them wrong. Elizabeth took electrical training and would have liked to move into electronics but that was not available at KCC and the move to Winnipeg was too intimidating. When the correctional centre was built in The Pas, Elizabeth worked on the wiring and today points out that she has "left her mark" on the criminal justice system.

She also took welding, carpentry, and woodworking courses and trained as a heavy-duty-equipment operator. Her daring and adventurous spirit was back; she challenged her own perceived limitations and was always successful. When Churchill Forest Industries was established at The Pas she operated one of the bulldozers clearing the land.

On the home front, however, life was not proceeding as well. The first three years of her marriage had been good ones but then it began to disintegrate. Elizabeth stayed two more years but recalls that they were difficult years for her. When she told Brian that she was leaving the partnership he was skeptical about her ability to survive on her own. That was just the kind of challenge she needed to break away from the unhappy life she was leading. She moved to Brandon with her two children with very little idea of what she would do when she got there.

Elizabeth had come a long way in charting her own life, but the underlying pain that was causing chaos in her life lay dormant, ready to flare at any moment. She was at a loss about what to do. Many Aboriginal students were attending Brandon University so Elizabeth decided she might as well try that, too. It was to be one of the best moves she made in her life. She met an Aboriginal professor, Dr. Art Blue, who taught Native Studies courses and who was also a psychologist. A friendship developed and over the years he was to be invaluable in helping her come to terms with who she was as an Aboriginal person. He helped her see that what had happened to her was not her fault and she need not be ashamed. He also helped her to understand that her mother, too, had been victimized.

Another serendipitous event occurred when she saw an advertisement for a course entitled "Seminar in Native Women's Issues." Out of curiosity she enrolled and found to her surprise that many of the issues she had thought of as being unique to Aboriginal women were common to all women. She learned that there were concerned men taking the course as well. She learned how colonization, and especially the Indian Act, had played havoc with the traditional balances in Aboriginal cultures. She found the course a safe place to express opinions, and her ideas, expressed from the front row, were respected by both the students and professor. She made some lasting friendships. However, she continued to repress the demons that lay deeply imbedded in her psyche. It was not the time or the place to bring them out.

When Elizabeth graduated with a bachelor of arts degree she moved back with Brian, hoping the relationship might have improved with the separation. Her stay only lasted two months. With the new insights she had acquired about what a family could be and into her mother's behaviour she decided to try to establish a relationship with her mother. She phoned her and asked her for train fare home. She told her mother, "I am thirty-six years old. I have given you two of my children to raise. You will help *me* now." The railway gave Elizabeth a ticket on credit with her mother's pledge to pay for it, while the children stayed in The Pas with their father.

Back in Pukatawagan, Elizabeth was initially given a job as a probation officer. Human resource development workers were a new community concept. Elizabeth felt it was work she was qualified to do but could not get a job without specialized training. She went back to the classroom, this time with the New Careers program—a government-funded program designed to provide onsite training for community workers in areas such as health, social work, or recreation. It was highly unusual for a university graduate to take New Careers courses. After graduation she spent two years working in the community. It was a time of healing for her as she reconnected with her estranged siblings and her relationship with her mother improved. There were times when Elizabeth felt that her mother actually approved of her.

She attempted reconciliation with Brian again when their daughter became pregnant. Both she and Brian felt they had not provided much of a life for their children, and they wanted to do better for their grandchildren. However, when her daughter was accepted in a dental therapist program in Prince Albert, Elizabeth took the opportunity to leave the partnership again, this time permanently. She accompanied her daughter, to give moral support and to help with the care of her grandson. Elizabeth found work at the Pine Grove Correctional Centre in Prince Albert almost immediately. As she worked with the women at the centre she learned about abuse such as she had never before imagined. She was able to put her own life into perspective and realized that there were others whose lives had been much worse than hers. She treasured the interactions with the women but suffered great personal turmoil. Today she says her little grandson was the lifesaver who enabled her to carry on and not break down in the face of so much grief and her own repressed feelings.

When her daughter's course was finished they moved to Thompson where Elizabeth was hired as Assistant Director of Health for the Keewatin Tribal Council. Eventually she became the Health Transfer Coordinator. She enjoyed her work and revelled in a kind of freedom she was experiencing for the first time in her life. She was proving herself capable of directing her own life, dependent on no one, and especially not on an abusive man. When she was invited to become director of the Nikawiy Health Centre by her band, she returned to Pukatawagan, finally feeling that she did indeed have a home.

In the 1980s the issue of residential school abuse became public as Phil Fontaine, then Grand Chief of the Assembly of First Nations, spoke publicly about the abuse he had suffered. The consequences of this revelation led to intense media coverage as non-Aboriginal Canadians were finally ready to listen to what was by no means new information. Released from years of silence, residential school survivors gathered to share their experiences, console each other and hopefully begin a process of healing.

One of the first gatherings of former residential school students took place at Guy Hill School; this gathering was to become an annual event. The building had been demolished and the site was administered by Parks Canada. Parks Canada allowed the use of the grounds for the gathering, and eventually the Opaskwayak First Nation at The Pas claimed the site as part of their treaty land entitlement. In the summer of 2000 the survivors erected a memorial to Helen Betty Osborne at the entrance to the grounds.

Elizabeth participated in all the gatherings at Guy Hill. Slowly she was able to come to terms with her grief and fears as she and others shared their memories and attempted to exorcize the demons that still haunted them. After the dedication of Helen Betty Osborne's memorial she wrote:

> You would have thought my tears have run out by now ...
> but that is not the case. I still have buckets of tears when
> it comes to sharing about the residential school. I believe
> it's because I not only feel for myself but for others ...
> Even though I felt different emotions when seeing the
> Osborne family and having to listen to the details of
> Helen's passing ... at the end of it all ... I felt very much
> alive and thankful that I *can* feel like that.

Elizabeth understood that the relationship with her mother could never improve until her mother, too, revisited her residential school days. After two summers of healing for herself, Elizabeth convinced her mother to re-examine her experience. She agreed, and

Elizabeth arranged a trip to Sturgeon Landing for her mother, unaccompanied by any family members.

When she returned, support workers sat with her in a circle, drinking tea and making non-threatening conversation. It would have ended there if it had been her mother's choice. At first her mother spoke lightly of the experience, mentioning that the foundation was still there and how she had walked through it, placing herself in various locations. Her support group shared their feelings about the "coming out" experience and how they had all felt like helpless children again. They all agreed that they had to force themselves to relive the horror as they had experienced it as children, and they had to share it with others to be purged. They had learned from each other and were helped in the healing process since people who have not been in residential school cannot possibly understand their feelings.

Elizabeth's mother had always stated emphatically and unequivocally that the residential school system had not made her angry. However, the more she talked about the memories she had recalled in the haunted presence of the old foundation, the more agitated she became. She talked of the laundry room and how she had to seek out that room among the rubble because she had so often been sent there for punishment. She began to bang her fist rhythmically on the table in front of her, harder and harder. Finally she told the assembled women that her brother had been beaten so severely in that room that he had died of his injuries, a fact she had vowed she would never divulge to anyone. Spent, she reached over and caressed Elizabeth's hair, a maternal gesture Elizabeth had never before experienced in her life.

The relationship between mother and daughter has grown and no hard feelings remain. Her mother now believes what Elizabeth tells her of her school experiences. I asked Elizabeth about her attitude toward the church since they cannot be separated from her feelings toward her mother. She became thoughtful and did not answer for a long time. The small A-frame building at Pukatawagan is the focal point of the community, especially for the older people. It's importance is demonstrated by the immaculate grounds, the grotto between the church and lake, the well-kept cemetery under tall pine trees, and the weekly events that are a high point for many.

Elizabeth feels that today the Catholic Church has lost a great deal of its power to attract and control young people. She attends traditional sweats regularly and has an aunt who is a Medicine Woman. The eagle has become the symbol of the traditional spirituality. Her mother, like other older people who attended the schools, treats the traditional ceremonies with disdain, saying she will not be caught "praying to a Creature."

For Elizabeth there is no contradiction between the church and traditional ceremonies; she participates in both. When she is home on the reserve she loves to go to church with her mother for the closeness it brings. It is a childhood tradition that she respects and honours. She particularly enjoys singing in the choir. She loves the rich language of the Bible readings. The ambience is peaceful and nonthreatening as she is surrounded by what she has finally come to recognize as her own people. There is no coercion, harshness, or sadness associated with the little church in the community that has experienced so much heart-breaking grief.

But her manner changes as she talks about the Roman Catholic Church in The Pas, an elaborate cathedral flanked by an equally elaborate bishop's residence. She states that she could never bring herself to enter that church since it epitomizes the wealth of the Catholic Church, the inequities among people, and the destitution of the people it purports to serve. The dishonesty and hypocrisy of the institution weighs heavily on her mind, and she struggles to maintain a calm demeanour. She admits that she struggles with her emotions every time she passes the church. And pass it she must since it is located on the main highway through The Pas. It reinforces, time and time again, the condition of powerlessness of ordinary people against a huge, rich bureaucracy. She has to guard against becoming once again the frightened child, controlled to the point where her spirit was almost destroyed. She is very angry with the church for making her mother the compliant, apathetic person she is and is forever thankful that through some miracle she herself has emerged relatively intact. She feels she has been able to free herself of the pit dug by the church that mired so many Aboriginal people in self-destructive lives.

She also is exasperated with herself because she cannot control her anger at the church. "Every time I drive though The Pas I'm mad!" she exclaims. "I wish they would raze that building to the ground so we could get on with our lives." With increasing agitation she recalls Father Lacombe's chart, the colourful chart that was integral to every catechism lesson. It showed Indians descending into hell, illustrated in lurid, devilish detail. On the other side of the chart white people were climbing the stairs to heaven, adorned with angelic beauty. The message was clear. No Indian was ever going to heaven, and since there was nothing they could do about being Indian, the terrified, isolated children knew they were destined for hell. No matter how good, quiet, hard working, docile, or acquiescent they were, they were still Indians. Elizabeth says, "I don't believe today that there is such a thing as hell. How could such horrors be awaiting innocent Indian people who had never even heard of Christianity?" But after a pause she says tiredly, "But if there is hell, then for sure Father Poirier, Sister Ogre, and Sister Porky are burning in it right now!" But this is small comfort as she remembers, tears coursing down her cheeks, the forsaken child she once was with the threat of hell forever hanging over her head.

The future is bright for Elizabeth Bear, and she looks forward to each new day. For a time she lived with her daughter and grandchild at Pukatawagan, and her relationship with her mother gradually became better than she had ever dreamed possible. There never had been positive family interactions among the large group of siblings. They had spent little time together as children, and they dealt with events in their lives in different ways, but they have spent the last few years healing and getting acquainted. All want a family but they feel they really do not know what a family is. Slowly, patiently, they are dealing with the past and are drawing closer together as they search for a better future.

Because of a new and stable relationship, Elizabeth eventually left Pukatawagan and moved to The Pas. It was not long before she was hired by the Opasquiak Cree Child and Family Services as team leader for the Mathias Colomb Band, a job that entails frequent travel back to Pukatawagan. Her roots are firmly established in the community she now calls home.

Sara and Beverly Sabourin

Sara Sabourin was born in 1930 at Heron Bay, Ontario, a small community about six hundred kilometres east of Thunder Bay. When she was born it was a reserve community of twenty to thirty extended families with a total population of approximately eight hundred people. The people lived largely by hunting, fishing, and trapping, but some worked at the Ontario Paper Mill on Lake Superior, sixteen kilometres south of the community. Some also worked as loggers, floating logs down the Pic River to the mill. Others, such as Sara's grandmother, farmed, raising cows, chickens, and horses. They had huge gardens that provided the family with potatoes and other produce. Her grandmother also did beadwork, knitting, and quilting, and tanned moose hides; she made snowshoes, dance costumes, traditional *tikanagan* (cradle boards), and wigwams.

Sara's father made canoes of birch bark or cedar, since travel was largely by water. He had travelled extensively, going as far as Thunder Bay by hugging the shoreline of the vast lake all the way. In wintertime he travelled by dog team using sleds he had made himself.

Sara belonged to a family of twelve children, though a sister had died at birth and two brothers died before reaching the age of twelve.

Sara was supposed to have been born in 1929 but she was slow in coming. On New Year's Eve, while the rest of the community celebrated the coming of the New Year, Sara's mother laboured on. According to her mother, Sara was stubborn and would not make her appearance in the world—not until community members fired their guns into the air to celebrate the arrival of 1930. With the crack of the first gunshot, Sara was born.

Life at Heron Bay, as in the rest of Canada, changed dramatically with the advent of the Second World War. Rationing affected all Canadians but had a drastic effect on remote communities. The supplies to which the community had grown accustomed simply no longer appeared on the store shelves. Life became increasingly difficult since many had moved into the community and no longer had the skills to live off the land. Adding to the hardships were the military recruiters. When they arrived in the community they told the men that they had to enlist or they would face a jail term. In fact, by law, Status Indians were not required to enlist since they were not considered to be Canadian citizens. They were considered wards of the state and did not, for example, have the right to vote in either federal or provincial elections. Many of the community members were unable to read and most were unaware of exactly what their rights were. They had become accustomed to the paternalism of the Department of Indian Affairs as represented by the Indian agent and rarely questioned decisions of the government. To protest or question could have negative consequences, often in the form of fewer rations or rations that were withheld altogether. It was simpler to accept, with as good grace as they could muster, the controls of the department.

When the recruiters came there were those Ojibway men who enlisted willingly since the prospect of adventure has always appealed to the restless; in other cases the prospect of a regular paycheque for their families would ease difficult living conditions. Many, however, objected strongly to a war that they felt was of no concern to them. Some escaped into the bush and hid until the recruiters left. Others were taken forcibly, with little regard for age as long as they were strong and healthy and looked old enough. Several of Sara's uncles were underage when they were drafted; one was only fourteen years old. Sara believes they were tricked into enlisting.

Likely unknown to them as it was to many other Status Indians at that time, was the fact that enlistment also meant automatic enfranchisement. This meant that they no longer were legally "Indians." They lost all their treaty or status rights, such as the right to live on a reserve, receive reserve housing, health care, support payments in times of unemployment or ill health, or funding for an education. If they were married their wives and children would also lose these rights. In exchange, they had the right to vote, to drink legally, and to lay down their lives for their country.

Once the war was over the Canadian government provided retraining programs for returned servicemen or helped them get established on farms or in businesses. The Department of Veterans' Affairs did not provide adequately for the Indian men because they were considered to be the responsibility of the Department of Indian Affairs. When the Status Indian men returned home they found they could no longer access band services, nor did they get any compensation from the Department of Indian Affairs since its position was that they were the responsibility of the Department of Veterans' Affairs. This injustice was not rectified until late in the twentieth century when a large percentage of Indian veterans had already passed on.

The Great Depression had created hardships for many Canadians but was even more devastating on Indian reserves unless the people living on them had the ability to go back to the land. Life became so difficult for the Sabourin family at Heron Bay that Sara's parents decided to move back into the bush. This decision was prompted by another overriding consideration. Sara's father, Patrick Sabourin, was adamant that the children would not be sent to residential school.

Patrick Sabourin knew about church-style schooling. He had been sent to school in Thunder Bay, hand-picked for the priesthood, and learned to read and write in both Ojibway and English. He left the school, and the training he had received resulted in strong anti-education feelings that persisted all his life. He did not like learning about things that were not relevant to his life, and he did not like learning about other people. His experience had been that non-Aboriginals were usually coercive in their education practices, and, in all cases, he was expected to give up his culture and his spirituality.

He left the school and returned to Heron Bay where he lived a very spiritual life, on the land as much as possible. Though he was a devout Christian, he had been able to meld his traditional beliefs with the new Christian religion. The family never went to church but he read Bible stories that had been translated into Ojibway to his children every night, and prayers were said in Ojibway. He also was the area medicine man and healer. He had been given the surname "Sabourin" by missionaries because it vaguely resembled his Ojibway name. His descendants adopted the name, but birth certificates down through the years show a variety of spellings.

He knew that the residential schools would not be good for his children. His philosophy of life was that he never talked about negative things if he could help it. He was a firm believer in the power of positive thinking. Many students from that area were going to the residential school in Thunder Bay, then known as Port Arthur, and Sara's father did not like what he saw when they returned. He did not talk about the deleterious effects of the school, but he was doubly determined to keep his family together. He simply told his family, "It is for the best for us to go in the bush."

At one point in their life the family did not have enough money for food. They had run short of everything. They had a little flour but no baking powder or fat of any kind. In desperation Sara's mother used cod liver oil to make a barely edible bread. That was the low point in their lives, and a move back to the bush appeared to be the only option.

They did have a destination in mind. Ontario Paper had bush camps for the loggers and Sara's father asked to be sent to the bush. He went ahead, promising his family he would clear a place for their camp, and then he would send for them.

In the meantime, Sara's mother prepared the family to move. At this time there were eight children, ranging in age from two to thirteen years. Only some of the children had coats and shoes, and it was the dead of winter. Sara's mother and grandmother set to work to equip the children for life in the bush. They cut up blankets to make each a coat and wrapped the children's feet in pieces of cloth, which they tied into place.

Finally the day to leave arrived. Sara's grandfather accompanied them as they travelled by train into the forest north of Heron Bay. Their father had arranged for the family to travel in the caboose at the end of the train. He had written a letter to the conductor with precise instructions about the milepost at which he was to stop the train and let the family off. Their mother prepared the children before they reached the designated milepost. She told them there would be nothing but bush and the only way to survive the cold would be for them to keep moving until they could reach the camp their father had prepared.

When they got off the train, huge snowbanks lined the sides of the railway. They waited on the tracks for their father. The children were happy to be active after the long train ride and did not suffer from the extreme cold as they played on the tracks. To Sara's young mind it was a long time before their father came, but eventually he did arrive on snowshoes. Had they climbed over the high snowbank, they would have seen the trail he had made for them, and they could have followed it to the camp. Their mother, however, would not let the children climb the banks since arrangements had been that they would wait on the track for their father.

After a joyful reunion with their father, the family followed him down the trail. In the clearing were a wigwam, a big fire, and plenty of rabbits ready for roasting. Sara's mother immediately set about preparing food for the hungry family.

Thus began a happy sojourn in the bush that Sara still recalls with considerable pride. Her father and brothers built a bigger wigwam with logs around the bottom part and canvas on top. Food and furs were plentiful. Sara recalls, "We got wealthy in the bush."

With his first paycheque her father took the train back to town in order to buy supplies, especially clothing for the children. Their diet of wild meat was supplemented by leftovers that their father brought home from the logging camp kitchen at the end of the day. Other than the supplemental food, they were self-sufficient. Sara's father and brothers hunted, trapped, and fished. Her mother used her considerable skills to tan hides and make clothing. The children all had rabbit-skin bonnets and blankets. The children participated in the life of the camp and learned all the traditional skills from their parents. Two more children were born in the bush and Sara recalls that no one was ever sick.

Several years later they were joined by more families and subsequently the community of Mobert was established on the site. After the war many of the families went back to Heron Bay but Sara's family stayed on in the bush. Pressure to educate all Indian children increased, which motivated many of the families to move into town. When family allowances were established they were paid only if children were in school.

Sara's father was adamant. "To hell with school," he said. "It wouldn't be good for them to go to school. We don't know what will happen to them there." None of the older children ever went to school. Sara's father made the deliberate decision to stay in the bush and hide his children from authorities. He was well aware of the fact that he was breaking the law and was risking imprisonment if the authorities chose to close in on him. Had the authorities chosen to prosecute him they would have had considerable difficulty even finding the family. Her father felt it was a risk well worth taking, considering the damage he was seeing in children who had returned from the residential schools.

Just because the children did not go to school did not mean that they were uneducated. They had daily Bible lessons and many stories, both legends and other oral narratives. They were expected to learn, by observation and practice, all the skills of their parents. They were educated in the traditional ways of life, particularly how to survive and to be connected to their cultural ways. This was a more important and more relevant education than what the school system was offering. They had a radio and there was much singing and music in their lives. Over time they acquired guitars, violins, and an accordion and were self-taught musicians. Their father made a point of bringing home comic books, and as soon as the children were old enough they learned to read in English.

In some areas, especially on the prairies, this defiance of authority would not have been tolerated. There, families were relentlessly hunted down and children were forcibly taken to school, if necessary. All this was done quite legally within the terms of the Indian Act. Punishments were severe and swift for recalcitrant parents. One documented case from the school near Lestock in southern Saskatchewan tells how the school truck would come every fall to pick up the children. The Indian agent would notify the parents when to bring their children to a specified location. The parents were still transient, living in tents, and in one case the father got his weeks mixed up. He did take his children to meet the truck, but it had already come and gone. A few days later two policemen and a priest came to apprehend both the children and the father. The children were sent to the school and the father was sent to jail. His son recalls, "He never understood why he had been sent to jail." [56]

This coercion did not seem to be the case at Heron Lake, not by Indian Affairs or the church. Likely the difference in attitude stemmed from the fact that the Saskatchewan prairies were being cleared of Indians to make way for settlers whereas the bush of northern Ontario was not coveted by anyone. Later, when Mobert was designated reserve land, relationships with the Indian agent were generally cordial.

When the family allowance system was established Sara's father would have nothing to do with it, though her younger siblings would have qualified. A woman came to the bush camp with papers for him to sign but he refused to do so. He realized that family allowance would give the government control over his family, which he refused to relinquish. On more than one occasion he escorted government officials out of his campsite. He warned his wife over and over again not to sign anything when he was not at home.

When Sara's youngest siblings were school age, Mobert had been designated a reserve and a day school was established. The early grades were taught on the reserve, though students still had to go to residential school if they wished to continue beyond grade eight. The family lived in the village during the week, though their father had a great deal of difficulty accepting an Indians Affairs house, and went back to the bush on the weekends. Summers were spent in the bush.

Sara's siblings all married and had families. The men worked as hunters, seasonal guides, firefighters, tree planters, line cutters, surveyors, railroaders, and one became a miner. Two of the girls married men who had been enfranchised because of their military service and had to leave the community. Two other sisters married non-Aboriginal men and also left the community.

Two of Sara's younger brothers died when they were living in Mobert. One had appendicitis, was operated on in Thunder Bay, and was put on a train for home by some health workers. However, it was the wrong train. An aunt recognized him on the train and so arranged for a transfer back on the right train. He died shortly after he got home; he was only ten years old. A baby sister died at birth and a second brother also died at Mobert, but Sara is not sure of the cause; she thinks it might have been a ruptured appendix.

Sara says there was a time when she "tried to get married." Her father definitely did not approve of church marriages, nor did he approve of the man Sara was intending to marry. In the small community there were many jealousies and intrigues and the romance was undermined. Eventually the man married someone else. Sara was angry at everybody in the community as well as at her father and so she left. She soon became pregnant and her daughter Beverly was born, followed by two sons.

Sara's ability to support herself was very limited. She spoke little English: she could read reasonably well but she could not write. Her job options were limited to cooking in bush camps and other menial jobs. After her third pregnancy she had matured enough to understand that she was hurting no one but herself and her children so she went home to her parents to raise them. She says that since she made that decision she has devoted herself to raising her children and giving them the good upbringing she herself had experienced.

For much of her life she harboured resentment against her father for denying her the opportunity to get an education. Though there were members of the community who went away to school and were devastated by the experience, Sara just assumed that if she had gone to school she would have had a good experience. But her father had forbidden it. She carried this resentment into her adulthood. It was so very difficult for her to make a good life for her children with her limited skills, and she felt that she had never been able to fulfil her own personal dreams. She lived with her parents in the bush camp or in Mobert until Beverly finished grade eight at the Mobert School. Sara was determined that her children would have the opportunities she had never had. Residential school was out of the question because Sara was well aware of the devastating effects on the children from the community who had been sent away. When they came home from the school for holidays they got into a great deal of trouble. They did not want to go back at the end of summer. When they finished school at age sixteen they seemed lost in the culture and community but did not seem to belong in white society either. Nor did Beverly want to go to the residential school at Port Arthur because it was too far from her grandparents. Sara enrolled Beverly in the provincial high school in the nearby town of Screibner, and, since she could not conceive of being separated from her daughter, she moved as well. After two years they moved to Thunder Bay.

Once Beverly was settled in a public high school in Thunder Bay, Sara enrolled in Confederation College to upgrade her English writing skills and attain a high-school standing. She really enjoyed mathematics and attracted the attention of her professor with her enthusiasm. He gave her extra help but some of the other Aboriginal women in the class resented this. They bullied and harassed her, both in and out of school, and eventually she quit.

Sara found life in Thunder Bay very difficult in other ways as well. Racism was rampant and she was often harassed on the street. On one occasion a young boy followed her, calling her a dirty squaw and other names. Suddenly she stopped, turned on him abruptly, landed a solid punch, and said, "Here's your squaw!" He fled from the scene. Working in bush camps, she had learned to fend for herself physically. Even there, her ability to fend for herself created animosity among the other women. One big, overweight woman with long, straight hair, as Sara remembers her, told her children to throw stones at Sara. Sara ignored the children but she attacked the surprised woman by grabbing her long hair and whipping her head back and forth. Sara's spare five-foot frame could carry a considerable wallop!

Today Sara is a practising Catholic. She began to attend the Catholic Church in Mobert when the children were little and has retained her relationship with the church ever since. She is deeply involved in church work and is a Eucharistic minister as well as an Aboriginal Elder.

Beverly finished her grade twelve in Thunder Bay, went to Confederation College, and received a diploma, then moved on to Trent University to specialize in Native Studies. She had spent most of her childhood in the bush with her parents, grandparents, younger aunts and uncles, and her younger siblings. She learned skills from her mother and grandmother in much the same way as her ancestors had taught them since time immemorial. She is fluent in English and Ojibway and can speak and write some French.

Her first job arose from an unfortunate experience she and her mother had in Thunder Bay. Sara found it hard to rent an apartment because when a prospective landlord realized she was an Indian they told her the apartment had been taken. Yet when Beverly phoned to make inquiries the apartment was still available. They registered a complaint with the Human Rights Commission and though they had a well-documented case, Sara decided to drop it because she was nervous about possible consequences. Staff at the Human Rights Commission, however, were impressed with Beverly's abilities and offered her summer employment that eventually led to a fulltime job as human rights officer.

Beverly enjoyed the work, but her first love was counselling. When a position became available she took a job as regional counsellor in the Territorial Students Program for the Ontario Ministry of Education/Ministry of Communication and Social Services. After two years on the job she took a job as regional consultant with the National Native Alcohol Abuse Program in Thunder Bay, and then became a Native Indian Student counsellor with the social service division at Confederation College in Thunder Bay. At this time she was also on the board of directors of the Ontario Native Women's Association. In this capacity she became acquainted with Peter Globensky, who was the district manager for Secretary of State, the government department that funded and provided training for the association. Though they met in 1977 they did not get married until 1986 because to do so would have meant that Beverly would have lost her Indian status.

Beverly's subsequent career path was determined by her husband's moves as he worked for governments in various capacities. She had begun a bachelor of arts at Lakehead University in sociology, and she finished it at the University of Calgary. She took a job with Native Students Services at the University of Calgary, which she held for five years.

Another move took her to Ottawa, where she was hired as a social service development officer with the Secretary of State. She did this for two years, then she moved back to Thunder Bay to be coordinator of student support services at Lakehead University followed by a year as the consultant for the Mahmowenchike Board of Directors, where she did research and designed the development of a major operational proposal for the Family Development Centre. She also did board training and development and acted as community agency consultant and liaison. A move to Montreal enabled her to acquire a bachelor of social work from McGill University followed by a master of social work degree. She became the executive director of the Quebec Native Women's Association.

In 1996 she established, and became president of, Beverly Anne Sabourin and Associates (BASA Inc.). This is a consultancy devoted to assisting institutions, organizations, and individuals with the dynamics of corporate and social change, strategic planning, and intervention strategies. BASA excels at program conception, design, implementation, and evaluation. A major research project resulted in the publication *The Language of Literacy: a National Resource Directory of Aboriginal Literacy Programs.*

Currently Beverly is the director of ACCESS Model programs at Red River Community College in Winnipeg. The ACCESS programs were established in Manitoba in the 1970s in order to provide affirmative action programs designed to begin the arduous task of remedying the historic miseducation of the Aboriginal people of Manitoba. They have functioned continuously at Brandon University, the University of Manitoba, and Red River Community College since that time. Besides her job history, Beverly's community and consultancy profile indicates her involvement in many aspects of Native women's organizations, friendship centres, and various education issues. Today Beverly lives in the Tuxedo area of Winnipeg with her husband, who is director general of the Council of Ministers of the Environment, an intergovernmental agency, and her teenage son, Jesse.

Beverly feels that she was very lucky to always find the kind of work she wanted to do in spite of their frequent moves. Though luck may have had something to do with it, the dramatic change in opportunities for women, especially Aboriginal women, was also in her favour. Beverly's commitment to equality for Aboriginals, her vision, her enthusiasm and hard work, coupled with a profound spirituality instilled by her grandfather in the forests of northern Ontario and nurtured throughout her life by her mother, ensured that she was ready and able to take on new challenges wherever she went.

Both Beverly and Sara have lived lives far removed from residential schools. No one in their immediate family attended a residential school; both grew up in secure and loving environments, surrounded by stable, significant others. Yet both feel that the residential school system has had a profound impact on them.

When her children grew older and Sara had more time away from family responsibilities, she began to attend healing ceremonies as an Elder. The healing circles, as practised by Sara's culture, use pipe ceremonies and burning sage and tobacco in their rituals. As she became more involved, Sara came to understand the terrible rifts in Aboriginal cultures that have been created by the residential schools. The widespread use of alcohol as a crutch and the horrendous suicide rates are symptoms of deep pain. Over and over again Sara is hearing people with growing or grown families expressing the pain they have buried for many, many years. She hears what she calls "awful" stories of straps, sexual abuse, denial of food, loneliness, and despair. Her role is to counsel people, to help them talk their way through their pain, to share, to cry. She also understands how the pain inflicted by the schools has become intergenerational, as children of traumatized parents suffered in turn, and how the schools and their aftermath have impacted on all Native cultures today.

Sara has also reached a better understanding of the dynamics between the Ojibway traditional cultural practices and mainstream society during her formative years. She realizes now how the power of her Ojibway culture was cut off because people were threatened with lifetime jail terms if they performed the ceremonies. She understands now why they hid their drums and paraphernalia in the bush when she was a child. She recalls the chagrin of Indian Affairs and other government officials when they had apprehended an Indian person and then that person was released from prison in short order. The officials did not understand that it was a tribal custom to perform secret ceremonies to get these people out of jail. The non-Aboriginal people never did understand the effectiveness of the medicine the Ojibway people practised. Or perhaps they did and that was why any traditional ceremonies and beliefs were so ruthlessly suppressed. Sara also cautions that the medicine can be very harmful if used for evil purposes, but that was never her father's way.

Today Sara goes wherever she is called. It may be to speak about Native culture at Catholic Churches as far flung as Winnipeg or Montreal, or it may be a healing ceremony in a small community near Thunder Bay. She participates in healing, women's, and pipe ceremonies, and she is a traditional powwow dancer. Most important to her are the healing ceremonies, to heal both her own people and the churches who are attempting to cope with this terrible legacy from the past. Sara admits that she carried hurt and anger at her father for many years for not allowing her to go to school, but today she cannot repeat often enough: "Dad, I'm not angry at you anymore. I am so *thankful* you did not allow me to go to residential school!"

As a researcher, counsellor, academic, administrator, or community volunteer Beverly is constantly confronted with the devastation created by a brutal system that was determined to break up Aboriginal family life and disrupt the transmission of cultural values. Had the government and the churches succeeded in their scheme there would be no viable First Nations cultures in Canada today. The older generations would have passed away; the younger generations would have no knowledge or memories of their roots. Had the schools succeeded in the education of Aboriginal children, theoretically they would be equal to other Canadians today and would be represented in all walks of Canadian life and occupations. One can only speculate what the identity of these cultureless people would have been, since their roots would have been obliterated. They certainly did not belong to the predominantly Euro-Canadian society of the times, either.

The grand assimilation plans failed in every respect, as they were doomed to do, since the very racist nature of Canadian society at that time precluded any possibility of equality for First Nations people. Not only did the scheme backfire, but the legacy it has left haunts all Canadians to this day. The Indian students were deliberately and ruthlessly educated to become a permanent underclass without cultural identity or cohesiveness. If the legacy does not consciously haunt all Canadians, it certainly has an impact on every Canadian because of the horrendous social costs that must be redressed today. Disrupted lives and social ills that resulted as a consequence of the family and cultural destruction are seen in the overrepresentation of Aboriginals in jail populations, poverty statistics, unacceptably high infant mortality rates, poor health, city gang life (which had its genesis in the residential schools), sexual confusion, the high rates of substance abuse, and the high rates of suicide.

Residential schools were not the only factor in the creation of these deplorable statistics. Land loss, a cavalier disregard for Aboriginal rights, and the paternalism of the Department of Indian Affairs have played roles, as well, but no other government policy was as devastating as the deliberate attack on the heart and soul of a people. The deliberate destruction of families and the education of children without nurture and without an understanding of roots or family values were unnatural and cruel acts. Though the physical and sexual abuse that many children suffered is horrendous, the psychological and spiritual abuse *all* children suffered has likely left a more lasting impact on Canadian society. The miracle is that there are some who survived relatively unscathed, though it was not easy for any residential school survivors to painstakingly piece their lives back together again.

Beverly Sabourin's life has been devoted to working with First Nations people as they struggle to overcome the tremendous handicaps of the past. Most of her work has been devoted to helping students cope with educational institutions that have been established for mainstream students whose life experiences have been dramatically different from First Nations students. Non-Aboriginal staff in mainstream institutions, though they may have been well meaning and caring, have had little knowledge or understanding of the background experiences First Nations students bring with them. The most common method of coping with First Nations history is what Professor D. Bruce Sealey called the "blackout" method.[57] To simply ignore and never ever refer to Aboriginal realities was the simplest approach, which continued to undermine student identities as they felt there was no niche for them in Canadian society. Little has been done by mainstream society to acknowledge that the residential school era is as much a part of Canadian history as is the building of the railway, the Great Depression, or the internment of the Japanese during the Second World War.

The residential school era has had a profound impact on all First Nations people. As the twenty-first century begins, it is possible to examine the era, talk about it freely, and seek redress and healing. Though public understanding, formal apologies, and compensation payments are helpful, it is only from within the cultures that real healing will come. Sara and Beverly Sabourin concur with Sister Dorothy Moore (see pages 70–86) that they are "right up to [their necks] in correcting past harms."

End Notes

1 Paula Gunn Allen, *The Sacred Hoop: Recovering the Feminine in American Indian Traditions* (Boston: Beacon Hill, 1986) 190.

2 Author's Note: I used Eleanor Brass's book, *I Walk In Two Worlds* (Calgary: Glenbow Museum, 1987), to verify some specific information she had passed on orally.

3 *Ibid.*, 5.

4 *Ibid.*, 36.

5 *Ibid.*, 37.

6 *Ibid.*, 59.

7 A. L. Getty and Antoine S. Lussier, eds., *As Long as the Sun Shines and Water Flows* (Vancouver: University of British Columbia Press, 1983) 126.

8 *Ibid.*, 126.

9 Agnes Grant, *No End of Grief: Indian Residential Schools in Canada* (Winnipeg: Pemmican Publications, 1996) 297.

10 Cecil King, "Cross-cultural Teacher Education: A First Nations' Perspective," in *Journal of Professional Studies* (Volume 3, Issue 1, 1995) 3.

11 *Saskatchewan Indian Federated College Calendar* (Regina, 1976) 1.

12 *Ibid.*, 43.

13 In Kent Gooderham, *Notice, This is an Indian Reserve* (Toronto: Griffin House, 1972).

14 Rita Joe, *Song of Rita Joe: Autobiography of a Mi'kmaq Poet* (Charlottetown: Ragweed Press, 1996) 9.

15 *Ibid.*, 13.

16 *Ibid.*, 25.

17 *Ibid.*, 32.

18 Rita Joe, *Song of Eskasoni* (Charlottetown: Ragweed Press, 1988) 55.

19 *Song of Rita Joe*, 80.

20 *Ibid.*, 101.

21 *Ibid.*, 139.

22 *Ibid.*, 142.

23 Alice French, *My Name is Masak.* (Winnipeg: Peguis Publishers, 1976).

24 *Ibid.*, 38.

25 *Ibid.*, 105.

26 Alice French, *The Restless Nomad* (Winnipeg: Pemmican Publications, 1991) 4.

27 *Ibid.*, 13.

28 *Ibid.*

29 *Ibid.*, 30.

30 *Ibid.*, 50.

31 *Ibid.*, 51.

32 *Ibid.*, 92.

33 *Ibid.*, 164.

34 Isabelle Knockwood and Gillian Thomas, *Out of the Depths: The Experiences of Mi'kmaw Children at the Indian Residential School at Shubenacadie, Nova Scotia* (Lockport, Nova Scotia: Roseway Publishing, 1992).

35 Shirley Sterling, *The Grandmother Stories: Oral Tradition and the Transmission of Culture* (Vancouver: The University of British Columbia, 1997, unpublished Ph.D. dissertation) 10.

36 Marie Battiste and Jean Barman, eds., *The Circle Unfolds: First Nations Education in Canada* (Vancouver: The University of British Columbia, 1995).

37 Shirley Sterling, *My Name is SEEPEETZA* (Vancouver: Douglas and McIntyre, 1992) 36.

38 *Ibid.*, 14.

39 *Ibid.*, 25.

40 Celia Haig-Brown, *Resistance and Renewal: Surviving the Indian Residential School* (Vancouver: Tillacum Library, 1989) 72.

41 *Ibid.*

42 *Ibid.*

43 Jack Funk and Gordon Lobe, ... *And They told Us Their Stories* (Saskatoon: Saskatoon District Tribal Council, 1991) 68.

44 *My Name is SEEPEETZA*, 83.

45 *The Grandmother Stories*, 21.

46 John S. Milloy, *A National Crime: The Canadian Government and the Residential School System, 1879-1986* (Winnipeg: The University of Manitoba Press, 1999) 149.

47 *Out of the Depths*, 75.

48 *Maclean's*, 17 May 1999.

49 *Ibid.*

50 *Ibid.*

51 Northland School Division No. 61, *New Employee Orientation Package* (1998).

52 *No End of Grief*, 75.

53 Linda R. Bull, "Indian Residential Schooling: The Native Perspective," in *Journal of Native Education* (18 Supplement, 1991).

54 Maggie Hodgson, "Rebuilding Community After the Residential School Experience," in *Nation to Nation: Aboriginal Sovereignty and the Future of Canada*, Diane Englestad and John Bird eds. (Concord, Ontario: House of Anansi Press, 1992) 103.

55 *A National Crime*, 236–7.

56 ... *And They Told Us Their Stories*, 69.

57 D. Bruce Sealey and Verna Kirkness, *Indians Without Tipis* (Agincourt: The Book Society of Canada, 1973) 99.

About the Artist and Cover Art

Joane Cardinal-Schubert, LL.B (Hon), studied painting, printmaking, and multi-media at the Alberta College of Art and obtained a Bachelor of Fine Arts degree from the University of Calgary in 1977. From 1978–1985 she was a Curator at University of Calgary. A member of the Royal Canadian Academy of Arts since 1986, Cardinal-Schubert is also a writer, curator, lecturer, poet, and activist for First Nations' artists and individuals engaged in the struggle for Native sovereignty. She has received numerous scholarships, grants, and awards for her work, including the Commemorative Medal of Canada in 1993, and most recently, the Queens Golden Jubilee Medal for her contribution to Canada, as well as to her community. Cardinal-Schubert lives and works in Calgary, Alberta, where she continues to address her family's history and place in southern Alberta.

According to Cardinal-Schubert, "Pow Wow Dream" is a self-portrait, painted after meeting a young woman at the Plains Indian Cultural Survival School, Calgary, who was graduating and had been invited to dance at the Grad Pow Wow. When the student took a break, she sat beside Cardinal-Schubert, and though they never spoke, there was an instant "transference"—of pride in culture, pride in her dance, and her obvious happiness to have been invited to dance with the traditional women. This reminded Cardinal-Schubert how important it is to know who you are and where you belong, and resulted in "Pow Wow Dream."

About Fifth House

Fifth House Publishers, a Fitzhenry & Whiteside company, is a proudly western-Canadian press. Our publishing specialty is non-fiction as we believe that every community must possess a positive understanding of its worth and place if it is to remain vital and progressive. Fifth House is committed to "bringing the West to the rest" by publishing approximately twenty books a year about the land and people who make this region unique. Our books are selected for their interest to readers, quality, saleability, and contribution to the understanding of western-Canadian (and Canadian) history, culture, and environment.

Look for the following Fifth House titles at your local book store:

Inside Out: The Autobiography of a Native Canadian
by James Tyman

Just Another Indian: A Serial Killer and Canada's Indifference
by Warren Goulding

Loyal till Death: Indians and the North-West Rebellion
by Blair Stonechild and Bill Waiser

The People: A Historical Guide to the First Nations of Alberta, Saskatchewan, and Manitoba
by Donald Ward

Prison of Grass: Canada from a Native Point of View
by Howard Adams

The World Is Our Witness: The Historic Journey of the Nisga'a into Canada
by Tom Molloy with Donald Ward